Creating Culturally Competent
Services for Children and Families

of related interest

Therapy in Colour
Intersectional, Anti-Racist and Intercultural Approaches by Therapists of Colour
Edited by Dr Isha Mckenzie-Mavinga, Kris Black,
Karen Carberry and Eugene Ellis
ISBN 978 1 83997 570 7
eISBN 978 1 83997 571 4

Working Within Diversity
A Reflective Guide to Anti-Oppressive Practice in Counselling and Therapy
Myira Khan
ISBN 978 1 83997 098 6
eISBN 978 1 83997 099 3

D.I.V.E.R.S.I.T.Y.
A Guide to Working with Diversity and Developing Cultural Sensitivity
Vivian Okeze-Tirado
ISBN 978 1 83997 631 5
eISBN 978 1 83997 632 2

Black Grief and Healing
Why We Need to Talk About Health Inequality, Trauma and Loss
Edited by Yansie Rolston and Patrick Vernon
ISBN 978 1 83997 327 7
eISBN 978 1 83997 328 4

Creating Culturally Competent Services for Children and Families

CULTURAL DIVERSITY AND SOCIAL
JUSTICE IN HEALTH AND SOCIAL CARE

Edited by **Iyabo Fatimilehin**
and **Hasan Waheed**

FOREWORD BY **ADAM DANQUAH**

Jessica Kingsley Publishers
London and Philadelphia

First published in Great Britain in 2026 by Jessica Kingsley Publishers
An imprint of John Murray Press

2

Jessica Kingsley Publishers
Carmelite House
50 Victoria Embankment
London EC4Y 0DZ

www.jkp.com

John Murray Press
Part of Hodder & Stoughton Ltd
An Hachette Company

The authorised representative in the EEA is Hachette Ireland, 8 Castlecourt
Centre, Dublin 15, D15 XTP3, Ireland (email: info@hbgi.ie)

To God be the Glory.

Contents

Foreword

Just Psychology Community Interest Company (CIC) has been making psychological services accessible and meaningful for Black and minority ethnic children and their families for close to 15 years. In a landscape of statutory services that have become stretched to breaking point, Just Psychology has remained a landmark of inclusive, innovative and impactful practice. It has made a difference not only to children and families, but also to how we do and think about psychology provision in Greater Manchester, be that co-production and leveraging lived experiences to develop strengths-based approaches to cultural diversity, building culturally competent capacity in the local healthcare and education systems, or facilitating family reunion following serial migration. Just Psychology is the realization of the vision that psychology and mental health provision can be avowedly and effectively socially just.

Just Psychology needed a book, and Dr Iyabo Fatimilehin and Dr Hasan Waheed have duly delivered. As the founder, Iyabo has poured a near-professional lifetime's work into these pages, assisted by Hasan, whose own professional journey has remained closely connected to the organization. In doing so, they have made Just Psychology's ethos and approach accessible and implementable to health and social care practitioners who would like to develop services – perhaps their own – that align with such values.

I am so glad Iyabo and Hasan have edited this book. I came to know Iyabo as a non-executive board member for Just Psychology, supporting her to steer the organization through the turbulence of the Covid-19 pandemic. It was here I came to understand fully the reach of the organization's work, having previously been aware of their reputation. Prior to that I was already aware of Iyabo's contribution to psychology more generally, having trained as a clinical psychologist on the University of Manchester doctorate. Iyabo has been researching and writing about racialized identities and experiences for a number of years, especially from a developmental perspective and with attendant service development in mind. She has also not shied away from incorporating the complexities of the concept of culture and our multiply determined identities, citing Professor Ann Phoenix's psychological research into intersectionality as an inspiration (Carmichael-Murphy and Danquah 2022). In a wider discourse often characterized by fixed and rigid categorization, Iyabo's work bears out Edward Said's contention that:

> No one today is purely one thing. Labels like Indian, or woman, or Muslim, or American are not more than starting-points, which if followed into actual experience for only a moment are quickly left behind. Imperialism consolidated the mixture of cultures and identities on a global scale. But its worst and most paradoxical gift was to allow people to believe that they were only, mainly, exclusively, White, or Black, or Western, or Oriental. Yet just as human beings make their own history, they also make their cultures and ethnic identities. (Said 1994, p.408)

Iyabo is part of a critical tradition in clinical psychology, going back to David Smail and the Midlands Psychology Group, that foregrounds the contribution of social and material conditions to our psychologies. In the area of race and ethnicity, Iyabo takes a place alongside practitioners like Nimisha Patel, Maxine Dennis and Nick Wood, who have been challenging the profession from within for some years (see, for example, Patel *et al.* 2000). Iyabo made a significant contribution to antiracism and essentially decolonial praxis in British clinical psychology before the current widespread awareness of these approaches, and has done as much as anyone in the profession to force recognition and engagement with the full diversity of our clients. Iyabo's engagement with the diversity of children and families' needs – and the people behind these needs – and the many barriers to having them addressed through statutory services, led to her developing new ways of working (Fatimilehin 2007). Iyabo understood early the importance of intervening at the level of the system and building capacity in services to meet the needs of all client groups and communities (Kagan *et al.* 2012). Through cultural consultation, Iyabo has enabled people from a wide range of backgrounds to use their lived experience and expertise to enhance the practice of health and social care professionals.

By the time Hasan started his clinical psychology training at Manchester, I was working on the programme and had the privilege of supporting and observing his development. Hasan had already worked as an honorary assistant psychologist at Just Psychology, and professes to having been deeply influenced by Iyabo's leadership. It was clear to me that he already had a developed sense of social justice, not only in terms of wanting better outcomes for marginalized communities, but also in understanding how inclusive practice could bring these about and what part he would play in that work. The profession's blind spot for working with faith and spirituality was a particular focus of Hasan's, and it is good to see his developing practice contained within these pages. Hasan trained amidst controversy about racism in the profession (Patel *et al.* 2020) and during the pandemic and reaffirmation of Black Lives Matter. Hasan was able to stay in the eye of such storms, helping the programme team find perspective and better support trainees through his calm, clear-sighted advocacy and contribution to the Equality, Diversity and Inclusion (EDI) action plan. It is no surprise to me that Hasan is picking up the baton from Iyabo and emerging as a new leader in the field of socially just psychology.

The prevalence of mental health problems across the population and the inadequacy of the healthcare system for meeting this need has led to a *treatment gap* (Kohn *et al.* 2004). Just Psychology came from Iyabo's recognition as a consultant clinical psychologist working with Black and minority ethnic children and families in Liverpool that this overall problem of access was exacerbated for certain ethnic groups compared to others (Fatimilehin 2007). Iyabo and Just Psychology have been addressing this *cultural gap* ever since. Rather than focus solely on the counselling and individual therapy offer that characterizes statutory services and that belies a largely Eurocentric approach, Just Psychology encompasses a holistic approach that takes account of the range of social and economic factors contributing to poor psychological health. The ethos is open to the range of marginalized experiences, be that migration journeys, extended family systems, collectivist culture or spiritually orientated worldviews. This is underpinned by recognition that economic hardship and racial discrimination take an incredible toll on childhood development and communities' trust in external agencies. At the same time, there is recognition of resilience and that solutions can come from the very differences that set people apart in hostile environments – identity, belief, an appreciation of different cultural perspectives, and a wider range and depth of social support. Just Psychology helps children and families build on these strengths, and in the process develops a different, non-pathologizing narrative about marginalized communities – that they will be the authors of their own ascent. Simply put, it is an attempt to meet people where they are at.

Going beyond the consulting room, then, Just Psychology has trained professionals to develop their awareness, skills and confidence in working with Black and minority ethnic communities, coordinated family group conferences to help children contribute to their own care plans, supported children and caregivers to develop skills that help the children manage stressors in their lives, helped families separated by migration to rebuild relationships and avert family breakdown or the involvement of social services or family courts, and brought cultural competence and compassion to expert witness work. As a social enterprise, Just Psychology reports on the social impact of its work. The numbers tell an impressive story of reach and impact across the Greater Manchester area. Less tangible is how much of Manchester's culturally competent practice the organization holds, its connecting a network of associates, Cultural Consultants, practitioners, practitioners in training and creating capacity in services and communities. As Hasan and other practitioners would attest, Just Psychology has been a beacon for those coming up in the psychological professions looking for more nuanced, contextualized understandings of mental health problems and a wider range of approaches to engage communities in solving them. Just Psychology's ethos is embodied in its people, who are similarly drawn to working in meaningful and impactful ways to change lives:

We have a team of colleagues from different backgrounds and experiences all led by a passion for social justice.

It makes for an incredible sense of purpose and energy that has powered service provision to NHS trusts, housing trusts, city and town councils, schools and a university.

So, do we now have child and family services in the region that are fit to work with all children and families regardless of race, ethnicity and culture? Well, the challenges certainly continue. If anything, the national treatment gap has grown larger over Just Psychology's years of operation due to declining child mental health (see, for example, Mind 2024). At the same time, a rising tide of ethnonationalistic populism exploiting societal discontents has made for an increasingly hostile environment within which to redress healthcare inequalities. And yet, Just Psychology has continued to grow despite, and perhaps because of, such challenges. Indeed, it is only the organization's determination to stay true to its founding values that has stopped it taking the numerous opportunities to grow even faster. Despite shouting populists leading the current backlash against our common humanity, UK society has been quietly getting on with growing more diverse (ONS 2022) and tolerant with that (Kaur-Ballagan 2020). We need services that can keep pace with these demographic realities and social attitudes. This is not all Just Psychology's work to do, but it has played its part in demonstrating the viability of, as well as responding to the ethical imperative for, such work.

Iyabo's story is that with passion, knowledge frameworks and collective endeavour, you don't have to remain stuck in services that don't align with your values. In the time since I trained to now, private practice has moved from being a dirty word to almost a default supplement to work in statutory services, if not one's main source of income. In this market-driven landscape I know many practitioners are looking to work in a way that is socially just as well as more self-directed and freeing. Iyabo and Hasan's book can be read as a 'how to' for setting up a social enterprise, but one without illusions. They are upfront about the challenges of adequate pricing, recruitment, terms and conditions, maintaining an appropriately skilled and experienced staff team, and creating a culture. If marginalized communities bear the weight of hostile societal projections, then Just Psychology will be subject to additional strain in helping people throw these out. Just Psychology's having endured is testament not only to growing acceptance of the more culturally attuned care it has helped to promulgate, but its people's, particularly Iyabo's, stamina. The payoff for lasting out is the continuation of a rich, ultimately satisfying, professional journey that is improving so many children's life chances along the way. Apart from providing psychological approaches and instructive case material, the book is a rich theoretical resource. Practitioners can work out their own way, steadied by the depth of experience, rigour and research evidence across the contributors' chapters.

I hope the chapters in this book become blown seeds, inspiring practitioners, managers and commissioners across the country to develop psychology provision that is rooted in relationships, cultures and communities, as distinct from only individual subjectivities. I hope this work germinates on psychology and mental health trainings, so that its practice-based, co-produced wisdom informs the next generation of practitioners, and makes its rightful contribution to the lively conversation about a decolonized curriculum. Just Psychology needed a book. Those of us who intend to offer culturally competent services need to read it.

Adam Danquah, Professor of Clinical Psychology and Associate Dean for Inclusive Education and Engagement, University of Manchester

References

Carmichael-Murphy, P. and Danquah, A. (2022) *Hidden Histories: Black in Psychology*. https://dclinpsych.leeds.ac.uk/wp-content/uploads/sites/26/2022/10/Hidden-Histories_Black-in-Psychology.pdf

Fatimilehin, I. (2007) 'Building bridges in Liverpool: Delivering CAMHS to Black and minority ethnic children and their families.' *Journal of Integrated Care 15*, 3, 7–16. https://doi.org/10.1108/14769018200700017

Kagan, C., Micallef, M., Siddiquee, A., Fatimilehin, I., *et al.* (2012) 'Intergenerational work, social capital and wellbeing.' *Global Journal of Community Psychology Practice 3*, 4, 286–293. www.gjcpp.org/en/resource.php?issue=9&resource=125

Kaur-Ballagan, K. (2020) 'Attitudes to race and inequality in Great Britain.' Ipsos MORI, 15 June. www.ipsos.com/ipsos-mori/en-uk/attitudes-race-and-inequality-great-britain

Kohn, R., Saxena, S., Levav, I. and Saraceno, B. (2004) 'The treatment gap in mental health care.' *Bulletin of the World Health Organization 82*, 11, 858–866. PMID: 15640922.

Mind (2024) *The Big Mental Health Report 2024*. https://mind.org.uk/media/vbbdclpi/the-big-mental-health-report-2024-mind.pdf

ONS (Office for National Statistics) (2022) 'Ethnic group, England and Wales: Census 2021.' www.ons.gov.uk/peoplepopulationandcommunity/culturalidentity/ethnicity/bulletins/ethnicgroupenglandandwales/census2021

Patel, N., Alcock, K., Alexander, L., Baah, J., *et al.* (2020) 'Racism is not entertainment.' *Clinical Psychology Forum 326*, 2–19.

Patel, N., Bennett, E., Dennis, M., Dosanjh, N., *et al.* (Eds) (2000) *Clinical Psychology, 'Race' and Culture: A Training Manual*. Blackwell.

Said, E. (1994) *Culture and Imperialism*. Vintage.

Acknowledgements

Every chapter in this book has been written by someone who has been involved in Just Psychology's journey at some stage, and others have also been mentioned in the chapters (e.g. as case study authors or in the Conclusion). However, there are also people who have not been mentioned at all and who had a significant impact on the development of Just Psychology's work. Their support has been invaluable over the years, and we want to acknowledge them here:

Amor Perez Pavon

Anna Brunt

Babz (Oladamola Babalola)

Ben Willmot

Brenda Jones

David Cooke

Ebele Nwokoye

Fiona Whelan

Gabriel Wynn

Hannah Williams

Helen Besant Roberts

Henry Ngawoofah

Jacqui Nelson

Janet Mannion

Joanna Bricher

Jonathan Baker

Kate McGrath

Kelly Hylton

Ken McDonald

Maira Azam

Martin Nolan

Mary Rose Gunn

Maura Rose

Melanie Bryan

Mercy Lozi Chiwama Chikoti

Nadine Mirza

Nickala Torkington

Penelope Machin

Ruth Bennett

Sana Gill

Sharon Dixon

Introduction

IYABO FATIMILEHIN AND HASAN WAHEED

The Just Psychology approach

Just Psychology is a social enterprise, based in North West England, that aims to provide services and interventions that address the psychological and mental health needs of children, adults and families, and to improve the delivery of existing services, with particular emphasis on cultural diversity, cultural competence and social justice. We incorporated as a Community Interest Company (CIC) in 2011, with a clear statement of our vision, values, objectives and mission.

Vision

Our vision is the full participation of all Black and minority ethnic children, adults and their families in an equal and fair society through the achievement of a significant improvement in psychological health and mental wellbeing, and the prevention of problems with mental health.

Values

- We value principles of equality and social justice, and acknowledge the range of factors (including economic and social) that affect mental health.

- We value diversity and difference and the rights of people to be treated with respect.

- We value equality of opportunity and ways of working that address issues of discrimination.

- We value ways of working that preserve mental wellbeing and prevent deterioration in mental health.

- We value good stewardship (the efficient use of time and resources), the use of approaches based on best evidence and best value for money.

- We value the strengths and resources that people have developed throughout their lives, and believe that all people and all communities have the capacity to draw on personal, family and community resources and strengths.

- We value collaboration and the participation of local communities in the development of our work.

- We value learning and continuing development in all areas of our work.

Objectives

Our objectives are directly linked to our vision and values:

- To provide services that promote competence in addressing issues of race, culture, gender, sexuality, spirituality, religion, socioeconomic status and ability

- To provide support to parents and carers, children and families at their time of need (early intervention)

- To provide parenting support and intervention

- To build capacity in order to increase the accessibility and appropriateness of mental health and family support services for Black and minority ethnic children and their families; this includes engaging with statutory and public sector agencies to increase awareness and understanding, thereby building capacity to meet the needs of Black and minority ethnic children and their families

- To provide preventative services that address both the causes and effects of poor psychological health and improve mental wellbeing; this includes working with communities to address the range of factors (including social, familial, economic, etc.) that undermine wellbeing and impact on mental and psychological health

- To ensure we deliver services that are planned and developed in collaboration with local communities and local services

- To provide culturally competent expert witness assessments for private and public law proceedings

- To evaluate all outcomes and services delivered and to contribute to the knowledge base regarding the improvement of psychological and mental wellbeing in Black and minority ethnic communities.

Mission

Our mission is to be a key and preferred provider of evidence-based, effective and culturally competent interventions that address the psychological and mental health of Black and minority ethnic children and their families (including parents, other carers and adults) and improve mental wellbeing. We aim to achieve a significant improvement in the accessibility and appropriateness of services for Black and minority ethnic children and members of their families.

History

This book has been co-edited by two clinical psychologists, Iyabo Fatimilehin and Hasan Waheed. Here we outline our journeys and our personal and professional connections to the work that Just Psychology has undertaken since its inception.

Iyabo Fatimilehin

I am the founder of Just Psychology CIC and initially delivered 90 per cent of the services of the company when it was incorporated as a social enterprise on 1 April 2011 following the formation of an advisory board. All members of the board had worked with me previously when I was service lead for a specialist service for Black and minority ethnic children and families in Liverpool called Building Bridges. At that time, I was employed by Alder Hey Children's Hospital, and developed and led this innovative community-based service that was accessible and appropriate for Black and minority ethnic children and members of their families. Members of the advisory board were involved in delivering and evaluating the work of the service and/or had been strong advocates for the work. Essentially, Just Psychology's advisory board consisted of people who had a strong track record of working with Black and minority ethnic children, families and communities in Liverpool and Manchester in health, community and education settings.

I am passionate about social justice (hence the name of the company is Just Psychology), and have always been committed to the values of achieving an equal and just society. I qualified as a clinical psychologist in 1989 and was proud to work in the NHS as a service free to all at the point of access. I believe that it is necessary and possible for everyone in society to be mentally and psychologically healthy, and that this is a sustainable goal. The changing economic climate means that we have to be creative and develop new ways of achieving this goal, and hence my commitment to a social enterprise model that prioritizes both people and profit.

My personal background is one in which I grew up both in the UK and in Nigeria, and I therefore have experience of two very different societies and cultures. I do not believe that one is superior to the other but rather that there is much to learn from each in terms of factors that undermine or promote emotional health. Nigerian society is very entrepreneurial, and this was part of my early life experience. I am also aware of the pernicious effect that socioeconomic disadvantage and social deprivation can have on people's choices and behaviours, and on family functioning. I am a parent, and my personal and professional experiences inform my passion and commitment to issues of equality and social justice and to making an impact on society.

I left the NHS in 2008 in order to pursue my dream of providing innovative and responsive services and interventions that focus on issues of social justice. My skill and passion converge when working with others to alleviate and prevent psychological and emotional distress. Therefore, the founding members of the advisory board were people who shared my passion, values and principles with regard to working with children, families and communities. I have been responsible for developing the organization to meet its long-term goals to become a thriving social enterprise.

Hasan Waheed

I often tell people that I have come full circle with Just Psychology, and much of this journey has been deeply influenced by Iyabo's leadership. By that, I mean, I started my career as an honorary assistant psychologist and returned as a trainee clinical psychologist before rejoining the organization as a clinical psychologist. At the time of returning to the organization, I was also under the employment of East Lancashire Children and Adolescent Services where I worked as a clinical psychologist delivering psychological services to children, young people and adolescents in the Blackburn with Darwen area. I have since left the NHS and taken up other roles in the voluntary community and social enterprise sector – for example Ihsaan Therapeutic Services CIC, which deliver specialized faith-based therapies in Bradford, and Freedom from Torture, a charity organization that offers trauma-focused therapy to survivors of torture. I have also served as a board member for the British Psychological Society's Equality, Diversity and Inclusion Strategy.

I have had the opportunity to stand on the shoulders of giants in the clinical psychology field and learn from their experiences, which, in turn, has shaped my thinking in how healthcare should be delivered to those from culturally diverse backgrounds. Throughout my time working alongside Iyabo, both as a trainee and later as a clinical psychologist, I have continually drawn inspiration from her ability to build community-centred services that prioritize equality and inclusion. Her leadership encouraged me to look beyond traditional service models and explore creative, tailored and sustainable ways of delivering psychological interventions. Watching her navigate the challenges of creating a social enterprise taught me that serving disadvantaged communities requires not only cultural competence but also persistence and innovation. I am aware that the conversation of cultural competence and social justice has been ongoing for decades, as illustrated by Iyabo, and I am therefore very conscious that I do not want to reinvent the wheel or continue the same conversation about 'what needs to change'. Rather, I am very much motivated to put ideas into practice and serve those from disadvantaged communities. As a second-generation British-Pakistani Muslim male, I appreciate the impact of culture, migration and identity on how we make meaning of the world and our relationships. This perspective has, in turn, allowed me to disrupt and challenge the status quo within clinical psychology and healthcare services more broadly, but, more importantly, to highlight that the way in which we are taught to think and practise clinically is ultimately culturally niched. Finally, I strongly believe that we should be working towards prevention and early intervention while valuing the strengths, skills and resources that exist across all cultures.

Our hopes for this book

This book provides an overview of the work of Just Psychology and the services that we have developed and provided that align with our vision and values. We hope that it will provide practitioners working in the health and social care sectors with ideas about how they can develop their own services to ensure cultural competence, appropriateness and accessibility.

The rest of this introductory chapter will outline some of the underlying concepts, definitions and terminology that are used in the book, and the approach we have taken to structuring each chapter. It will end with an outline of the book.

Terminology and concepts

The terminology used within the arena of race, ethnicity and culture is constantly evolving and changing. This is linked to changing political and societal contexts across the world. *Race* has been defined as: 'a human group defined by itself or others as distinct by virtue of perceived common physical characteristics that are held to be inherent' (Cornell and Hartmann 1998). This definition emphasizes biological or genetic differences that are minimal (e.g. skin colour, hair type) when compared with the physical similarities between people of different 'races'. In essence, 'race' is a social construct with no scientific basis, founded on notions of superiority and inferiority.

Definitions of *ethnicity* largely focus on a sense of community. Phoenix (1996) defined ethnicity as 'a collectivity or community which shares common attributes to do with cultural practices and shared history', and this can include attributes such as language, religion and patterns of behaviour or belief (Cornell and Hartmann 1998).

Culture is defined as a more socially interactive and changing process. Greenfield *et al.* (2003) describe it as a socially interactive process of construction comprising two main components: shared activity (e.g. cultural practices) and shared meaning (e.g. cultural interpretation). The emphasis is on shared beliefs and values that influence individual experiences and actions.

The labels that are used to describe people from diverse racial, ethnic and cultural backgrounds are highly contested and have changed over time as a result of migration, colonization and political resistance. The terms 'Black, Asian and minority ethnic' or 'Black and minority ethnic' have been used widely in the UK for a couple of decades, but these are not without critique. 'Black' is a term that grew out of the American civil rights movement as a resistance to the term 'coloured' that was used to describe African American people. In the UK, it became a term under which people of different cultures and ethnic backgrounds rallied against racism from the 1960s to 1980s. More recently, it has been used mainly to describe people of African descent.

The term 'Asian' is used mainly to refer to people of South Asian descent within the British context. This includes people whose ancestry is related to India, Pakistan and Bangladesh. The way in which the term is used largely excludes people from other parts of the Asian continent (e.g. Japan and Singapore). Basically, the term Black, Asian and minority ethnic splits out African and Asian ancestry, and places all other non-White British people within a general 'minority ethnic' category.

The term 'minority' has also been subject to criticism with concern that it is part of a process of disempowerment that locates people as being 'done to' rather than resisting. There are similar concerns about the use of the term 'minoritized' (e.g. racially minoritized, ethnically minoritized). More recently, antiracism campaigners have begun to introduce and promote the term 'Global Majority'. This is in recognition of the fact that the people who are minoritized on the basis of race or ethnicity are actually the majority in the world. This approach fosters a more positive self-identification and includes people who have been categorized as Black, Asian, Brown or of multiple heritage and are Indigenous to the Global South. It emphasizes solidarity with the global antiracist struggle (DaCosta *et al.* 2021).

Our experience is that terminology is also contested at a regional level in the UK. For example, in Liverpool there was a period of resistance to the term 'ethnic' due to its roots in the notion of paganism and its association with the foreign or exotic. People of African descent have lived in Liverpool for hundreds of years and often refer to themselves as 'Liverpool-born Black' instead of 'Black African' or 'Black Caribbean' on official documents. This issue of heritage is equally pertinent and resonant for people of mixed racial/ethnic heritage (Fatimilehin 1999). In the US, the 'one drop rule' meant that any person with any known Black ancestry was defined as a Black person even if their single African ancestor was several generations earlier. While this legal definition has not been used in the UK, the use of a definition based on minority heritage is widespread (as in other parts of the world).

As Alexander and Byrne (2020, p.11) note: 'questions of terminology are complex, politically charged and shift historically. Racialized and ethnic identities are socially constructed and therefore mutable and changing. They are produced both through racist structures and discourses, as well as through processes of resistance and community-building.' In this book, we do not aim to identify a single term that will work in all contexts. Instead, we want to recognize diversity and aim to acknowledge the range of terminologies that fit with the context of the service being delivered.

Cultural competence

The concept and pursuit of cultural competence has driven the development of Just Psychology and the services it delivers. Cultural competence has been defined as:

> a set of problem-solving skills that includes (a) the ability to recognize and understand the dynamic interplay between the heritage and adaptation dimensions of culture in shaping human behaviour; (b) the ability to use the knowledge acquired about an individual's heritage and adaptational challenges to maximize the effectiveness of assessment, diagnosis and treatment; and (c) internalization (i.e. incorporation into one's clinical problem-solving repertoire) of this process of recognition, acquisition and use of cultural dynamics so that it can be routinely applied across diverse groups. (Whaley and Davis 2007, p.565)

It is acknowledged to be a journey as opposed to a destination, and that all practitioners should strive for a continuous development approach to cultural competence. There is a danger of assuming that one can become competent in working with people from a specific culture, but, as the definition of culture shows, this is an impossible goal as cultures are continually changing (Fatimilehin and Hassan 2016). Some researchers (e.g. Lekas, Pahl and Lewis 2020) propose that cultural humility is a separate concept to cultural competence, but we view cultural humility as part of the journey towards competence.

Our experience in practice shows that working with the values and beliefs of White, British, upper-class families is significantly different from working with White, British, working-class families, and these beliefs and values have shifted over time. Thus, we espouse a more nuanced approach that involves the use of frameworks and emphasizes the complexities and dimensions of human diversity. This includes frameworks such as individualist/collectivist (Greenfield *et al.* 2003), multidimensional comparative (Falicov 1995) and Social GRRRAAACCEEESSS (Burnham 2012). These frameworks incorporate intersectionality (e.g. race, gender, sexuality, class, acculturation, family organization and migration history) and fluidity. Alongside frameworks we also value a process of co-production and consultation with people with lived experience of specific cultures and developing strengths-based narratives that rise above the problematized approach to cultural diversity in beliefs and values.

The UK has an increasingly diverse racial and cultural population (Census 2021).[1] There was an increase in the Black, Asian and minority ethnic population (excluding the Irish group) between 2001 and 2011 (Shankley and Williams 2020). In 2011 nearly 11 million people (19.5 per cent) of the population were said to belong to a minority ethnic group (Census 2011). It has been estimated that this figure will double by 2050 (Sunak and Rajeswaran 2014).

Nonetheless, research consistently shows:

- High levels of socioeconomic deprivation within Black, Asian and minority ethnic communities (a House of Commons Briefing Paper showed that unemployment rates were 4.5 per cent for people from a White ethnic background compared to 9.5 per cent for people from a minority ethnic background – see Murray 2024)
- Low rates of access to early intervention services
- High rates of admission to crisis services.

Yet the approaches that are used to support the psychological and mental wellbeing of children, families and communities are largely Eurocentric. They have been researched and validated by WEIRD (Western, Educated, and from Industrialized, Rich Democracies) communities and are used with disadvantaged and diverse communities that have different beliefs and values.

It is increasingly recognized that participants in psychological research are predominantly from WEIRD communities, and that many research findings may not generalize to other populations. One study (Rad, Martingo and Ginges 2018) sampled articles published in a psychological journal in 2014 and their participant groups. The authors found that 57.76 per cent were drawn from the US, 71.25 per cent were from English-speaking countries (including the US and UK), and 94.15 per cent sampled Western countries (including

---

1   www.ons.gov.uk/census

English-speaking countries, Europe and Israel). The impact of this is that many of the beliefs and practices that are consistent with collectivist cultures are viewed as unusual or 'abnormal' within Western health and social care services, despite these being practised by the majority of the world's populations.

This has also led to the colonization of non-Western cultures to fit European/American values and belief systems about psychological and mental wellbeing (Watters 2011).

Social justice

The social and political contexts in which health and social care services are delivered have a direct impact on their accessibility and appropriateness for diverse communities. This diversity includes, for example, social class, race, ethnicity, gender, disability, sexuality and socioeconomic status.

Social exclusion is a complex and multi-dimensional process. It involves the lack or denial of resources, rights, goods and services, and the inability to participate in the normal relationships and activities, available to the majority of people in a society, whether in economic, social, cultural or political arenas. It affects both the quality of life of individuals and the equity and cohesion of society as a whole (Levitas et al. 2007).

Therefore, it is about being unable to access, or being prevented from accessing, the resources that are available to others, and this has an impact, not just on the individual, but on society as a whole.

Experiences of discrimination and disadvantage result in significant barriers to the use of statutory services by people from minority ethnic groups. Government and independent research on mental health services for Black, Asian and minority ethnic adults shows that rates of admission to hospital were up to ten times higher than expected for some Black and minority ethnic groups (e.g. Black Caribbean, Black African, Other Black, White/Black Caribbean, White/Black African), and that referrals from general practitioners (GPs) and community mental health trusts were lower than expected for some of these groups (Commission for Healthcare Audit and Inspection 2007). Black people were four times more likely than White people to be detained under the Mental Health Act in 2019–20. These disparities have persisted over time (see Chapter 2), with some fluctuations.

Child and Adolescent Mental Health Services (CAMHS) are more accessible for some ethnic groups than others, with African Caribbean families experiencing more coercive routes to referral and Bangladeshi and other South Asian families less likely than White families to self-refer or seek treatment for mild or moderate difficulties (Goodman *et al.* 2008; Messent and Murrell 2003). A study by the Afiya Trust (Malek 2011) stated that professionals give insufficient consideration to the mental health needs of Black, Asian and minority ethnic children and young people because of their age and ethnicity, and this omission disregards the fact that Black, Asian and minority ethnic children and young people are overrepresented in the youth justice system, looked-after provision and school exclusions. All these indicators have links with poor mental and psychological health.

Discrimination and being treated differently and less advantageously in society can be related to a number of social characteristics such as gender, race/ethnicity, social class, disability, sexuality and age, among others. However, these groups are not homogenous in composition and experience. For example, there may be areas of social life in which some sections of a group are doing relatively well, while for others there is stark disparity. Our work in Just Psychology is aimed at increasing social justice and social inclusion. We acknowledge that many modern approaches to health and social care increasingly locate pathology within the individual and not in the system around them.

The incidence of mental health problems in the Western world is rising (WHO 2022), and a report from the Organisation for Economic Co-operation and Development (OECD) (2023) showed increases in anxiety, depression and suicide rates from 2019 to 2022. The rise in numbers of people with mental health problems is partly due to better methods of assessment or detection, but social and environmental factors, such as isolation, family breakdown, poverty, social media and trauma, have also been implicated.

Over the past 50 years, there has been a corresponding rise in the numbers of professionals who have trained to work with people with mental health problems. For example:

- In 1921, the Royal College of Psychiatrists (or Royal Medico Psychological Association, as it was then) had about 600 members, but by 2009, it had over 15,000 members (Royal College of Psychiatrists 2022).

- The American Psychological Association (APA) had 5391 members in 1948, and by 2010 it had 67,254.

- The British Psychological Society (BPS) had 77 professional members in 1948, and by 2010 it had 10,000 clinical psychologists alone, without including educational psychologists, counselling psychologists or other practitioner psychologists.

- Similarly, the British Association for Counselling and Psychotherapy (BACP) was reported to have over 33,000 members in 2012.

Our response in Just Psychology has been to take a systemic approach and draw on a number of models. Bronfenbrenner's ecological systems theory (1992) outlines the microsystems, mesosystems, exosystems, macrosystems and chronosystems that impact on individuals and shape their development. In line with this we draw on community psychology, and narrative and systemic approaches that are grounded in co-production and the identification and utilization of people's strengths in addressing the challenges they face. We also value prevention and early intervention, and the importance of collectivism as an approach to working with difficulties/challenges across the micro-to macrosystemic levels. The aim is for a balance of individual and community/collective rights to achieve the best outcomes for all.

Outline of the book

This book aims to describe culturally competent approaches to working with children, young people and their families. It is aimed primarily at health and social care professionals in the UK, and outlines pertinent issues regarding accessibility and appropriateness of services. It examines how cultural competence and social justice can be embedded across a range of services including prevention, early intervention and tertiary intervention.

The book focuses on the four key themes in Just Psychology's work, including capacity building, therapeutic interventions, community development, and family justice and legal work.

The first chapter begins with reflections on the journey that Just Psychology has made, and the impact of changes in the social, political and economic landscapes, nationally and locally. Part 1 introduces some of the fundamental themes and concepts that have been incorporated into Just Psychology's work. This includes racism, spirituality and faith, and systemic and strengths-based approaches to working with children, families and communities. Each chapter addresses intersectionality and diversity across Global Majority communities.

Part 2 consists of chapters that describe the key services that Just Psychology has delivered. These include psychological assessments in the family courts, family group conferences, cultural consultancy, emotional health and wellbeing services, family reunion and parenting work, and capacity building (internal and external). Each chapter provides an overview of the research and theoretical underpinnings of the work followed by a description of the service delivered. All the chapters provide case studies and reflections and, where appropriate, also address co-production and intersectionality.

All the chapters are co-authored by practitioners who have been involved in developing and delivering Just Psychology's services.

CHAPTER 1

Just Psychology

The Evolution of an Enterprising Organization

CAROLYN KAGAN AND IYABO FATIMILEHIN

Carolyn: I was a non-executive director of Just Psychology from its inception until 2022, and was a part of the team discussing the need for and formation of Just Psychology.

Iyabo: I have been the executive director of Just Psychology since its inception, and brought together the team of people who helped create the organization.

Overview

In this chapter we take a community psychological and organizational perspective on developing a social enterprise that crosses the boundaries of health, social care and community development. The core of the analysis is of a values-based, small organization, carving out and developing a unique place within the delivery system of post-bureaucratic services and welfare pluralism in the Global North (Greater Manchester in the UK in particular). We move from describing the context of Just Psychology over the last 10 years and beyond (ideological and policy, organizational and resource contexts) to describing its organizational structure(s) and operations. In doing this we will show how Just Psychology has changed over time. We address the skills and responsibilities of managing and staffing Just Psychology, highlighting points of tension and strain – both for the organization and for its people. In conclusion we propose recommendations for other small social enterprises in this arena. Although we inevitably focus on the UK, the framework can be applied elsewhere.

Introduction

The origins of Just Psychology lie in the experiences of an earlier project, Building Bridges (Fatimilehin, 2017), and from the feedback given by various participants in that project over a number of years. We, and others involved from the start, drew on these experiences to establish the need for Just Psychology, that is, the lack of culturally appropriate services supporting the wellbeing of Global Majority families and communities that experience considerable strain.

Those of us who came together to explore the viability of establishing Just Psychology (the infant advisory board) had a range of skills and expertise that were mainly in the fields of psychological practice, research and psychotherapy (including clinical, community/counselling, social psychology and art psychotherapy). We spent a lot of time discussing the nature of this need and the boundaries around the issue to be addressed, and thereby the boundaries within which Just Psychology could exist – an essential first stage to any attempt at organizational and systems change (Peirson *et al.* 2011).

From these discussions Just Psychology was born as a locally focused social enterprise combining Global Majority expertise with evidence-based interventions, tailoring clinical, legal and community health and social care services to an individual or family's cultural context in order to produce preventative interventions and effective, long-lasting health and social care outcomes that enable families to function well.

Organizations do not exist in a vacuum and must be understood as part of a wider system – as a complex, soft system of interconnected elements (Mulder 2018) – but also as a nested system of different levels of influence and connection. Figure 1 illustrates one rendering of such a nested system, rather like the layers of an onion, through which the progress of Just Psychology can be understood. At its core is the values-based small social enterprise, Just Psychology. Its efficacy depends on the skills and responsibilities of its staff, which are, in turn, linked to the choices made about organizational structure and form. All this has to be understood in terms of the wider context in which Just Psychology emerged over the last 10 years and in which it is embedded.

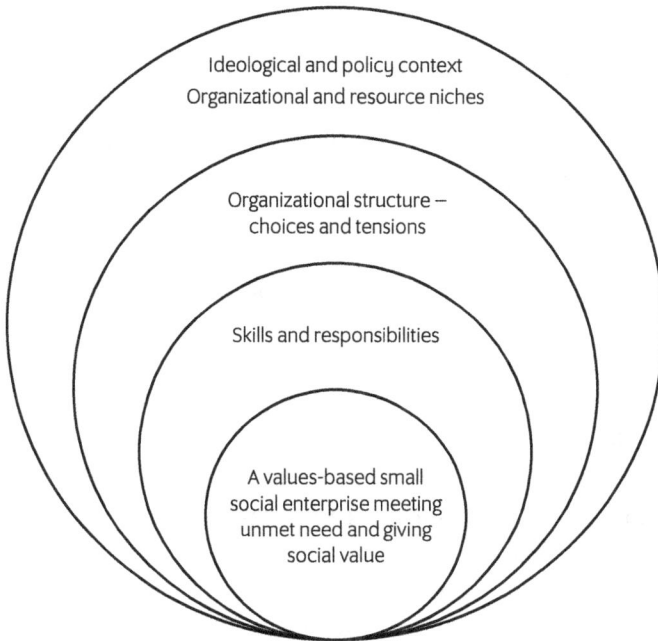

Figure 1: A multilayered health and social care system in which Just Psychology is embedded

Let us start with the wider context. We have suggested elsewhere (Burton and Kagan 2003) that it is helpful to have in mind the extent to which the wider context reflects and provides (a) a favourable ideological and policy climate; (b) organizational niches; and (c) resource niches.

An ideological and policy context creating organizational and resource niches

Just Psychology began in 2011, but we need to go back a little further to understand the ideological climate that framed those social policies that were the organization's bedrock. In particular we will draw on three ideological eras: Thatcherism (1979–97), New Labour

(1997–2010) and the austerity era (2010–current). Over this period there has been an ideological and policy shift away from the state-organized, collectivist policies of the post-Second World War welfare state to policies that promote welfare pluralism and that stress individual and community responsibility for health and wellbeing. Each era has created the conditions in which Just Psychology could come into being and influenced how it has taken shape. These are complex and multifaceted contexts, and our account will inevitably be brief and selective, highlighting those elements that have had the most impact on Just Psychology.

Thatcherism (policies from 1979–97, and onwards)

Thatcherism is the term used to describe the raft of neoliberal political strategies that, among other things, promoted free market ideology in all areas of public life, including financial deregulation, trade liberalization and, importantly, the privatization of public goods and services – including health and social care services (Scott-Samuels *et al.* 2014). These strategies were accompanied by an increasingly racialized discourse that continues today. Here, we will identify key aspects of this international neoliberal policy agenda that are most relevant for the emergence of Just Psychology.

Thatcher's public sector reforms applied business principles to the welfare state, introduced the 'quasi' market of purchasers and providers, underpinned by the introduction of 'new public management', and prepared the National Health Service for being broken up and open to privatization. These reforms were associated with substantial increases in socioeconomic and health inequalities. Between 1975 and 1985 there was a near doubling of poverty rates in the UK, from 6.7 per cent to 12.0 per cent, and along with this a rise in spatial inequalities. As Scott-Samuels *et al.* (2014, p.12) put it, 'Thatcherism bears historical and contemporary responsibility for making Britain a less healthy and more unequal place than it might otherwise be.' This legacy contributed to the need for Just Psychology's services, based as they are in North West England, one of the most deprived regions in the UK.

One of the first attacks on public services was the policy of contracting out, or outsourcing, in 1983, whereby health authorities were required to set up competitive tendering arrangements for their cleaning, catering and laundry services. Additional non-clinical services were later added to the list. Very quickly this led to the fragmentation of service provision itself, which laid the ground for more pluralism in service delivery.

Thatcherism created the conditions wherein successive administrations have looked for ways to further dismantle public services, including health and care services. Part of this strengthening of neoliberal policies has been to place the responsibility for health and wellbeing on individuals, making whole systems, preventive work in the public sector virtually impossible.

New Labour (1997–2010)

The New Labour project (along with other administrations worldwide) built on Thatcherism's adoption of, and enthusiasm for, what became known as 'new public management' (NPM), fed by neoliberalism. New Labour continued with the Thatcherite rhetoric that 'public sector provision was inefficient and often ineffective; that it led neither to cost containment nor to quality improvement' (Dawson and Dargie 2002, p.34). We will take a deeper look into NPM and its relevance for Just Psychology.

Hood (1991) highlighted some core features (he calls them 'doctrines') of NPM adopted by New Labour and that directly affect the way Just Psychology has operated. These include:

- A shift to the promotion of competition in the provision of public services, underpinning the move towards welfare pluralism and opening the way for greater involvement of the not-for-profit sector, now known as the voluntary, community and social enterprise (VCSE) sector,[2] in tendering for service contracts

- A focus on hands-on and entrepreneurial management, as opposed to the traditional bureaucratic focus of the public

---

2   At this time the VCSE sector was more usually referred to as the 'third' sector, that is, not public and not private-for-profit. Just Psychology is a third sector organization.

administrator, opening the way for the development of social enterprises and different organizational forms

- Explicit, changing standards and measures of performance, underpinning reporting requirements (which were then included in public sector contracts won by Just Psychology)

- An emphasis on output controls (Just Psychology has had to understand its outputs and report these to grant, investment and more fully to contract funders)

- The importance of disaggregation and the decentralization of public services – which created the conditions that were ripe for the VCSE sector to deliver more direct services

- A stress on private sector styles of management and their superiority, which made working in the public sector less attractive and doing preventive work almost impossible (providing the impetus to establish Just Psychology)

- The promotion of discipline and economy in resource allocation, which, to this day, has directly affected the tight funding available through grants and tenders for the delivery of services, with no requirement to focus on social inequalities.

New Labour presided over further disaggregation of public services. In 1998 they introduced the voluntary and community sector Compact as:

a device for "unifying" the various strands of New Labour's programme of marketizing public service delivery, increasing the emphasis on local or regional delivery of policy, promoting trust and combating social exclusion and environmental degradation. (Zimmeck, Rochester and Rushbrooke 2011, p.4)

The Compact was intended to change the nature of the relationship between the government and the voluntary and community sector, and to establish a set of 'rules of engagement' through which they could interact. Most importantly it was intended to open up public services to delivery by the VCSE sector via a system of public contracting and competitive tendering. While there are critiques of the policy and its implementation, it did open the way for public sector commissioners to tender widely for work and award contracts to the VCSE sector. Competitive tendering did (and does) not favour small organizations. Over time this created distortions in the VCSE sector itself, with large charitable organizations winning contracts and then subcontracting to smaller organizations that had been part of the delivery matrix all along. New Labour's *Best Value* approach recognized that quality services commissioned by the public sector were achieved, not through competitive tendering alone (introduced in the Thatcher era), but rather through partnership approaches. The partnerships were, themselves, compromised in a shift towards targets and outcome measurement, ossifying the separation of commissioners and providers.

Rochester and Zimmeck (2011) suggest that the Compact policy failed, largely due to the volatility of the political environment in which it operated. The optimistic days of 1997, when policy was seen to be driven by a vision of partnership, gave way to increasingly top-down, target-driven programmes based on prescription rather than trust. In the process, the policy model of partnership with the VCSE sector gave way to contracting and commissioning. And a plethora of new initiatives – such as local strategic partnerships – displaced local Compacts as the main or only way of managing the relationship between local authorities and the voluntary sector in their areas. The lasting legacy of the Compact and NPM for Just Psychology was to create the conditions wherein charitable (and later on, all VCSE sector) organizations could bid for public sector contracts.

New Labour, then, used those principles underpinning NPM to forge ahead with creating a matrix of providers delivering public services, further fragmenting the public sector and opening it to VCSE sector organizations, including social enterprises, which were now able to compete with private sector organizations for contracts. This market-oriented public service delivery vehicle was augmented by the austerity coalition and Conservative governments that followed (Chaney and Wincott 2014).

In its early years, New Labour did, however, focus on addressing inequalities and introduced a number of funded, place-based initiatives, not only around urban regeneration but also around health and education – Health Action Zones (HAZs) and Education Action Zones (EAZs). These were innovative attempts to draw in a range of different agencies, working in partnership with local communities and institutions, to find creative and innovative interventions. They afforded opportunities for public sector organizations to work with others in new, dynamic and creative ways. Indeed, it was a HAZ that funded Building Bridges, the NHS-based parent project to Just Psychology. Once these delivery vehicles ran their course, though, funding ceased. As public services contracted, it was difficult to find funds to continue those innovative and preventive ways of working; HAZ-funded projects were not necessarily incorporated into mainstream services (Barnes *et al.* 2012).

The austerity era (2010–current)

New Labour presided over greater welfare pluralism and fragmentation of public services, but – initially at least – with a view to positive partnerships between the state and the VCSE sector, based on shared values and mutual respect. Successive governments, though, not only pursued NPM principles, but returned to Thatcherism in a quest to fragment and reduce public services – not just those that were State-delivered, but in total. They did this through imposing the 'necessary austerity', which, they argued, was required following the financial crash of 2008. This political choice had dire consequences for public mental health (McGrath *et al.* 2016) and resolving inequalities. Local authorities, which were mandated to commission many of the public health and wellbeing, as well as family support, services, had their government grants cut severely and became ever more financially stretched. This has continued to the present day, with budget cuts upon cuts imposed.

During this period, the VCSE sector was increasingly expected to be self-financing, and any public commissioning of services was very tight, with the assumption that introducing competition into the market would deliver better efficiency and value, not just of money, but of social value too. The Public Services (Social Value)

Act 2012 (that came into force in 2013) required all those commissioning public services to think about how they could also secure wider social, economic and environmental benefits for their money. Social enterprises were well placed to deliver social value, but this requirement put even greater stresses on a sector that was already squeezed through the pricing of public service contracts that undercut the costs of public and private provision. At the same time, the Conservative government's 'Big Society' agenda[3] sought to place more of the effort to meet the needs of citizens on to citizens themselves, through building social capital, and away from government, in the name, not so much of communitarianism, but of reducing the size of the state (Szreter 2012).

Over time, interest in the 'Big Society' waned as neoliberal forces proved incompatible with producing social capital (Ferragina and Arrigoni 2017). While attempts to transfer responsibility for health and wellbeing to individuals and communities via the Big Society initiatives failed, somewhat paradoxically in the same period the rhetoric was strengthened around service user participation in health and welfare, via a different kind of partnership in service delivery – co-production (Sorrentino, Sicilia and Howlett 2018). There were a number of different antecedents to co-production in the UK. We should be in no doubt that, as Beresford (2019, p.5) argues, rather than being a progressive implementation of the demands made by social movements for greater participation in all sorts of social institutions, participation in health and welfare in the UK during this period 'reflected the consumerist/managerialist ideology significantly underpinning such state or service system driven schemes for involvement, increasingly rooted in market sector thinking'.

Nevertheless, the way was opened for an approach to service development that was grounded in the experiences of communities for whom the services were designed. One of the features of Just Psychology has been our commitment in theory and practice to community voice, reflecting the communities of Greater Manchester. We have built culturally safe services and embrace cultural diversity in

---

3   The 'Big Society' was promoted in the Conservative party's election Manifesto in 2010, and thereafter implemented by the Coalition government – Conservative and Liberal Democrat – from 2010 to 2015.

every aspect of the organization, from membership of the advisory group and executive board to staff recruitment and service delivery. It is not easy to achieve this, and women, young people and people of colour are underrepresented on boards of all types of organization (FCA 2022), including that of Just Psychology. It is hard enough to recruit executive board members for any small VCSE sector organization, and to seek diversity on top of this is time consuming and requires good networking and use of IT skills. We have sought advice from some of the organizations supporting wider Global Majority participation in governance and best recruitment practices, but it is still hard.

Thus, we have come full circle from the neoliberal ideology underpinning Thatcherism in the 1980s to the start of a more socially oriented ideology with New Labour, but which shifted towards market (and neoliberal) policies, and back to the fully neoliberal austerity era with its severe contraction of local government and public services. Income inequality has expanded during this period, and so have levels of poor health and mental health, especially among those communities with lower income levels (Bansal *et al.* 2022; Marmot *et al.* 2020; Wilkinson and Pickett 2017). The need for psychological services, particularly those for Majority Global families and communities, has never been greater.

Levels of poor health and mental health have increased further, and so have inequalities in health and mental health outcomes following more recent political events, the first being the major policy decision to leave the European Union – Brexit. Poor levels of mental wellbeing have been found to be both a cause and a consequence of leaving, and overall mental distress has increased following Brexit (Hervy *et al.* 2022; Powdthavee *et al.* 2019). Another event is, of course, the 2020 pandemic, which has had a major and unequal impact on mental health and family functioning (Marmot and Allen 2020; Marmot *et al.* 2021; Mind 2021; Proto and Quintana-Domeque 2021).

Alongside these events has been the growth of technology, particularly social media, affecting the health and wellbeing of young people. Abuse within social media, often by former friends and acquaintances, but also by grooming gangs, has led some young people to experience anxiety, depression and body dysmorphia, even trauma, at a time when public services have contracted (Plackett, Sheringham and Dykxhoorn 2023).

Over the last 40 years, then, political and policy shifts have prepared the ground for Just Psychology to operate within the market-oriented VCSE sector. They have also created organizational niches enabling particular organizational forms to emerge.

Organizational niches

In the early 2000s New Labour introduced social enterprises as a way of doing business that would benefit the community. Social enterprises are businesses with social and environmental purposes. From their outset, social enterprises were seen, and institutionally supported, as businesses and as part of the market. Over time this has changed, and they are now seen as part of the VCSE sector alongside incorporated voluntary groups and charitable organizations. In 2023 the umbrella organization, Social Enterprise UK, described them thus:

> Social enterprises are businesses which trade for a social or environmental purpose. There are more than 100,000 social enterprises in the UK, contributing £60 billion to the economy and employing around two million people. Social enterprises demonstrate a better way to do business, one that prioritizes benefit to people and planet and uses the majority of any profit to further their mission. Social enterprises contribute to reducing economic inequality, improving social justice and to environmental sustainability.

By 2005, New Labour recognized that a new, more flexible than hitherto legal organizational form was necessary in order to deliver the partnerships and growth of the social enterprises they craved. What was needed was an organizational form that contained an asset lock and remained a not-for-profit organization, that had a duty to provide community benefit, that restricted the levels of payouts to directors and was independent from the public sector. This was the Community Interest Company (CIC).

The CIC was ideal for Just Psychology. Before this organizational structure was introduced, the not-for-profit sector was dominated by mutual organizations such as cooperatives. CICs opened the way for non-mutual businesses, which were not charities, to operate and trade within a not-for-profit shell and to be eligible to deliver public services. The CIC provided a legal structure within which Just Psychology could operate.

While CICs were and are mostly set up as companies limited by shares or by guarantee, they also have an asset lock, ensuring that any surpluses are used to further the company mission, and they are required to show how they benefit the community. They are, therefore, one of the legal forms recognized as social enterprises. If a CIC was a company limited by shares, then a proportion of its assets could be paid out to directors; a company limited by guarantee pays no dividends and is eligible for a wider range of funding. We deliberated long and hard about the best legal form of incorporation for Just Psychology. Initially, we were advised that Just Psychology should be established as a CIC limited by shares due to our focus on trading and public sector contracts. However, it soon became clear that we would need to access much-needed grants for preventative projects (see 'Resource niches'). We changed our constitution to be a CIC company limited by guarantee, thereby rendering us eligible for diverse forms of funding.

So, Just Psychology is both a non-charitable social enterprise and a CIC, a company limited by guarantee. A CIC is required to satisfy what is called the community interest test, that is 'if a reasonable person might consider that its activities (or proposed activities) are carried on for the benefit of the community' (BEIS 2016). Each year we must submit a community interest report to the CIC regulator to show we are still benefiting the community and engaging appropriately with our stakeholders in carrying out our activities. While this is an additional reporting requirement, it has proved useful for ensuring we have all the up-to-date information we need in one place, both to report to the board and our community stakeholders and for funding bids. One of our sources of funding has been social investment and we have had to report our social impact quarterly, to form the basis of a meeting to discuss our progress. This is in contrast to requests for social value statements from public sector commissioners, who then have not followed this up with any comment or feedback.

The CIC statement, then, acts as a statement of social value, which we have had to be able to demonstrate whenever we submitted a tender for services or applied for a grant. Huckfield (2021) argues that social value reporting was pioneered in the cooperative movement that initiated social accounting and social auditing in the 1970s. He contends that these were the roots of social enterprises. Social auditing and social value or impact reports are very similar processes (for an example of our social impact, see Just Psychology 2018).

From the outset, Just Psychology has emphasized services that have a particular focus on cultural competence. Its location in Manchester, in North West England, places it in a multicultural place where approximately 200 different languages are spoken (Multilingual Manchester 2013). A limited number of other services that focused on particular ethnic groups existed, but none that sought cultural competence for all. A large part of the way we have worked is to find common cause with other organizations, and we work together to meet children and families' needs. Thus, rather than attempting to deliver all services alone, we have successfully worked in collaboration with other VCSE sector organizations, seeking opportunities to work at the organizational 'edge', where energies and human resources are augmented (Kagan 2007), as illustrated through the services outlined in other chapters.

The organizational niches we have found for Just Psychology are linked to the wider policy context discussed, and it is not possible to understand our progress without some understanding of these niches. Organizational niches cannot be filled without adequate resources, and we turn now to resource niches.

Resource niches

We have seen that the context in which Just Psychology has operated is one of contracting public services, increased welfare pluralism and social policies that have resulted in greater need for services supporting the health and wellbeing of children and families.

In the New Labour years funds were available for innovation in areas of greatest social need, via, for example, the HAZs. Once that funding ceased, and in light of public service cuts, the NHS had to focus more and more on crisis interventions. Any resources available from the NHS were to provide services that were already defined, and were mostly about delivering direct psychological services on an individual or group basis. Having said this, during the time of Just Psychology, health services in Greater Manchester have undergone massive and turbulent change.

In 2017 health and social care became the responsibility of the newly devolved Greater Manchester Combined Authority (GMCA). Initially, these changes brought no additional resources to the region – for health and social care in general (although additional resources have since been obtained), and certainly not for innovative ways of working with marginalized communities. National government, local health and social care commissioners and the GMCA have all been responsible for identifying priorities for funding and commissioning services to address them, and we have bid for some public sector contracts that fall within our remit.

Just Psychology was accepted onto the Troubled Families[4] register of providers (a central initiative from the austerity era, which sought to provide intensive services to those families with multiple and complex needs in order to save money in the longer term), ensuring that we were in a position to tender for work within this programme. Public sector tenders were often written with very short deadlines, putting pressure on the organization. The competitive tendering process drove down costs, making it difficult to cover infrastructure costs beyond the duration of the time-limited projects. Public sector contracts placed heavy demands – particularly on Iyabo as the executive director – for regular, detailed reporting, with very little discussion or feedback following the reports. The difficulties faced by small VCSE sector organizations partnering with the public sector have recently been recognized by the government (Perspective Economics 2022); whether anything changes, we shall have to see.

Amidst all this turbulence, we had to look outside the public sector for funding for the preventive work that is consistent with

---

4   From March 2021, known as the Supporting Families programme.

Just Psychology's mission. We took opportunities to apply for grants from the National Lottery Community Fund to fund the innovative Cultural Consultants Project, for example. Other grants have been from local trusts, social enterprise support funds and from social investment organizations, which provide a mix of loans and grants.

From the outset, training and expert witness services have been provided on a fee basis. Not only did these provide some funds for core functions, they were both important in the early years as a means of building the reputation of Just Psychology, thereby placing us in a good position to tender for those relevant services commissioned by the public sector.

Over the first five years, then, we built a business model that had diverse funding streams, each with its own advantages and limitations. Early on we relied on grants and commissioned services, with training and expert witness work supporting core costs not covered through other means. Later we included social investment loans. During the 2010s, as social enterprises grew, so did social investment. Some grant programmes diversified to become grant and/or social investment. It was becoming clear that it was impossible to rely on contracts to fulfil Just Psychology's mission, and the only way we could grow was through social investment; in recent years social investment has been added to the financial mix.

There has never been a chance to get long-term public sector funding for infrastructure, partly because of the way in which the VCSE sector was viewed through the different policy eras, and partly because our mission to serve families from Global Majority communities through preventive work has not been seen as a priority (although we knew there was still a substantial unmet need for both mental health and social care services).

Some of the difficulties we have faced in securing a solid resource base include the following:

- Funding was and is easier to secure for start-up projects than for continuation of service provision.

- With most commissions and grants being tightly funded for specific initiatives, longer term funding was difficult to find.

- The only way that Just Psychology could fulfil its mission was to spend considerable time networking in order to collaborate with other groups and organizations for project funds, and it proved difficult to build the costs for this time into specific projects.

- Integrating co-production approaches into the development of services, done properly, takes time, and again these development costs are rarely accepted into commissioned or grant-funded work (Boyle and Harris 2009).

- The only way we found of addressing the resource shortfall for working in a collaborative and co-produced way was to increase the unit costs of providing services or the fees for training and expert witness work. Over time, we have got better at doing this!

- The time needed to secure funding, both for projects and for networking, takes time and attention away from service innovation – where is the thinking time and funding for this?

Various government-funded initiatives appeared and went, with a great deal of rhetoric about the importance of the VCSE sector, not always matched by additional funding. The Black Lives Matter protests that erupted in 2020 raised the profile of both the history and reality of living in the UK as a Global Majority citizen, but concern was not matched by sustainable resources to boost the much-needed health and wellbeing services. The movement did, however, feed into the zeitgeist of concern for the experiences of being Black in the UK, highlighting the relevance of Just Psychology and increasing the demand for training and capacity building.

In 2020 the pandemic produced additional strain, not only for children and families, increasing the demand for services, but also for Just Psychology itself. We were able to access support grants and resources provided by VCSE infrastructure organizations (e.g. the School for Social Entrepreneurs), easing some of the organizational challenges we faced during the pandemic.

The short-term nature of most funding, along with a lack of continuation funding, has made it difficult to grow the organization and navigate the challenges of short-term staff contracts, filling vacancies as well as maintaining IT systems. Furthermore, all the reporting requirements to funders, public sector commissioners and to the CIC regulator are unrelenting. The reporting requirements of public sector commissioners are particularly onerous. We have had more control over grant and social investment funding: once projects are agreed there is no deviation. In contrast, we have found that the landscapes, priorities and requirements of public sector commissioning have shifted *within* specific contracts, creating more pressure for us. Furthermore, contracts can be withdrawn at any time, leading to considerable uncertainty within the organization. Sometimes, if there is slippage in public sector budgets, work has been commissioned at very short notice. It then seems there is little accountability or interest in how the money has actually been spent, which is disheartening.

It is not just the reporting requirements that take time. Contracts with the NHS demand that monitoring data are fed into the Mental Health Services Data Set (MHSDS), but the time for this is not part of the contract brief. As public sector priorities change, these are cascaded down to contracted organizations that may not have the resources to implement new requirements. These demands have meant that public sector commissions have both dominated our operations and also diverted us from our core purpose towards the changing priorities of commissioners. Moving forward we are unlikely to tender for public sector work, instead returning to building trading (via fees for training and expert witness work, for instance) and grants.

In sum the resource niches have shifted over time. It is difficult for a small but agile organization like Just Psychology to find resources for the longer term, and a great deal of time and energy has gone into securing financial support and supporting staff on short-term contracts. It has been crucially important to maintain dialogue with other VCSE sector organizations in the same field, to share experiences and cost-effective solutions to organizational pressures.

Organizational structure and operation

In the first three years of development, considerable attention was paid to defining the need for culturally competent services and scanning the environment to better understand the national, regional and local contexts of operation. From 2011 onwards, a flexible, continually modifiable business plan was produced.

The organizational structure in the early years was very simple (see Figure 2).

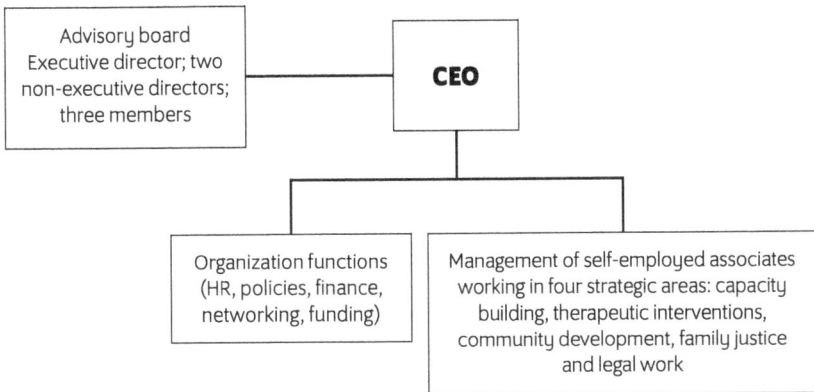

Figure 2: *Organizational structure of Just Psychology in 2011*

Then, Iyabo, as CEO, oversaw all the operations. There were four strategic areas of practice; namely:

- Capacity building (including training and consultation)
- Therapeutic interventions
- Community development
- Family justice and legal work.

Somehow, within all this, Iyabo was also responsible for networking, making funding bids, financial monitoring, the development of relevant organizational policies, the servicing of the advisory board (which consisted of some of those who had had the initial discussions about the viability of such a social enterprise), and for appointing staff, all of whom were fully qualified and joined Just Psychology as associates.

Just Psychology is committed to being a learning organization, and over the years we have held several organizational development days and a thorough Organizational Review in 2020–21. In 2020 it was decided to split the executive functions of the advisory group from its advisory functions, to form a more formal executive board, and to retain an informal advisory group with wider membership from diverse communities. For some time, IT and HR functions had been delivered by external organizations rather than in house.

Over time, Just Psychology has grown, with some projects coming and going on completion, and others enduring longer. The complexity of staffing has also grown – by 2021 there were 14 staff employed directly on various projects, 21 associates and 2 trainees, 2 assistant psychologists, 5 board members and 9 advisory group members. Capacity building was mainly undertaken through training, either general or bespoke, and shared across project practitioners; there were direct interventions via individual spot therapy contracts and also two longstanding services for families funded by local authorities and the clinical commissioning group; community development was delivered through the Cultural Consultant programme; and legal services had dwindled somewhat but were being rekindled by a dedicated expert witness lead and a bank of associates.

Iyabo, as CEO, still had an enormous amount of work – developing projects, supervising staff and maintaining quality – but by 2021 there were experienced staff supporting and managing the delivery of the different services. At the same time, the pressures of working through the pandemic were taking their toll. During the pandemic there was considerable stress within the organization, with staff resignations and career moves and all the difficulties of home working while still keeping services going. Iyabo called a series of 'crisis meetings' with the board and this resulted in some organizational changes and an Organizational Review was agreed. Following board development sessions that were externally facilitated, a pause on the growth and development of Just Psychology for a six-month period was agreed until vacancies had been filled and a senior management team formed.

By 2023, the organizational structure had changed (see Figure 3). Just Psychology remained a relatively flat organization, but there are clear lines of management and accountability.

Contractors/consultants
IT
Accountants
HR
Bookkeeping
FGC consultant
Business manager
Bid writer

Board of directors

CEO

Advisory group

Senior leadership team

Operations manager	Trafford Sunrise lead	FGC service lead	FRAP/cultural consultant lead	Expert witness lead	Training
Senior administrator	Psychological practitioners/ mental health practitioners	FGC coordinator	Clinical psychologist	Associate expert witnesses	Associate therapists
Monitoring and evaluation administrator	Assistant psychologists	Associate FGC coordinators	Assistant psychologist		
Administrator					

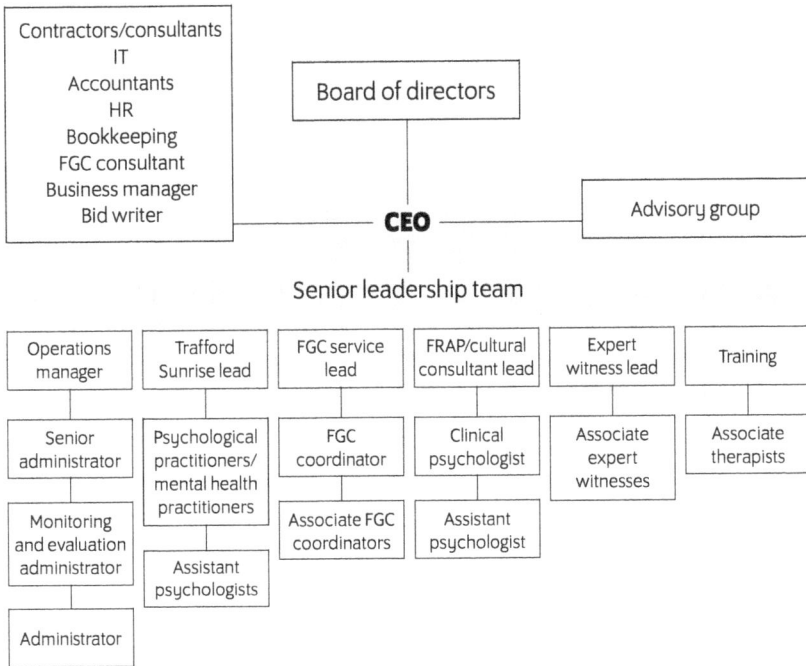

Figure 3: Staffing and structure of Just Psychology in 2023

The chapters in this book describe the projects and services that Just Psychology has developed over the years and currently delivers. These include:

- Legal work (Chapter 5)
- Family group conferences (Chapter 6)
- Cultural consultancy (Chapter 7)
- Emotional health and wellbeing services (Chapter 8)
- Family reunion and parenting (Chapter 9)
- Capacity building (Chapter 10).

In any organization, but particularly so in values-based small organizations, a positive culture within the organization leads to greater satisfaction at work and more effective internal communications and service delivery. This is, in part, linked to the organizational structure and role descriptions that enable all staff to be clear about lines of accountability while still allowing for flexibility. Ultimately, the responsibility for organizational climate and culture lies with the CEO, but all staff have a part to play.

Skills and responsibilities

Organizational development, change and growth creates significant shifts in the skills and responsibilities of staff. As we have seen, the majority of the work was initially delivered by Iyabo, the CEO and consultant clinical psychologist, in conjunction with some associate practitioners. The CEO skills required extended beyond those required in public sector organizations that are backed up by finance, IT and HR departments. They go beyond the professional, client-facing clinical psychology and management skills. Right from the start, business acumen and planning, strategic thinking, systems analysis, resilience, resource procurement and self-awareness were needed. As time went on, technical skills of financial planning and accounting, good HR practices and organizational policy development, collaboration and networking became paramount, and marketing of services and for associates underpinned direct service delivery. Throughout, CEO time had to be spent on networking with other social enterprises, allies and services with overlapping interests, as well as with commissioners and project funders. Skills of good communication, persistence and a range of management styles have all been needed, buttressed by a commitment to Global Majority families and a vision to ensure the success of Just Psychology.

In the early stages of development, it was particularly difficult to provide remuneration for the CEO that was commensurate with her roles and responsibilities and linked in any way to the public sector benchmarking levels. Initially we priced services too low to adequately cover Iyabo's salary; over time we increased our costings to provide better remuneration, but have still not been able to provide an NHS benchmarked salary. Pricing needs to be bold, and commissioners and funders need to understand the real cost of service provision.

As more projects and workstreams were developed, the need for more HR, including performance monitoring and disciplinary proceedings, IT, finance and corporate governance knowledge, increased significantly. Some of these functions have been outsourced, reducing the time that Iyabo spends on them, but there is still a lot of time spent monitoring the outsourcing!

It has been imperative for Iyabo to take up opportunities herself for learning and development, and these occasions have also been good for networking. She has been a part of 11 different networks, some of which attracted funding. These have included masterclasses on finance and marketing, business coaching or consultancy, different groups for peer learning, mentoring, networking, Covid-19 recovery grants, and bid writing and legal agreements. Opportunities have arisen in universities, as well as in the VCSE and private sectors, some of which are focused particularly on social enterprises, and others on business development more generally.

In addition, Iyabo has joined nine different social enterprises or mental health networks (e.g. as Fellow of the School for Social Entrepreneurs), but capacity issues mean she has been unable to keep up with them all. She joined the board of two organizations with similar values and learned a lot about social enterprise governance. The problems facing organizations of having so many different relevant networks have been recognized in the region and a new 'alternative providers' network has been set up; this promises to be a useful forum.

Just Psychology's first employees were administrative staff who ran the office and provided support to the associates and CEO. Our first public sector contracts enabled us to employ service delivery staff and this led to a corresponding increase, not only in undertaking recruitment and appointments, but also in the responsibilities of the organization.

Recruitment of staff is challenging when in competition with public sector organizations that can offer longer term contracts with better terms and conditions (such as higher salary levels, sick pay and annual leave). Short-term project funding meant that staff had little in the way of job security, and despite attempts to provide continuity from one project to the next, this was not always possible to achieve, and staff (understandably) frequently moved on to more secure jobs with other organizations. As the pressure was always to keep costs low, many of the staff were in the early stages of their careers, and they moved on to jobs that paid better and gave more career progression routes. In other words, it was not always possible to apply best HR practice for the retention of staff. In order to attract and retain staff, we have had to rely on our values and mission, and this is, in turn, closely linked to ensuring that knowledge about Just Psychology is spread widely, in part through networking and the delivery of projects.

Brexit and Covid-19 both resulted in a shortage of public sector NHS staff, with the health service carrying many vacancies for psychologists and other professionals working in children and family mental health and wellbeing, which made it even more difficult to recruit to Just Psychology. This workforce shortfall is a significant concern for the capacity of the health and social care system to deliver good quality health and wellbeing services, and also to embrace small social enterprise organizations. This links back to the ideological and policy context described earlier in this chapter.

We have sought staff whose values align with those of Just Psychology, and it has been challenging to recruit administrators with a good fit with the organization. However, their ability to bring their lived experience into their work has certainly contributed to the development of Just Psychology.

We cannot emphasize too much that maintaining an appropriately skilled and experienced staff team is extremely difficult when working with short-term contracts/funding. Recruitment and induction of staff takes time, and we have seen that if there is no new project to move on to and no financial cushion (as in larger organizations), staff have left for more stable jobs elsewhere. The recruitment and induction of staff takes time, and the implementation and delivery of a worthwhile project with sustainable outcomes takes more than a year.

In a small organization like Just Psychology, while roles were defined, it was essential for there to be some flexibility in staff supporting each other and filling gaps in light of staff absences, if necessary, beyond their own role descriptions. In the earlier years of development, informal flexibility was necessary as the organization grew; more recently it has had to be introduced more explicitly as an essential part of the organizational culture following the introduction of remote/hybrid working during the pandemic. In addition, the implementation of the senior leadership team following the 2020–21 Organizational Review has enabled more flexible working to be supported.

One of the things we, in Just Psychology, were good at was encouraging a strong sense of organizational identity as well as a positive working atmosphere. We were also good at recognizing when the climate was under strain and at taking steps to improve it. During the Covid-19 pandemic, for example, a staff support group was established with external facilitation and more frequent staff meetings encouraged.

Culture is determined not only by clarity of roles and behaviours within, but also in the use of symbols and symbolic practices. In Just Psychology, the logo is an Adinkra textile symbol from Ghana, representing wisdom, creativity and the complexities of life: the colours of purple and White run through all communications and Just Psychology's materials. Team meetings have been held regularly, and annually (except in the Covid-19 years) a whole systems event, around a meal, has taken place – staff, volunteers and other stakeholders with an interest in the work have come together in celebratory fashion. All these mechanisms served to create cohesion through symbolic means.

Remedial steps were taken when staff anxieties were high – as, for example, during the pandemic – and mechanisms were put in place for additional staff support. On occasion, tensions between staff negatively impacted on good working relationships; this was picked up and dealt with speedily, thereby avoiding grievances and the potential for disgruntled employees. The growth of the organization necessitated changes in management roles and responsibilities and the introduction of the senior leadership team.

The organizational strategy, now, is to enable Iyabo, the CEO, to spend more time on innovation and development of the organization instead of on day-to-day operations, using many of those organizational development skills she developed in the early days of Just Psychology.

Conclusion

The organizational development of Just Psychology is a case study of a developing and evolving social enterprise, taking place within a particular policy, organizational and resource context. It is an organization that has experienced tensions but that has worked collaboratively and clarified its boundaries over time, finding ways to adapt and adjust to external flux and sometimes turmoil. Strain at organizational and management levels has been evident, and lessons can be drawn about ways in which small organizations can support each other and exploit opportunities together.

There are a number of recommendations for the survival of small VCSE sector organizations like Just Psychology. These include:

- Work to understand the historical and current policy and resource contexts as well as the shifting support infrastructure and possibilities in which your organization exists, in order to make best use of opportunities and to understand and overcome obstacles you may face.

- Network to understand the social enterprise support infrastructure and how to get involved. Face-to-face contact is important. Building relationships takes time and contiguity. Collaborations need good relationships.

- Collaborate with other small organizations – but there is a need to be careful because these same organizations are sometimes competitors. Access to funding is highly competitive, and rather than encouraging collaboration, organizations are often pitted against each other for contracts and funding.

- When collaborating, offer something (such as time, expertise, experience or networks); do not just take learning from other organizations.

- Maintain a willingness to learn from other sectors, including the private and public sectors – use local resources like university or college staff and students, support organizations and other social enterprises.

- Your operating space is between the charity and public sector. You may encounter tensions and animosity expressed against the public sector, particularly in the face of severe public sector service cuts. It is helpful for someone senior to have experience of working in the public sector in order to fully understand what both the public and VCSE sectors are trying to do and how they complement each other.

- Note that contracts for services in the VCSE sector will be far cheaper than in the public sector, so it is important to have some trading income alongside the services.

- Most of all, be steadfast in your mission and values, keep a sense of perspective and humour – and develop a thick skin!

PART I

FOUNDATIONS AND KEY CONCEPTS

CHAPTER 2

Racism

ROHAN MORRIS AND IYABO FATIMILEHIN

Overview

The impact of racism on the physical and mental health of people from Global Majority communities in the UK has been documented over the past few decades. This chapter seeks to provide and explore information about what racism is, factors that influence experiences of racism and the impact of racism on physical and mental health. We contextualize the chapter by reflecting on our own experiences of racism. The chapter also provides recommendations for ways in which services can address the implications of racism, at both direct and systemic levels.

Introduction

We all have unique experiences that shape our perspective of the world. With a topic as emotive and often personal as racism, we believe that it is useful to contextualize this chapter by describing some of our own experiences. We hope that this will allow the reader to consider how this might have shaped what we have chosen to write and highlight our (at times involuntary) life-long engagement with this topic.

We have both had experiences of direct and overt racism, including experiencing racist verbal abuse, being spat on and being assaulted in racist attacks. We have also experienced treatment by others that was influenced by conscious and unconscious racial bias. One example of this is our experience of racial stereotypes (both positive and negative). Iyabo has had the childhood experience of her teachers trying to push her towards sport, much to their disappointment, once they realized this was not her forte. Rohan has had the experience of being accosted by two police officers, asking him 'What are you doing here?' while playing tag in a school friend's garden, in a mostly White area.

When reflecting on the differences between experiences of overt racism and experiences we believe were influenced by racism, we were both in agreement that we have found some of the less overt experiences more challenging. We both have felt confusion, suspicion and self-doubt while trying to understand and navigate situations where we believe that we have been treated differently because we are Black. We both reflected on how at times these less overt experiences of racism have left us feeling uncertain within some of our relationships, and almost wishing that the more subtle signs of racism were presented by people in more overt ways.

Throughout the course of writing this chapter we have reflected together about the intersectionality of gender and racism. For example, we thought about how this may account for the fact that Rohan has had more experience of racist violent assaults and negative interactions with the police, while Iyabo has found a greater experience of social exclusion (e.g. by parents of her children's peers).

We have also both experienced racism in our professional careers, and at times attempted to find ways to work around the barriers this has presented. We reflected on the ways in which we have anticipated racism and racist assumptions by preparing ourselves beforehand – for example, the challenges of interviews for jobs and knowing that there is a good chance that the interview panel members will have assumptions about us based on our race and ethnicity. Therefore, we developed a range of approaches to putting the panel members at ease and not seeing us as a threat (e.g. telling jokes that fit with British subcultures), and using language that both shows our familiarity with British culture and also our academic/professional knowledge. We attempted to humanize ourselves and appear more relatable. Nonetheless, this has not always been effective. For example, Rohan had an experience in a job interview where he received feedback from the interviewer that one of the interview panel felt uncomfortable when he stood behind them, which left Rohan questioning if they would have responded this way to a White woman.

We also reflected together on our gratitude towards the systems of support that have been developed to tackle racial inequality and the allies we have worked with over the years. We discussed the changes that we have seen in the representation of the Global Majority in trainee clinical psychologists. We also reflected on what has helped us to navigate issues of race and racism during our clinical psychology training courses. Rohan reflected that when he began training in 2016 it was helpful that these topics were discussed openly and could be talked about. This was encouraged by the course staff and other trainees. It was more likely to be seen as 'everyone's business' and not just limited to those from Global Majority backgrounds. Iyabo's experience in the 1980s was different, and as the only racially minoritized trainee in her year, she was usually the one who raised the issues. However, she became a member of the Division of Clinical Psychology's Race and Culture Special Interest Group, and members of the group provided her with significant support in managing issues of race, culture and ethnicity during her training. Therefore, the structures and systems around us are extremely important for addressing racial discrimination.

What is racism?

There are many definitions of racism in the literature, but one that works well for our focus in this chapter is by Paradies *et al.* (2015, p.2), who state: 'Racism can be defined as organized systems within societies that cause avoidable and unfair inequalities in power, resources, capacities and opportunities across racial or ethnic groups.' The emphasis on the avoidability of racism and its inherent unfairness are key concepts in our understanding and analysis of racism, and our belief that racism must be reduced and eliminated.

There are also different 'types' of racism to consider, such as xenophobia, Islamophobia and antisemitism, as described in the Racial and Religious Hatred Act 2006. Racism operates at multiple levels across society, including:

Internalized racism, which is the incorporation of racist attitudes, beliefs or ideologies into one's worldview. This is evident for people from both racially and ethnically minoritized communities as well as those from majority White backgrounds. For people from minoritized groups it refers to the acceptance and endorsement of derogatory and oppressive stereotypes about one's racialized group and other minoritized groups (Lewis-Smith *et al.* 2023; Mokuria *et al.* 2023). People from racially and ethnically minoritized backgrounds can believe they are not as clever or as attractive as those from majority White backgrounds (Dabiri 2023).

Interpersonal racism, which occurs through interactions between individuals and is also known as direct racism. It includes behaviour that directly maligns and degrades individuals based on their minoritized status (e.g. through insults, exclusions and physical attacks) and through the enactment of internalized racism (e.g. physical and verbal interactions based on stereotypical beliefs).

Systemic/institutional racism, which is defined by Patel *et al.* (2000, p.31) as

> the reproduction within institutions of practices of power which discriminate against people on the grounds of their perceived "race". These practices maintain the status quo in institutions and can be practices both in the commission of racist acts and in the omission of acts which would redress the situation.

They state that this resistance to change at a systemic level includes the racist control of and access to labour, material, economic and symbolic resources within a society. Common responses that perpetuate and maintain racism include denial and focusing on blaming rogue individuals.

The Macpherson report (1999) following the death of Stephen Lawrence outlined the impact of institutional racism in public sector organizations. It concluded that institutional processes, attitudes and behaviours result in the '*collective failure*' of organizations to provide appropriate and professional services to people from minoritized racial and cultural backgrounds. This can be detected in the outcomes in educational settings where children from specific Global

Majority backgrounds (e.g. Black Caribbean, Pakistani) have lower levels of attainment than others (e.g. Chinese, Indian) (Alexander and Shankley 2020; Department for Education 2023).

In social care, children from some Global Majority backgrounds are overrepresented in parts of the system (Edney, Alrouh and Abouelenin 2023), and children from Black and other racially minoritized backgrounds are overrepresented in custody in the criminal justice system (Shankley and Williams 2020). These disparities have existed for decades (with some nuanced changes) despite a raft of government policies and initiatives – for example, Delivering Race Equality in Mental Health Care (DRE) was a response to the death of David Bennett, a 38-year-old African Caribbean patient who died on 30 October 1998 in a medium secure psychiatric unit after being restrained by staff. However, there continues to be a disproportionate use of restraint against racially minoritized people in mental health settings (Pedersen *et al.* 2023), and disproportionate numbers of racially minoritized people are continuing to die as a result of constraint in police custody (Shankley and Williams 2020).

Various surveys and reports have collated the beliefs, views and experiences of people in the British population over the last 40 years. Although there have been some positive changes (e.g. people surveyed are more likely to endorse interracial marriages with Black or Asian people, and believe that migration is good for the economy and cultural life; see Kelley, Khan and Sharrock 2017), there are still significant issues regarding experiences of interpersonal racism. In each British Social Attitudes Survey since 1983, at least 25 per cent of the British population have described themselves as racially prejudiced (Kelley *et al.* 2017). A *Guardian*/ICM survey in 2018 found that people from ethnically minoritized groups were almost three times more likely to report being denied access to restaurants, bars and clubs (Booth and Mohdin 2018).

In addition, 38 per cent of ethnically minoritized people reported being wrongly suspected of shoplifting compared with 14 per cent of White people (Booth and Mohdin 2018). Reports of direct racial discrimination have also risen, with an increase from 58 per cent to 71 per cent between 2016 and 2019 for Black and Asian people (Booth 2019). The British Social Attitudes Survey indicates that between 2014 and 2021 there have been more positive attitudes towards immigration; however, post 2021 there has been a decrease (Humphrey, Wilson and Ford 2024). Nonetheless, there are nuances in the data that is being collected, and suggestions that our understanding and perception of the persistence of racial discrimination is being affected by social media and technology, specifically relating to the polarization of views and mass communication of negative beliefs (Begum and Williams 2023).

Changes in sentiment over time – local, national and world events

In the wake of local, national and global events of social, economic and political significance there are sometimes changes in sentiment towards particular ethnic or religious groups. In some circumstances this results in an increase in hate crime. For example, following an Islamic terrorist bombing in the Manchester Arena it was reported that Islamophobic hate increased by 500 per cent (BBC News 2017), and national surveys in the UK showed that Islamophobic attacks were at one of their highest points in a decade around the time of the Brexit referendum (Tell MAMA 2023). Similarly, following the escalation in the conflict in Gaza in 2024 there was a reported increase in antisemitic hate crime of 1350 per cent (Dodd 2023). It is clear that events can change public sentiment towards particular groups, and it is possible that these shifts in public sentiment are largely predictable. We believe that it is possible to address these shifts and take steps to counter the developing racist narratives and provide support for people who are increasingly likely to be victims of racism.

The advent of new technology may also result in changes in how racism is experienced and delivered. The rise in popularity in social media has increased our access to other people as well as our ability to deliver communications in an anonymous or pseudonymized fashion. This may increase people's exposure to experiences of discrimination with online racism being relatively commonplace. A 2021 survey in Canada suggested that 72 per cent of 18- to 29-year-olds had seen racist comments or content online (Canadian Race Relations Foundation 2021), and data indicates that racist material posted online leads to an increase in racist crimes committed offline (M. Williams *et al.* 2020).

The iconic Milgram experiments (De Vos 2009) demonstrate that a person is likely to be less empathetic to the suffering of others and do things that may harm others if they cannot physically see the victim's response. In our opinion, technology can produce a more polarized (online) society, which is reinforced through an echo chamber. While there can be positive effects through online campaigns, this can have a negative impact through perpetuating in-group, out-group positions, and can mean that people rely on shortcuts for understanding the world (schemas). Therefore, we believe that it is important to monitor the impact of the advent of new technologies and how this may play a role in people's experiences of racism.

Racism and power

As racism cannot exist without a power imbalance, it is important to consider the different types of power that exist. One theory of understanding mental distress has described seven different types of power that may have an impact: biological or embodied power, coercive power (or power by force), legal power, economic and material power, social or cultural capital, interpersonal power, and ideological power (Johnstone *et al.* 2018). These categories provide us with one way to explore how racism can exert an influence through many different aspects of someone's life.

Biological or embodied power is related to someone's embodied attributes and the cultural significance of this. Skin tone is one area in which racism can intersect with biological power. For example, one review concluded that there were increased experiences of discrimination and bias for people with darker skin (Adams, Kurtz-Costes and Hoffman 2016). Research has also indicated that among people of African descent, darker skin tone is associated with a greater incidence of mental distress and mental health difficulties (Hamler *et al.* 2022).

Coercive power or power by force involves the use of violence or threats of violence, which can be for the purposes of intimidation or compliance (Johnstone *et al.* 2018). Coercive power can play a role in ethnic differences in experiences of services. For example, people of Black African and Black Caribbean descent are significantly more likely to experience coercive pathways into mental health services (Mann *et al.* 2014). This also relates to *legal power*, the power to apply legal sanctions, where legal powers such as the Mental Health Act are used disproportionately higher on Black people in comparison to White British people (Mann *et al.* 2014).

Economic and material power is the power to acquire goods and services (e.g. housing), and to restrict others' access to them. Audits from the Office for National Statistics (ONS) suggest racial disparities in housing, with Arab, Bangladeshi, Black African and Pakistani people experiencing higher rates of overcrowding in comparison to White British people (ONS 2023b).

Social or cultural capital is power related to a variety of social identities and the networks of relationships that exist between people. It can also intersect with ethnicity. For instance, there is limited data to suggest that lower levels of social capital may account for a proportion of the ethnic differences in mental distress (Bamford *et al.* 2021).

Interpersonal power is the power to look after someone, to be looked after by someone or to be protected, including undermining or supporting someone with their beliefs or identities. Interpersonal power also intersects with ethnicity – for example the development of a positive self-identity about one's ethnicity may serve as a protective factor against the ethnic disparity in health outcomes (Rivas-Drake *et al.* 2014).

Ideological power is the power to develop narratives through the control of language and meaning, including the development of stereotypes. Ideological power intersects with ethnicity and racism in many ways, including in the use of language in media representation of ethnic groups, which contributes to the development of stereotypes (Ramasubramanian, Riewestahl and Ramirez 2023).

Each of these different types of power may intersect with racism and ethnicity. In order for racism to exist, then, it must exist in the context of power, which is not exclusive to one skin tone or ethnic group. For example, the Chechens, who find their origins in the Caucus mountain region and thus may be considered to belong to the Caucasian ethnic group, often experience high levels of racism in Russia (Kakişim 2019). This example highlights that racism exists in a system of power (which can be separate to skin tone), and is linked to the social, political and historical context, which, in turn, translates to different levels of racism (e.g. internalized, interpersonal, systemic) that can be experienced by the individual.

Impact of racism

Research on health inequalities shows the impact that racism has on access to health, social care and education services and the experiences of physical and mental health difficulties.

Physical health inequalities

Ethnicity is highly implicated in indicators of social exclusion and racism in the UK. Data from the 2021 Census shows that those who report poorer health tend to identify as White: Gypsy or Irish Traveller and Bangladeshi. While age was a factor in those from mixed or multiple ethnic groups (e.g. White Asian) reporting better health than average, this did not account for the poorer health reported by White: Gypsy/Irish Traveller or Bangladeshi people.

Year 6 children from a Black ethnic background from the most deprived areas are more likely to be obese than those in the least deprived areas compared to White and Asian children in Manchester (Allerton and Bullen 2021). Childhood obesity across ethnic backgrounds is also linked to other health issues, such as early-onset diabetes, asthma, depression and low self-esteem, which can all lead to long-term health issues in adulthood.

Differences in health vary across ethnic groups, with higher rates of diabetes in all non-White groups, higher rates of heart disease among Bangladeshi and Pakistani people, and higher rates of hypertension and stroke in Caribbean and African people (Chouhan and

Nazroo 2020). However, some of the ethnic disparity in physical health data may be explained by the clear link between health inequalities and socioeconomic inequalities (which is impacted by racism) (Chouhan and Nazroo 2020). Both in terms of the development of health inequalities and also in terms of the delivery of health and social care services, people from minority ethnic groups report poorer experiences with services than White British people (e.g. general practice services). Chouhan and Nazroo (2020, p.79) state that 'there is also a growing body of evidence that both physical and mental health are adversely affected by: experiences of racial harassment; fear of experiencing racial harassment; experiences of discrimination; and the belief that there is general prejudice and discrimination against ethnic minority people'. They identify stereotyping, discrimination, racism and cultural incompetence as key factors.

Experiences of racism and discrimination are widely recognized as an adverse childhood experience (ACE; Bernard, Smith and Lanier 2022). The links between ACEs and poor physical health outcomes are well established, with data suggesting that ACEs increase the risk of cancer (Holman *et al.* 2016), heart disease (Su *et al.* 2015) and diabetes (Deschênes *et al.* 2018), among other physical health problems. The ACE of discrimination is independently associated with poor physical health outcomes and has been associated with cardiovascular disease and poorer self-rated physical health (Chen and Mallory 2021), elevated blood pressure and higher inflammatory markers (Goosby *et al.* 2015), a higher Body Mass Index (BMI) (Goosby and Heidbrink 2013), and many other physical health concerns (Hutchins *et al.* 2022). This is thought to occur through a process of sensitizing the body's stress response system via the hypothalamic-pituitary-adrenal axis (Goosby, Cheadle and Mitchell 2018). The data clearly indicates that the impact of experiencing discrimination in childhood can have a lasting impact and adversely change the course of someone's life.

Mental health inequalities

There are significant disparities in accessibility and pathways into mental health services for children, young people and adults, and in the effectiveness of interventions provided.

Studies in the UK and the Republic of Ireland report that children from Global Majority backgrounds are more likely than White British children to be referred to Child and Adolescent Mental Health Services (CAMHS) through compulsory or coercive pathways such as social care, youth justice and education services as opposed to voluntary or primary care pathways such as family doctors (Edbrooke-Childs *et al.* 2015; Edbrooke-Childs and Patalay 2019; Skokauskas *et al.* 2010). In a study in South East London, Chui *et al.* (2021) reported that Black African children/young people were twice as likely to be referred through secondary health or social/criminal justice pathways than White British children/young people. They were also more likely to be referred to inpatient or emergency services. They conclude that children and young people from Global Majority backgrounds were two to six times more likely to be referred from social/criminal justice services than through a GP (family doctor). This was regardless of migration status, gender, household composition, year of referral and psychosocial functioning.

There is also research that addresses the representation of children and young people from Global Majority backgrounds in CAMHS. For example, in one study, Black and Asian children/young people were underrepresented in CAMHS while others (e.g. those of mixed ethnicity) were overrepresented (Arogundade *et al.* 2023). Those from Asian backgrounds and from areas of high deprivation were also less likely to be accepted into the service when referred.

There is little research regarding the effectiveness and outcomes of treatments and interventions provided to Global Majority children. However, one study undertook a regression analysis controlling for age, gender, referral source, presenting difficulty and case closure reason, and concluded that children and young people from Asian and mixed race backgrounds were less likely to report measurable improvements in mental health difficulties compared to White British children (Ruphrect-Smith *et al.* 2023). Furthermore, data indicates ethnic differences in the development trajectories of mental health difficulties throughout childhood, with Black Caribbean children showing more marked problems across a range of difficulties (Bains and Gutman 2021).

There are higher prevalence rates of many different mental health difficulties in ethnically minoritized groups. For example, Black women were significantly more likely to be diagnosed with a common mental health problem than White British women (Home Office 2018). Schizophrenia is one of the most well documented mental health diagnoses with ethnic differences in diagnosis rates. For example, a meta-analysis highlighted the relative risks of being diagnosed with schizophrenia were much higher among other ethnic groups in comparison to White British people (Halvorsrud et al. 2019).

In addition to differences in diagnosis rates there are ethnic differences in care pathways for people experiencing psychosis.[5] In the UK, in comparison to White British people, Black Caribbean, Black African and South Asian people with psychosis are more likely to experience compulsory detention, and Black Caribbean and Black African people are more likely to experience police contact and criminal justice system involvement, but less likely to have their GP involved (Halvorsrud et al. 2018). Similar findings have been highlighted among first-generation migrants in the UK, where many different ethnic groups who experienced psychosis were significantly more likely to experience compulsory admission in comparison to White British people, with African and Caribbean people experiencing the highest risk (Rodrigues et al. 2020). This finding is not limited to the UK, with similar data emerging from Canada (Anderson et al. 2014; Knight et al. 2021) and in the US, where care pathways of Black people are characterized by an increased exposure to contact with police and prison services prior to contact with mental health services (Oluwoye et al. 2021). Moreover, Black people are more likely to have experienced adverse (traumatic) life events and experience delays in treatment (Oluwoye et al. 2021). Duration of untreated psychosis is known to be a potent determinant of poor mental health outcomes (Howes et al. 2021).

Ethnically minoritized adults with psychosis also experience different care. They are more likely to experience restrictive practices and coercive treatment including seclusion, restraint and rapid tranquilization (Pedersen et al. 2023). Black people are also more likely to

---

5   Psychosis is an umbrella term that is typically considered to encompass a range of experiences and is related to several different mental health diagnoses including schizophrenia, schizophreniform disorder, delusional disorder, schizoaffective disorder, etc.

experience physical and chemical restraint (Smith *et al.* 2022) and a longer duration of restraint (Singal *et al.* 2023). Black people are more likely to receive their medication via a depot injection (Das-Munshi, Bhugra and Crawford 2018). In New Zealand, Māori people are significantly more likely to experience seclusion than non-Māori non-Pacific people (McLeod *et al.* 2017). In addition to experiencing more coercive and restrictive care, minority ethnic people are less likely to experience recommended treatments. For instance, in the UK, Black people are less likely to receive treatment in line with national guidelines and Asian people are less likely to receive copies of their care plans (Das-Munshi *et al.* 2018). Black Caribbean and Black African people are less likely to be offered or receive psychological interventions as recommended by national treatment guidelines (Das-Munshi *et al.* 2018). Some research has suggested that the ethnic differences in treatment may be accounted for by ethnic differences in other factors such as self-harm, suicide attempts or symptom profiles (Gajwani *et al.* 2016). However, even when controlling for these factors, research has indicated that Black Caribbean and Black African people are less likely to receive national guideline-recommended psychological intervention (Morris *et al.* 2020).

Ethnically minoritized people are more likely to have poor mental health outcomes. For instance, Irish Travellers are six times more likely to die as a result of suicide than non-Travellers (Bignall *et al.* 2019). From ONS data (which does not break down categories for Irish Travellers), men from mixed or multiple ethnic groups were at the highest risk for suicide (ONS 2023c). Black Caribbean and Black African people with psychosis experience worse clinical and social outcomes than White British people (Morgan *et al.* 2017), with Black Caribbean people from the same cohort highlighting their experiences of powerlessness and a cycle of disempowerment throughout their journeys with mental health services over a 10-year period (Lawrence *et al.* 2021).

To summarize, the data indicates that Black African and Black Caribbean people are more likely to be diagnosed with a mental health problem, and specifically what is often referred to as a 'severe mental illness'. Black African and Black Caribbean people are more likely to experience coercive pathways into services and to experience coercive treatment. However, they are less likely to receive treatment in line with national guidelines, and when they do receive psychological intervention it is possible that this may be less effective. The data also indicates that ethnically minoritized people experience worse mental health outcomes.

It is possible that more coercive pathways into services exist due to the 'circles of fear', where Black people are more likely to fear and mistrust services and therefore be less likely to willingly engage with treatment, and professionals are more likely to be fearful of Black people and resort to more coercive treatment options (Keating, Robertson and McCulloch 2002). Delays in seeking help for mental health difficulties are known to lead to worse outcomes (Howes *et al.* 2021), so it is possible that ethnic inequalities in access to primary healthcare (Ajayi 2021) results in people from minority ethnic communities being more mentally unwell (necessitating more restrictive treatment options and pathways) by the point at which they come into contact with services.

The treatment options presented in mental health services are based on research. People from Global Majority groups are disproportionately represented in the participants of health research, despite there only being slight differences in willingness to participate in research (Smart and Harrison 2017). A particular group of societies – Western, Educated, Industrialized, Rich and Democratic (collectively known by the acronym WEIRD) – have been found to represent 96 per cent of study participants from a collection of psychology journals, despite only representing 12 per cent of the global population (Arnett 2008; Henrich, Heine and Norenzayan 2010). This low representation in research studies means that treatments are often designed, implemented and evaluated without considering ethnic differences in effectiveness and the psychological impact of racism.

One of the most widely acknowledged factors determining good outcomes from psychological intervention is the therapeutic relationship between the client and therapist, with the ability to appropriately culturally adapt therapy being a factor that may also determine good outcomes (Wampold 2015). One factor that determines the development of a therapeutic relationship is client–therapist match, which ethnicity and cultural background is part of (Noyce and Simpson

2018). However, Global Majority people are proportionally underrepresented in the profession of clinical psychology (York 2019). Therefore, it is feasible that due to underrepresentation of Global Majority people in the psychology profession, minority ethnic people may receive less effective treatment. Therapy, specifically cognitive-behavioural therapy (CBT), has been reported to be less effective for non-White people (Huey *et al.* 2023), although contradictory evidence exists (Cougle and Grubaugh 2022). The impact on healthcare due to the lack of representation in the psychology professions is acknowledged by Health Education England (HEE), who are implementing an action plan to improve access to the psychology profession for Global Majority people in an attempt to improve ethnically minoritized people's experiences of mental healthcare (HEE n.d.).

Psychological impact of racism

There are many different possible explanations for the ethnic differences in diagnosis rates, treatments and outcomes. One such plausible explanation is the impact of racism at both a systemic/societal level and interpersonal level. For instance, the development of mental health difficulties is associated with adverse life experiences including experiences of racism (Bernard *et al.* 2022); this may, in turn, lead to an increased incidence of mental health problems among those most likely to experience racism.

Over the past decade, an increasing number of research studies (including meta-analyses) have investigated the impact of racism and racial discrimination on mental health and wellbeing of adults and children. Paradies *et al.* (2015) reviewed 293 studies, mainly carried out in the US, and concluded that racial discrimination has a significant negative impact on the mental health of adults. They further noted that more recent studies were showing stronger effects of racism on mental health, and speculated that this could be explained by a number of factors such as a greater awareness of inequalities and improvements in the measurement tools being used. Although people are more aware and less accepting of racial discrimination, this does not mean that it has ceased to exist, and it is likely that it has become more covert. It is also possible that covert racism is more challenging than overt racism because it results in people continuously reviewing and reflecting on experiences. This can have a high toll on mental and emotional wellbeing (Kinouani 2021).

Priest *et al.* (2013) and Lazaridou *et al.* (2023) reported the outcomes of international reviews that showed that there is a strong association between racial discrimination and mental health of children and young people (including anxiety, depression, self-esteem and behavioural difficulties). These studies found that children are more likely to under- than overreport racial discrimination, especially in the case of internalized or systemic racism. However, experiences of internalized racism increase the risk of negative mental health outcomes.

A growing body of research evidence is also demonstrating strong associations between maternal/paternal experiences of direct racial discrimination, maternal perinatal mental health and adverse social, emotional and developmental outcomes for children (Bécares and Atatoa-Carr 2016; Kelly, Bécares and Nazroo 2012). Intergenerational trauma means that the experiences of parents have a direct impact on the development of their children, whether this is transmitted biologically/physically or through the use of parenting practices that have a detrimental effect on the parent–child relationship (Kelly *et al.* 2012; Kim *et al.* 2018; Recto and Champion 2020). There are also generational differences in the experience and interpretation of racial discrimination. For example, parents who migrated to the UK may be more likely to accept some forms of racial discrimination (especially the more covert variations) than their children who were born in the country and perceive themselves as entitled to the same rights as their co-citizens.

Research studies have also focused on the factors that can reduce the impact of racism on mental health. These include a stronger ethnic identity, positive parenting, social support, more interethnic contact and bicultural identities (Beiser and Hou 2006; Chun and Lee 2006; Hwang, Wood and Fujimoto 2010; McDonald and Kennedy 2004).

Implications for practice and service delivery

The evidence for changes to practice and service delivery is compelling. In order to achieve better outcomes for children, adults and families from Global Majority communities in the UK, it is imperative that we implement changes at individual/direct and systemic levels. The strategies outlined here are based on the literature that we have reviewed as well as on our own experiences.

Direct work

In many different therapeutic approaches, one of the therapist's roles is to consider and discuss their relationship with the client. Some of the factors that a therapist may typically consider are how the therapist and client may relate to one another and what the therapist may represent to the client. Therefore, one implication for practice is that there may be a benefit in acknowledging differences in ethnicity and the potential for differences in experiences due to ethnicity. When considering differences in characteristics (and what these characteristics may represent), the onus is not solely on the client to 'bring' these to therapy. We would recommend that a practitioner initiates conversations about differences (and similarities) in characteristics. We believe that this may help to minimize the power differences in the therapeutic relationship and present an opportunity for framing the client as the expert in their culture and cultural experience. We believe that by initiating conversations about difference this may make it easier to explore experiences of racism. Racism only exists within the context of power differentials. Consequently, it may be particularly important in working to eliminate power differentials within the therapeutic relationship for people who have experienced racism.

Trauma-informed care approaches suggest that practitioners should have an awareness of their client's trauma history. This includes racial trauma. In order to be adequately aware of a client's trauma history it may be necessary to explicitly explore a client's experience of racism and its impact. This falls in line with the power threat meaning framework (Johnstone *et al.* 2018) that seeks to reframe the narrative from 'What's wrong with you?' to 'What happened to you?' As part of acknowledging a client's experience of racism it may also be useful to consider childhood experiences of racism (among other ACEs) and pay particular attention to descriptions of parental or familial experiences of racism that may increase the likelihood of intergenerational trauma.

Practitioners will benefit from exploring their own biases, which may include racial biases. The exploration of these biases may take place in the context of clinical supervision or the practitioner's own therapy. However, we are not always aware of our own biases, and one way in which we can bring our awareness to unconscious biases is by using tests such as the Implicit Association Test (available freely online). This may help the practitioner to adjust their practice and learn to challenge their own assumptions.

Practitioners will also find it helpful to consider their own experience of privilege and how the experience of privilege, or absence of privilege, may alter life experiences. Privilege comes in many different forms, but of particular importance in consideration of privilege in the context of ethnicity is White privilege. It may be helpful for practitioners to consider any advantages that may have been conferred by their specific characteristics, which may increase insight into the experience of someone without those specific characteristics. There is a purported test of White privilege that is freely available online and contains many questions that may help to increase insight into the experiences of people who may not experience this privilege (Individual Differences Research Labs n.d.).

Individual practitioners may find it useful to engage in developing an understanding of the communities they serve by familiarizing themselves with these local communities. This may include visiting community venues, community events and local places of cultural, social and spiritual importance (e.g. religious venues). Individual practitioners can seek to improve their understanding of how to culturally adapt their practice or learn about non-Westernized branches of intervention (e.g. Islamic psychology) by seeking out specific training. In Just Psychology, we provide capacity building services that aim to increase the appropriateness and accessibility of services to Global Majority communities (see Chapters 7 and 10).

Systemic implications

Change within health and social care services is essential at individual practice level and systemic level. We have presented evidence that social and economic disparities are closely linked to racism and discrimination at both direct individual and indirect institutional levels. Most government initiatives have addressed change at the direct individual level (e.g. increasing access through promoting services in community languages), but this has not resulted in improved outcomes for people from Global Majority communities (Chouhan and Nazroo 2020). Government policies such as DRE failed to improve outcomes and did not directly address the link between social and economic inequalities and racism. Instead, there has been a focus on locating health inequalities within the culture or genetics of individuals and communities – for example, focusing on diet as an explanation for higher rates of diabetes in some ethnically minoritized communities when there might, in fact, be socioeconomic explanations such as not having the time or resources for exercise due to low income (Chouhan and Nazroo 2020).

Addressing health inequalities within health and social care systems includes acknowledging the manifestation of racism and discrimination at all levels. It is essential to improve the recruitment of diverse staff teams at senior and board levels that reflect the ethnic and racial backgrounds of the communities that are being served. At present, 22 per cent of NHS staff are from a minority ethnic background while only 6.7 per cent are in 'very senior management' roles and only 7.1 per cent are members of NHS trust boards. Racially and ethnically diverse senior leadership teams are more likely to develop a racially and ethnically inclusive organizational culture (Otaye-Ebede and Shaffakat 2023). Recruitment initiatives need to include blind application forms, skills-based assessments and advertisements in locations that are accessible to people from Global Majority communities (e.g. community venues). However, there is also a need to provide developmental opportunities for people from minoritized backgrounds (especially younger people) so they can gain the knowledge and skills that their more affluent and connected White British counterparts have access to. In order to embed these changes in recruitment and organizational development practices, it is essential to have a number of processes in place including data analytics, work-force planning and development, and equality monitoring. These must then be linked to actionable change.

Within organizations, there can be a tendency to send Black and minority ethnic/Global Majority staff into teams in order to support and assist them with addressing racism/cultural competence. We believe this is neither advisable nor sustainable. There are issues of power, expectations and safety that need to be considered across teams and organizations. The responsibility for change lies with everyone within an organization, and the concept of allyship must be promoted in order to remove the burden for achieving change from those who are minoritized. Recommendations for developing more racially and ethnically inclusive organizations also include the identification of a specific team of staff with the power to devise and implement antiracist policies, procedures and practices (Otaye-Ebede and Shaffakat 2023) as well as the provision of training and education for staff that includes multiculturalism, antiracism, allyship and cultural competence. They advocate that training is not a one-off event but takes place over time in order to embed it into the team's culture. They also recommend skills development initiatives and mentoring for racially minoritized staff members.

Community Psychology approaches emphasize the need to acknowledge and incorporate the impact of social and economic inequalities into models of service delivery. The Community Psychology Section (2022) produced guidance that highlighted the importance of co-production, collaboration and developing shared understandings between commissioners, practitioners, service users, community organizations and other stakeholders. They adapted the ladder of participation (Arnstein 1969) to advocate moving from a non-participatory approach to service design that assumes stakeholders and service users are passive recipients to a citizen power approach characterized by partnership, delegated power and citizen control. It is important to develop trusting relationships with communities, and this is more likely to occur when services are based within those communities. It also improves the accessibility of services and shows that it is not communities that are 'hard to reach' but the services themselves. Service development also includes acknowledging and incorporating an understanding of systemic influences such as social and economic deprivation on mental health and wellbeing and addressing that within service design and delivery – for example, bilingual advocacy and support workers, cultural consultancy/peer mentoring and employability skills workers who can provide support with negotiating benefits, housing and employment systems.

Conclusion and reflections

We believe that racism permeates all levels of society and is sustained and supported by power imbalances. In order for racism to exist, a power imbalance is necessary. Attitudes towards racism change over time, and the expression of racist attitudes is impacted by social, economic and political events. Racism impacts the physical and mental wellbeing of children and adults across ethnic groups, both in terms of the psychological impact and the pathways into services. In addition, children, young people and adults from Global Majority communities are less likely to experience effective culturally appropriate interventions. These issues must be addressed at individual and systemic levels within services with a clear antiracist position being at the centre of policies, processes and practice.

We hope that drawing on our personal experiences has made the experience of racism more personal and less abstract. The experiences we have described are not unique; they are experienced by all racially minoritized people, even when they are unable to recognize or acknowledge what has happened to them.

CHAPTER 3

In the Eye of the Beholder

Nurturing Spirituality and Faith in Young People

HASAN WAHEED AND MODUPE ODEBUNMI

Introduction

The world is a vibrant tapestry woven with threads of diverse cultures, beliefs and traditions. Each thread, unique in its colour and texture, contributes to the richness and complexity of the global landscape. Within this tapestry, children are the vibrant colours, their lives shaped by the intersecting forces of culture and faith. We will explore the relationship between spirituality and religion, and its integration into professional practice when working with children and young people.

We begin this chapter by offering positionality statements, reflecting on our personal and professional experiences, and sharing what motivated us to write such an ambitious chapter. We approach this topic by acknowledging the complex interaction between mind and body, and how spiritual and religious beliefs shape children and young people's worldviews. Both spiritual and religious beliefs act as a guiding compass and provide a sense of purpose, meaning and comfort during times of prosperity and hardship. They can influence a child's sense of self, their relationships and overall development. This means that we, as professionals, need to understand, respect and honour these beliefs, incorporating them into our practice in a culturally appropriate manner. We have both witnessed the power of spirituality and religion in the healing process and the impact it can have on an individual's wellbeing and life trajectory.

We begin with positionality statements in the hope that we can be transparent in sharing how our own backgrounds and experiences shape our understanding of this complex topic. As we reflect on our journey into exploring the integration of spirituality and religion into professional practice, we are reminded of the diverse paths that led us here. Growing up in a traditional Islamic family, my (Dr Hasan Waheed) connection to faith was fostered by my mother and learning to read the Quran at home. My early years in preparatory school were spent in the company of Muslims and Christians, shaping my understanding of religion and its place in our lives. Entering a new environment in state high school (aged 11–16) brought a new perspective and made me more consciously aware of this difference in my identity as I encountered different views from a more ethnically diverse cohort of young people from a range of socioeconomic backgrounds.

Coincidentally, this period of my life is where I was exposed to more formal Islamic education by going away on weekend retreats with my father and other members of our community. These retreats were more than just a religious experience; they were moments of bonding where spirituality became a shared journey between us. I navigated the cultural dichotomy of my dual identities, forming close friendships with individuals from different religious and cultural backgrounds. This expansion of my worldview prompted an introspection that would unknowingly influence my path as a clinical psychologist later in my life.

My co-author, Modupe Odebunmi, brings a different yet complementary perspective as a non-denominational Christian, Global Majority, Cultural Consultant, who is married with children. She believes in the Triune God and power of prayer. She relies on the Holy Bible for guidance in her life choices and decisions. Her belief in miracles, wonders and healings does not replace but rather complements medical and therapeutic interventions. Raised in a Christian family, faith was the cornerstone of her upbringing. Weekly church attendance and teachings of the Holy Bible provided a strong foundation for her spiritual journey. For many years, this was the only worldview she was exposed to, although she began asking deeper questions into her adolescent years. Her turning point came when she recognized the profound influence of biblical principles in her life choices and behaviours. The influence of mentorship within the development of one's faith cannot be understated, offering guidance and strengthening one's convictions.

Together, we recognize the impact of spiritual and religious beliefs on the lives of children and young people. We approach this topic with an open mind, and as we delve deeper into this exploration, we aim to provide insights and guidance for professionals to navigate this important aspect of holistic care.

The evolution of religion in the Western world

First and foremost, the evolution of religion in the Western world provides an interesting context for our exploration of spirituality and religion in clinical practice. It is a story of shifting ideologies, power dynamics and societal transformations. From the polytheistic and idolatrous roots of Greco-Roman civilization to the dominance of the Roman Catholic Church during the Middle Ages, the Western world has undergone its own religious and spiritual journey. The Renaissance, a period of intellectual and artistic revival, challenged the authority of the Church, encouraging independent thought and scientific inquiry, setting the stage for the Protestant Reformation and Enlightenment. These movements promoted scepticism and critical thinking, leading to a rise in atheism and shift towards scientific rationalism. Today, secular democracy reigns supreme in Western civilization, reflecting a cultural move away from traditional religious dogma.

Humans do not live in a vacuum; our beliefs, values and experiences are constantly shaped by the events and influences in society, from culture and media to social movements and community norms. We are mindful of the impact these shifting ideologies and power dynamics have on young people's spiritual and religious identities. The Renaissance, with its encouragement of independent thought and scientific inquiry, set in motion a chain of events that continue to shape the spiritual landscape of the Western world today.

The cultural shift away from traditional religious dogma can be disorienting for young people who are seeking to establish their own spiritual and religious identities (Philips 2007). By recognizing this change over time, we start to unlearn and relearn new ways of thinking, which can propel us to start providing culturally appropriate care that integrates spirituality and religion into our clinical practice. In our personal and professional practices, we have witnessed the struggles of young people navigating their spiritual and religious beliefs in a society that values individualism, materialism and scientific rationalism. For some, there is a real sense of dissonance between their inherited religious traditions and the prevailing secular culture, and this may, in turn, impact family functioning. They may question their beliefs, feeling pressure to conform to the dominant ideology or experience a cognitive dissonance when their religious teachings conflict with scientific discoveries or mainstream education. For others, their religious or spiritual beliefs may be a source of comfort, providing a sense of purpose and belonging in an increasingly uncertain world. By recognizing the impact of these historical and contemporary contexts, we can start to create safer spaces for young people to explore their beliefs, provide guidance and resources that respect their worldviews, and help them integrate their spiritual and religious identities in a way that is authentic and meaningful to them.

Modupe shares thoughts on the importance of our environment:

I grew up in a country [Nigeria] where religion was intertwined with every aspect of daily life. It was normal, just like breathing. Christians, Muslims and those of other faiths openly practised their beliefs and their rituals were accommodated by society at large. In school, my Muslim friends were given the space and time to pray, and no one batted an eye. I recall hearing the Islamic call to prayer in the mornings from mosques within the neighbourhood. The prayer rooms were always equipped with kettles and access to water for their ablutions. It was a beautiful display of religious harmony, with both Christian and Muslim religious celebratory events being deeply embedded in the community. We were accustomed to adjusting for Lent, Easter, Christmas, Ramadan, Eid al-Fitr and Eid al-Adha, with public holidays for the entire country – meaning no school or formal work on those days. This was a common practice as many extended families within communities had members who practised different religions. One interesting thing to note was that even in hospitals, there was a common phrase used by medical staff and sometimes inscribed as notices, which was "We treat, but God heals", placing a great emphasis on the influence of faith and spirituality in the treatment of patients and their recovery. This showcased the expression of my country's ability to embrace diversity.

However, when I moved to the UK, I noticed a stark contrast. Religion seemed to be a more private matter, and people were cautious about expressing their beliefs openly. It was as if they were walking on eggshells, careful not to offend anyone with their religious views. This seemed more glaring in schools – one of it being no bank holiday to celebrate Eid festivities. However, I realized that some schools permitted children to be off school to celebrate Eid festivities. Children were encouraged to participate in lessons about different practices, some of which contradicted their faith practices and beliefs. I recall one brave child asking why they were not taught about other communities with the same enthusiasm, and their question hung in the air, unanswered. I found that navigating this new cultural landscape was both alien and challenging, especially as a parent, which means I am doubly intentional about explaining to my children our faith, beliefs and rituals. I struggled to understand why things were so different. Why was it that in a country like mine, where religion was openly celebrated, we could coexist peacefully, but in the UK, there seemed to be a tension in religious expression? It appears that the media has disseminated varying narratives about different religions, leading to mixed reactions, including fear and prejudice. However, the negative characteristics attributed to certain individuals or groups should not be seen as representative of the entire community of people who practise those religions.

Faith and spirituality in child development

The role of faith and spirituality in child development is a complex topic that warrants deep exploration. It is essential to recognize that religion and spirituality are distinct yet interconnected concepts. Religion, with its structured framework of stories, symbols and rituals, offers guidance for people to navigate their lives. On the other hand, spirituality transcends religious boundaries, offering a broader perspective for interpreting life's challenges and encouraging personal growth (Kaiser 2016). These beliefs can shape how young people understand the world, their place in it and their relationships with others. For example, a child's concept of right and wrong may be influenced by religious teachings, impacting their moral development and sense of justice. It is also important to consider the potential challenges that can arise when integrating faith and spirituality into child development. Children may struggle with questions about existence, the nature of God or the interpretation of religious texts. They might also encounter conflicts between their religious beliefs and those of their peers, leading to feelings of isolation or confusion. As such, a safe and non-judgmental space beyond secular spaces (e.g. religious institutions) is crucial for young people to explore their spiritual and religious identities, encouraging open dialogue and fostering a sense of self-acceptance.

As we reflect on our experiences living in an individualist society, it becomes evident that delaying the introduction of abstract concepts of faith and spirituality until children reach a certain age is a misguided approach. A simple analogy comes to mind. A child in full-time education begins to learn about the human body. Despite not having physically seen or touched their own brain, they are certain of its existence. Similarly, a young person of faith may not have visibly seen God but chooses to believe and engage devoutly in practices such as reading, studying and praying. This suggests an acceptance that not all answers can be explained through scientific means; some may be experienced rather than logically induced. In Islam, this is considered through the concept of 'Fitrah', an innate natural disposition towards God (Skinner 2019). In fact, current thinking would suggest that parents who help raise young people risk socializing them away from religion if they do not nurture this natural inclination early on. The first seven years of a child's life are pivotal, and according to the Islamic tradition, this time should be devoted to play and relationship building. It sets the foundation for future learning and teaching. This aligns with Western psychology's understanding that children at this stage are not yet cognitively equipped to comprehend complex religious teachings. Instead, it's about providing stimulus and initiating them into positive behaviours, as well as teaching them how to interact and share with others. In the Christian faith practice, for example, children are taught in the church meetings, separate from the adults, giving them opportunity to ask questions, reflect, learn and explore the Holy Bible with adult guidance (teaching); more often the focus is emphasizing the Holy Bible being a moral compass for everyday living in a child-friendly way.

As we delve deeper into this topic, we are drawn to the works of renowned psychologists Piaget and Vygotsky, whose theories offer insights into the role of early experiences in shaping a child's faith and spiritual journey (Venter and Stoker 2020). Piaget's theory of cognitive development (Piaget 1952) suggests that the preoperational stage, from ages two to seven, is a critical period for introducing religious concepts. This is a stage where children are inquisitive and curious, often asking endless questions about the world around them. This curiosity extends to their understanding of abstract concepts, making it an ideal time to introduce religious concepts. Piaget believed that children in this stage are highly receptive to symbolic thinking, which aligns seamlessly with the stories, symbols and rituals often associated with religious and spiritual practices. This allows children to connect with and make sense of the complex and abstract ideas presented in religion. By exposing children to religious concepts during this critical period, they can develop a strong foundation for their faith and spiritual journey. This is because the preoperational stage is when children are developing their understanding of language and symbols, allowing them to grasp the concepts of religion in a meaningful way. As they continue to grow and develop, these early experiences and understandings will shape their beliefs and values, providing a solid foundation for their spiritual development.

Furthermore, the concept of guided participation and scaffolding in Vygotsky's social development theory (Vygotsky 1978) highlights the important role of social interactions and relationships in a child's spiritual development. Children learn and internalize the beliefs and practices of their caregivers and the wider religious community through these interactions, making them highly receptive to symbolic thinking. This allows for a natural incorporation of religious and spiritual concepts into a child's understanding of the world. These concepts provide children with a framework to make sense of the world around them, as well as a sense of connectedness and purpose. As they continue to develop cognitively, their understanding of these symbols and rituals will also evolve, allowing for a deeper and more meaningful connection to their faith. By providing a nurturing environment that resonates with a child's evolving cognitive abilities, caregivers can help foster a strong spiritual foundation that will guide them throughout their lives. This process, we believe, highlights the importance of a supportive and inclusive community in nurturing a child's spiritual growth. Individually, and collectively, we have witnessed the power of these early experiences in shaping the spiritual journeys of young people. Their interpretations of religious stories, engagement with symbols and rituals, and mentors from their faith communities all contribute to the development of their worldviews and can support young people to navigate the interplay between their spiritual and religious beliefs and their sense of self and place in the world.

Modupe shares her thoughts on nurturing religion and spirituality concepts with her children:

As a parent, I have seen my children grow in their faith, asking questions to clarify their beliefs and understand our beliefs and the basis of our morals and life choices. Our basic guide in obeying God is through the Holy Bible where it clearly directs parents to teach their children the laws written in them. In our belief system, what we learn in our lives as people of faith is expected to be shared with children. This is expressed through local church meetings, Children's Sunday School, where they are taught the Holy Bible and how it influences our lives daily. This includes reading, studying, meditating on and memorizing the Bible. This is reinforced by modelling to young people what this looks like. This does not mean that we as adults or parents have fully perfected our journey in faith, as it is always an ongoing process. It requires a huge dose of vulnerability and courage, being open to scrutiny and constructive criticism.

Interestingly, I grew up in a family who attended the Baptist Denomination, and in my late teen years into my early twenties, I began to question the beliefs as I wrestled with questions as follows: are these beliefs my personal convictions as a Christian, or is it something that I inherited because I was born into it? It took me a few years to figure out my own answers to this question. My parents were happy that I was on this personal journey as they believed that a child grows into the Christian faith based on their parents' own convictions, but then the child grows older and needs to discover their own faith convictions. One discovery from my experience was that each person's faith journey is unique, but when embarked on with sincerity and willingness to remain resilient in learning more about Faith, studying scriptures diligently, engaging with others whose faith has been transformed to a strong conviction, the remarkable transformation happens, from a belief to a life of conviction of faith.

Parenting and transmission of faith in the Western context

Parental influence is paramount in the transmission of faith to children. This also extends to grandparents, peers and mentors from their faith communities who play a significant role in shaping their worldviews (Smith and Adamczyk 2021). This combination of external influences, along with a child's own personal experiences, helps them to navigate their sense of self and place in the world. As children grow and develop, they are constantly exposed to new ideas and beliefs from those around them. However, it is through the guidance of parents and other influential figures that they learn to discern and filter through these beliefs, ultimately forming their own unique worldview. Parenting plays a vital role in the transmission of faith, as parents are often the first and most consistent source of religious teachings and practices for children. By instilling a sense of faith and spirituality in their children, parents not only pass on their religious beliefs, but also provide a foundation for values and a sense of purpose in life.

However, in the context of education within the UK, where children from the age of four spend the majority of their day in school, parents have a relatively small window of time to nurture religious and spiritual beliefs in their children. This highlights the importance of utilizing that time effectively and providing a strong foundation for children to form a connection with their faith. By doing so, parents can greatly impact their child's overall wellbeing and personal growth. They can also help their children navigate challenges and make important decisions by grounding them in their religious beliefs. It is therefore crucial for parents to prioritize their role as a guide and mentor in their child's religious journey. Through their loving guidance, parents can help children to form a strong and meaningful connection with their faith, which can have a profound impact on their overall wellbeing and growth as individuals.

Parents also play a critical role in guiding their children towards forming a meaningful connection with their faith. By actively participating in religious activities, children are more likely to adopt these behaviours and attitudes. Bandura's social learning theory (Bandura 1977) suggests that children learn through observation, particularly from their parents, including the enactment of their own religious beliefs and practices, crucial in shaping a child's religious identity. When parents provide loving guidance and support for their child's religious beliefs, it can have a profound impact on their overall wellbeing and growth as individuals. This is because religion offers a sense of belonging and comfort, and can provide guidance during times of difficulty.

For children, a strong connection with their faith can also provide a sense of purpose and direction in life. As they navigate through the challenges and uncertainties of childhood and adolescence, having a strong religious foundation can help them make sense of the world and make informed decisions. In contrast, a lack of parental engagement in religious activities can lead to ambivalence or rejection of these practices by the child. Without proper guidance and support, children may struggle to form a strong connection with their faith, which could potentially lead to feelings of confusion and uncertainty, potentially causing an identity crisis in their adolescence when they navigate their expectations of 'the ideal' in life's situations and relationships with their families and others. As a result, they may be more susceptible to different influences that impact on family functioning. When parents actively engage in religious practices, such as prayer and attending services, children are more likely to adopt these behaviours.

We have witnessed the profound impact of parental influence on the transmission of faith to children and have observed that when parents embody and consistently demonstrate these behaviours, their children are more inclined to embrace and internalize them. On the other hand, when there is a disconnect between parental beliefs and actions, children may struggle with ambivalence or even reject religious practices. This highlights the critical role of parental congruence in shaping a child's faith development.

Modupe illustrates this:

> It has been especially important for us as a family for our children to learn about our beliefs, understand it and how it influences our attitudes and values. This has meant that in my family, as a parent, I am modelling my faith through my attitudes, beliefs and values. The focal point being the importance of the Holy Bible informing our beliefs, attitudes and values. We go to church weekly; when there was lockdown, we joined church online because we do not neglect meeting together. The way we treat and interact with others is important because we are instructed to "Do to others, as you would like them to do to you". We spend time reading the Holy Bible and discussing areas of our lives that have been challenged by the Holy Bible, and ways to adjust and align accordingly, covering issues like Truth, Love, Faith, Trust in God, Kindness, Forgiveness, Patience, Honour, Respect.

Impact of globalization

The impact of globalization cannot be understated when examining the landscape of spirituality and faith, particularly in relation to children and their development. As the world becomes increasingly interconnected, diverse cultural and religious traditions are now more accessible and visible to young people. This exposure to a wide range of beliefs and practices offers both opportunities and challenges for children's spiritual and religious formation. On the one hand, globalization has fostered a greater awareness and appreciation of different faiths, encouraging children to explore and embrace a more inclusive and tolerant worldview. For example, through travel, the internet and cultural exchanges, children can now easily access information and connect with individuals from diverse spiritual and religious backgrounds. This exposure can broaden their perspectives, challenge preconceived notions and promote a more nuanced understanding of global spiritual and religious diversity.

However, the influence of globalization also presents potential challenges. The vast array of spiritual and religious options available can lead to confusion, especially for children who are still forming their identities. They may struggle with questions of authenticity and the interpretation of various teachings, especially when different beliefs and practices conflict. Additionally, the influence of social media and the internet can shape children's understanding of faith and spirituality, sometimes in ways that are difficult for parents and caregivers to monitor and guide. As clinicians, it is important to recognize these dynamics and support children and their families in navigating these complex waters. This places greater pressure on parents to focus their parental influence by consistently expressing their religious beliefs and practices at home as well as involving children in local faith communities, giving their children opportunities to ask questions and explore these beliefs with their parental guidance.

Addressing faith and spirituality

One of the most important aspects of integrating faith and spirituality into therapy with young people is the need for therapists to approach the topic with sensitivity and openness. This requires therapists to be aware of their own biases and be prepared to explore their clients' spiritual beliefs without imposing their own views. This can be a delicate balance, as therapists must also be mindful of the cultural and religious context of their clients' background in order to provide effective and respectful care. This poses a challenge for therapists in working with the unknown, as they must be prepared to set aside their own beliefs and approach their clients' own with an open mind. It requires a level of self-awareness and cultural competence to navigate this terrain successfully. Furthermore, therapists must be mindful of the cultural and religious context of their clients' background. This is crucial in providing effective and respectful care, as it allows therapists to understand the unique experiences and perspectives of their clients. It also helps to avoid imposing their own views on their clients, as they are able to approach their clients' beliefs with sensitivity and understanding. In order to truly support their clients' spiritual wellbeing, therapists must constantly strive to expand their own knowledge and understanding of different spiritual beliefs and practices. This not only allows them to provide more effective care, but also fosters a deeper level of connection and trust with their clients. It is a continuous learning process that requires therapists to approach each client with an open mind and a willingness to explore and understand their clients' spiritual beliefs and also to avoid making recommendations that are in direct opposition to the clients' spiritual/religious beliefs and values.

Using therapeutic techniques in the form of solution-focused questioning is a powerful way to help young people explore how their spiritual beliefs can be used as resources to solve their problems. By asking questions like 'How has your faith helped you?', therapists can help young people identify and utilize their religious beliefs and spiritual strengths as an asset and resource. These questions can also encourage young people to reflect on how their faith has shaped their worldview and coping mechanisms. Narrative therapy techniques are another effective technique for incorporating spirituality into therapy, through storytelling. By encouraging young people to share their stories about their faith journey, therapists can gain insight into their values and beliefs, and how these shape their identity and coping mechanisms. This can also provide a sense of validation and affirmation for clients, as their spiritual experiences are acknowledged and explored in therapy. Furthermore, incorporating mindfulness and meditation practices that align with spiritual traditions can also be beneficial in therapy. For example, incorporating prayer or scripture reading into sessions for young people, or using guided imagery and breathing exercises for clients from various spiritual backgrounds, can help them connect with their spirituality and enhance their overall wellbeing. These practices can also provide young people with a sense of calm and inner peace, which can be helpful in managing stress and anxiety.

RECOMMENDATIONS FOR PRACTICE

A nuanced approach is necessary when incorporating spirituality and religion into clinical practice for young individuals, taking into account their stage of development, cultural heritage and individual convictions.

– *Foster age-appropriate engagement.* Tailor conversations according to the developmental stage of the child or young person. Adapt discussions about spirituality and religion to the young person's age and maturity level. For young children, ask simple, comforting questions, like 'What makes you feel happy or calm?' With adolescents, engage in a more thoughtful conversation about identity, purpose and beliefs. This can be done through encouraging creative expression (e.g. art or play), which can be particularly impactful for younger individuals.

– *Assess spiritual needs*, using customized spiritual assessments. Ask questions suited to the young person's age. For younger children, ask about moments that bring them joy. For teens, delve into their sense of purpose or the things that help them feel connected to others. Encourage young people to share their spiritual or religious beliefs by asking questions, like 'What helps you feel strong when things are hard?' or 'Do you have any spiritual practices that are important to you?'

– *Respect autonomy and individuality.* Recognize emerging identity. Adolescents often start forming their own spiritual identity, which may differ from their family's beliefs. Support them by facilitating respectful, understanding discussions to help them explore and navigate these differences without negatively impacting on family functioning.

– *Involve family and community,* with family-centred discussions. With the young person's consent, involve their family in discussions to ensure that family values are considered, but also balance this with the child's own beliefs. Without this, professionals put themselves in a position where they can unconsciously and actively cause divisions and ruptures within family systems. Help connect the family to community-based spiritual or religious resources that align with their beliefs, ensuring these resources are safe and supportive.

– *Incorporate spiritual practices into care* with flexible care plans. Allow space for spiritual or religious practices within the care plan, such as prayer, meditation or attending religious services, based on the young person's preferences. Honour rituals and symbols. If specific symbols or rituals provide comfort, ensure they can be included in the clinical setting. This might involve providing items like a prayer mat, religious texts or other objects meaningful to the child.

– *Educate and empower.* Promote spiritual wellbeing. Educate young people about the link between spiritual wellbeing and overall health. Integrating this into broader health education helps them understand how spirituality can positively affect their life.

– *Consider ethics.* Maintain confidentiality. Respect the confidentiality of spiritual discussions, especially as young people may not feel comfortable sharing everything with parents or guardians. Be mindful of boundaries. Let both the child and the family lead conversations about spirituality, with your role as the professional being supportive rather than directive.

– *Create a welcoming environment* with youth-friendly spaces. Make the environment welcoming to young people from different spiritual and religious backgrounds. Encourage peer connections. Facilitate peer connections with others who share similar spiritual or religious interests. This peer support can be valuable during adolescence, when they may be seeking belonging and understanding.

Conclusion

Integrating spirituality and religion into clinical practice requires sensitivity, openness and a willingness to explore these dimensions with children and young people. By drawing on our lived experiences and the frameworks provided by existing models, we can better understand and support the diverse spiritual needs of those we serve. This chapter has offered insights into the role of faith and spirituality in child development, highlighted the historical evolution of religion in the Western world, and provided practical applications for clinical practice.

CHAPTER 4

Systemic and Strengths-Based Approaches

AMIRA HASSAN AND MICHAEL GALBRAITH

Overview

This chapter will examine strengths-based approaches focusing on systemic therapy, narrative therapy, solution-focused therapy and the family resilience model. It will explore their applicability across diverse cultures in addressing the needs of individuals, families and communities. We will give specific examples from our practice that illustrate the application of strengths-based approaches. These real-world examples highlight how focusing on clients' strengths and resources can lead to positive therapeutic outcomes. We aim to demonstrate the versatility and effectiveness of strengths-based approaches in diverse settings and with varied populations.

Strengths-based approaches in psychology focus on identifying and nurturing the inherent strengths and resources of individuals rather than concentrating solely on their problems or deficits. This positive psychology perspective, pioneered by figures such as Martin Seligman and Christopher Peterson, aims to promote wellbeing and resilience by building on what individuals do well (Seligman and Csikszentmihalyi 2000). Strengths-based approaches are particularly effective when working with culturally diverse populations. By recognizing and valuing the unique strengths inherent in different cultural backgrounds, these approaches foster inclusivity and respect. This culturally responsive framework helps clients from diverse backgrounds feel understood and valued, which can enhance therapeutic outcomes (Sue and Sue 2016). These strengths-based approaches are in contrast to problem-focused, pathologizing and often medicalizing approaches that have been dominant in Western mental health systems (Fernando 1991) – systems developed from colonialist perspectives that either have racist assumptions built into them (e.g. that belief in and communication with spirits is a form of psychosis) or they are used in racist ways.

Individualistic and collectivist cultures

Understanding the distinction between individualistic and collectivist cultures (Hofstede 1980; Triandis 2001) is crucial for psychologists, sociologists and other professionals working in multicultural contexts. These cultural orientations significantly influence behaviour, communication, values and social relationships.

Individualistic cultures

In individualistic cultures, there is a strong emphasis on autonomy and independence. Personal independence, self-reliance and individual rights are highly valued, and people are encouraged to pursue their own goals and desires. This cultural orientation places a high value on self-expression, personal achievements and self-fulfilment. Individuals in these societies prioritize personal space and privacy, viewing personal decisions and choices as inherent individual rights. Communication styles in individualistic cultures are typically direct and straightforward, with a preference for clarity and the expression of personal opinions. This linear communication approach underscores the importance of individual perspectives and honesty in interactions. For a discussion of the limitations of linear thinking and practice, see Gregory Bateson (2000), and for an illustration of a more systemic and holistic approach, see Nora Bateson (2023).

Collectivist cultures

Collectivist cultures place a strong emphasis on interdependence and community, prioritizing group harmony, family ties and communal relationships over individual desires. In these societies, the needs and goals of the group take precedence, and individuals derive their identity largely from their group memberships, such as family, clan or community. Decision making and responsibilities are shared among the group, with achievements and failures viewed as collective rather than individual. Communication in collectivist cultures tends to be more indirect and contextually based, relying on non-verbal cues and the preservation of harmony to convey messages and maintain relationships (Gudykunst, Yoon and Nishida 1987 explored the complicated differences in communication style between and within individualistic and collectivistic groups). Examples of collectivist perspectives include seeing qualifications and career success as reflecting the achievements of the family, not just an individual. Within a UK context a popular culture illustration would be when football managers say 'We win as a team and we lose as a team', especially when people are wanting to blame an individual's mistake for a defeat.

Implications for psychological practice

Recognizing these cultural orientations is essential for providing culturally sensitive and effective psychological services. In individualistic cultures, therapy may focus on personal growth, autonomy and self-actualization. In collectivist cultures, therapy might emphasize family harmony, relational dynamics and community support (Sue and Sue 2016). Therapists need to adapt their communication styles to match cultural preferences. Direct approaches might be effective in individualistic cultures, whereas a more indirect, context-sensitive approach may be necessary in collectivist cultures (Hall 1976). In collectivist cultures, involving family members and community in the therapeutic process can be crucial. This contrasts with the more individual-focused approach often seen in individualistic cultures (Falicov 2014).

Impact of migration

Migration has profound and multifaceted impacts on individuals, families and communities. These impacts can be both positive and negative, influencing various aspects of life including psychological wellbeing, social dynamics, economic status and cultural identity.

Migrants often experience a range of psychological and emotional challenges. The process of adapting to a new environment can lead to stress, anxiety and depression. This is often due to the loss of familiar social networks, the stress of acculturation and potential experiences of discrimination and xenophobia (Bhugra 2004). Migrants may also face trauma related to their migration journey, especially if they are fleeing conflict or persecution (Silove, Steel and Watters 2000).

Migration can significantly alter social dynamics and cultural identities. Migrants often find themselves navigating between their culture of origin and of their new environment. This can lead to cultural dissonance and identity conflicts, particularly for second-generation migrants who may feel caught between two worlds (Phinney, Horenczyk, Liebkind and Vedder 2001). On the other hand, migration can also lead to cultural enrichment and the creation of multicultural societies that value diversity and inclusivity. The concept of multiculturalism has come under attack recently for apparently leading to tensions and violence between people from different ethnic or religious backgrounds (see Watt and Mason 2015, commenting on remarks by Nigel Farage). Arguably these tensions come more from racist and xenophobic attitudes than by the contact between people from different backgrounds. There appears to be an assumption that you can only have so much cultural identity, and that the presence of other cultures will dilute or threaten that, whereas Charlemagne said, 'To have a second language is to possess a second soul.' Given that language and culture are inextricably bound, the same can be said for bi-, tri- and many-cultural competence.

The impact of migration on family dynamics is substantial. Families may be separated for extended periods, causing emotional strain and altering family roles and responsibilities (Expert Advisory Group on Migration and Population 2021) (see Chapter 9). Children of migrants may experience challenges related to language acquisition, educational attainment and integration into the new society (Suárez-Orozco and Suárez-Orozco 2001). However, migration can also strengthen family bonds as families work together to overcome challenges and build a new life in the host country.

Migrants may face barriers to accessing healthcare due to language differences, lack of knowledge about the healthcare system or legal status (Derose, Escarce and Lurie 2007). The stress associated with migration can exacerbate existing health conditions and contribute to new health issues. However, some migrants bring with them resilient health practices and community support systems that can positively influence their health outcomes.

Eurocentric approaches in mental health

Eurocentric approaches in mental health have historically dominated the field, primarily focusing on theories, practices and diagnostic criteria developed in Western contexts. These approaches often emphasize individualism, a biomedical model of mental health, pharmacological interventions and therapeutic practices that may not always align with the cultural values and experiences of people from Global Majority backgrounds (Watters 2011). While these approaches have been useful for some people for some situations, they also present limitations when applied universally, particularly in addressing the needs of culturally diverse populations.

Core characteristics of Eurocentric approaches

Eurocentric mental health approaches are characterized by an emphasis on individualism, highlighting individual autonomy, personal responsibility and self-actualization. This focus on individualism often contrasts with the collectivist values prevalent in many non-Western cultures (Triandis 1995). In fact, even within a Western scientific paradigm, the idea that people operate as individuals is being increasingly questioned – see, for example, social baseline theory (Coan and Sbarra 2015).

Additionally, Eurocentric models prioritize biomedical explanations for mental health conditions, focusing on biological and physiological factors and often favouring medication and biological treatments over holistic or culturally integrated approaches (Fernando 2010). Standardized diagnostic tools such as the *Diagnostic and Statistical Manual of Mental Disorders, Fifth Edition* (DSM-5) and the 11th revision of the *International Classification of Diseases* (ICD-11) are also central to Eurocentric approaches. These tools are based on reductionist assumptions and Western norms and may not adequately capture culturally specific expressions of mental health issues, potentially leading to misdiagnosis or underdiagnosis in diverse populations (Kleinman 1980).

The inbuilt reductionism in these approaches contradicts a core systemic concept, which is that 'the whole is greater than the sum of the parts' (to paraphrase Aristotle), especially when they ignore some of the parts like material circumstances and living in a racist, sexist, homophobic, able-ist society. To ignore these factors means that people's reaction to being oppressed gets labelled as 'depression' and their reaction to living in danger gets labelled as 'anxiety'. These psychological 'disorders' are seen to have their basis within individuals, either in terms of neuro-chemical imbalances from a psychiatric perspective, or problematic thoughts, behaviours and unexpressed urges from a psychotherapy perspective. Even the trauma-informed suggestion that 'it is not what is wrong with you, it's what's happened to you' can limit the focus to individuals (see Reynolds and Wilson 2024). It might be more accurate to say 'it's not what is wrong with you, it's what is wrong with the circumstances that you have lived and do live in'. The inherent limitations of the Western medical model have recently been critiqued by Gabor Maté (2022).

Challenges in meeting the needs of diverse populations

Different cultures have unique ways of understanding and addressing mental health, which may not align with Eurocentric perspectives. This discrepancy can lead to misdiagnosis, inappropriate treatment and mistrust of mental health services (Kirmayer and Minas 2000). In many African and Asian cultures, mental health issues are often understood through spiritual or communal lenses. Symptoms that might be classified as psychosis in a Western context could be interpreted as spiritual experiences or ancestral communications in these cultures (Gearing *et al.* 2013).

The expression of psychological distress varies significantly across cultures. Eurocentric diagnostic criteria may not account for these variations, leading to underdiagnosis or misdiagnosis of mental health conditions in non-Western populations (Bhui and Bhugra 2002). In some Latin American cultures, somatization expressing psychological distress through physical symptoms is common. This might be overlooked or misinterpreted in a Eurocentric diagnostic framework that prioritizes psychological symptoms (Escobar and Vega 2000).

Eurocentric models may inadvertently contribute to stigma and discrimination against people from different cultures by not recognizing or validating their cultural experiences and emotional expressions. This can deter individuals from seeking help and adhering to treatment (Corrigan and Watson 2002). For example, in many Middle Eastern cultures, mental illness carries significant stigma. The emphasis on labelling and diagnosis in Eurocentric models can exacerbate this stigma, making individuals less likely to seek mental healthcare (Al-Krenawi and Graham 2000).

Strengths-based approaches

Strengths-based approaches such as narrative therapy, solution-focused therapy and some of the contemporary systemic approaches emphasize the identification, maximizing and celebration of clients' strengths and resources – for example a child's knowledge of trains or dinosaurs rather than their social naivete, a person's ability to draw or sing rather than seeing them 'only' as a victim or survivor of sexual abuse. These approaches focus on promoting wellbeing and resilience by building on what individuals do well, rather than concentrating solely on their deficits or problems. Originating from positive psychology and social work, strengths-based approaches have become integral to various therapeutic contexts due to their empowering and holistic nature.

Core principles of strengths-based approaches

Strengths-based approaches in psychotherapy emphasize several core principles that collectively foster a positive and empowering therapeutic environment. First, they focus on empowerment by emphasizing clients' control over their lives and their ability to make positive changes (Saleebey 2012). This approach highlights resilience building by concentrating on clients' past successes and strengths, thereby enhancing their capacity to cope with future challenges (Lopez and Snyder 2009). Additionally, strengths-based approaches adopt a holistic view, considering the whole person, including their strengths, resources and contextual factors (Smith 2006). The therapeutic relationship is built on collaboration, viewing the client as the expert in their own life and working together to identify and leverage their strengths (Rapp 1998).

These approaches are inherently adaptable and can be tailored to fit the cultural contexts of different populations, making them crucial for addressing the unique values, beliefs and practices of diverse cultural groups (Ungar 2005). For instance, many cultures emphasize collectivism and community over individualism. Strengths-based approaches can be adapted to recognize and utilize communal and familial strengths, which are central to many non-Western cultures (Triandis 1995). Furthermore, these approaches help clients from diverse backgrounds to strengthen their cultural identity and pride. By focusing on cultural strengths and historical resilience, strengths-based therapy fosters a positive self-concept and community pride (Sue and Sue 2016).

Techniques of strengths-based approaches

Strengths-based approaches in psychotherapy utilize various techniques to empower clients and leverage their inherent abilities. The different stages of therapy will now be considered in turn: getting to know each other (assessment), making sense of things (formulation), trying something new (intervention) and seeking feedback and feedforward (evaluation and maintaining change).

Traditionally assessment protocols have concentrated on problems, difficulties and deficits, and while there can be some relief in voicing concerns to someone who doesn't judge or make assumptions, it may not open possibilities for future changes. In strengths-based assessments therapists collaborate with clients to also identify their strengths, talents and resources, including past successes, personal qualities and supportive relationships (Saleebey 2012). The use of solution-focused questions, which highlight clients' past achievements and future possibilities, might include 'What has worked for you in the past?' or 'What are your best hopes for the future?' (de Shazer and Dolan 2007). Additionally, narrative therapy techniques help clients re-author their stories to emphasize strengths and resilience, focusing on times when they have successfully managed challenges (White and Epston 1990). The aim is to develop a balanced picture of someone's burdens and brilliance.

This initial information would normally be used to make a diagnosis or formulation, the former being done by the clinician (usually a medic) and the latter constructed jointly between people, usually using a framework (like the '5 Ps' model) chosen by the clinician. The '5 Ps' model (mapping Predisposing, Precipitating, Presenting, Protective and Perpetuating factors; see Johnstone and Dallos 2013) generally focuses on Presenting problems concerning an individual, and four of the 'Ps' are about problems, with the only positive as Protective factors. A more strengths-based (and collaborative) approach would develop a shared way of summarizing, combining and contrasting the information gathered in the getting to know stage. This would privilege the frameworks for understanding people that people bring with them from their personal, family and social contexts.

In second-order systemic practice (Hoffman 1993) the distinction between the earlier stages of therapy and the 'intervention' phase are more blurred and fluid. It may be that highlighting strengths and abilities that had previously been overlooked, or putting an individual's experience into a social context, may be interventions in themselves. On other occasions there may be a period of rehearsing new ways of being, for individuals and the people around them. It is useful to maintain an orientation towards where they want to get to, what has been achieved and the effort in attempts made, rather than what is not working.

There is currently a strong emphasis on evaluating therapy, often using patient-rated standardized outcome measures. Unfortunately, most of these measures are symptom-based, drawing people's attention back to an individualized pathology concept. A rating scale based on someone's goals keeps the focus on their preferred destination (Law and Jacob 2015), and looking at skills that have been gained, refined and strengthened is more strengths-based.

Last but not least, there is the stage of preparing to move on from therapy. While trying to pre-empt and make plans for future challenges may have benefit, a complementary approach from narrative therapy is outsider witnessing. Clients are helped to identify who and how they can celebrate their achievements, for the story of their success to be witnessed by people inside and outside their social circle. This 'audiencing' makes their preferred identity more real as it involves an articulation of strengths, and this is heard and affirmed by significant people in clients' lives. It could be thought of as the opposite of a medical ward round or social care case conference.

Strengths-based approaches can be effectively applied in various settings, including individual therapy, family therapy, community work and organizational contexts. They are particularly useful in environments where empowerment and resilience building are crucial. For example, in educational settings, these approaches help students build on their academic and personal strengths, thereby improving motivation and engagement (Gilman, Huebner and Furlong 2009). In community mental health, strengths-based approaches empower clients by leveraging community resources and social networks, fostering a supportive and resourceful environment (Rapp and Goscha 2012).

Benefits of strengths-based approaches

Strengths-based approaches offer numerous benefits, including enhanced self-esteem and confidence as clients gain a more positive view of themselves and their abilities. They also increase motivation and engagement by focusing on strengths and successes, encouraging clients to actively participate in therapy and pursue their goals. Furthermore, clients develop greater resilience and the ability to cope with future challenges. Overall, strengths-based approaches are associated with positive therapeutic outcomes, including improved mental health and wellbeing, although the research evidence for this is limited. There are a number of reasons why the research evidence to support this is limited at present, and although there is not space to unpack this fully here, a brief overview is given. For a fuller description see *De-Medicalising Misery* by Mark Rapley, Joanna Moncrieff and Jacqui Dillon (2011).

Currently the gold standard for research is the use of randomized controlled trials based on reductionist assumptions (i.e. different aspects of people's lives can be separated, studied in isolation, and considering all the partial results will give you an understanding of the whole, and that therapists and researchers are a neutral influence, i.e. the technique is what makes the difference, not who is applying it). These assumptions contradict systemic and relational forms of therapy, setting up a contradiction between the therapy and research methodologies. Second, there is the difficulty of collating data on therapy that prioritizes client set goals, as these tend to be specific to them as opposed to a predetermined goal set in a research trial to reduce anxiety or depression say. Third, systemically aware approaches (including many strengths-based ones) bring social and political processes into consideration – they question the hand that feeds (or doesn't feed) them. Those in power tend not to fund research into the ill effects of that power. This is further complicated by the relationship between biomedical understandings of distress and the pharmaceutical industry, which has a vested interest in theories and treatments that locate problems within individuals (Watters 2011). Other ways of evidencing the effectiveness of strengths-based approaches are possible, but tend not to be given as high a status by official bodies like the UK's National Institute for Health and Care Excellence (NICE).

Strengths-based approaches are eminently applicable in culturally sensitive ways, as they respect and incorporate clients' cultural backgrounds, values and strengths. This cultural sensitivity makes them particularly effective in working with diverse populations, ensuring that therapy is relevant and respectful of each client's unique cultural context (Ungar 2005). By focusing on strengths within a cultural framework, therapists can build stronger therapeutic alliances and facilitate more meaningful and effective interventions.

Family and systemic approaches

Family and systemic therapies enhance mutual understanding and support within the family and broader connected systems like education, healthcare or religious organizations. These approaches grew out of a range of diverse theories: Bertalanffy's general systems theory, Bronfenbrenner's ecological model, cybernetics (Wiener and Bateson, among others) and social constructionism. Systemic psychotherapy focuses on understanding individuals within the context of their relationships and broader social systems. It sees beliefs, behaviours and feelings as arising from and being maintained by the interactions between people (usually family and close contacts, but can also include distant influencers like politicians, celebrities or fictional characters) rather than residing solely within the individual. This perspective is particularly valuable as it acknowledges the complexity of human behaviour and the influence of familial and social dynamics on people.

Core principles of family and systemic approaches

Gregory Bateson said, 'Without context, words and actions have no meaning at all' (2002, p.14). Family and systemic psychotherapies try to understand and facilitate change by including people's home, neighbourhood, political, historical, spiritual, physical and social contexts in the frame of reference (this is not an exhaustive list – there is always another context to consider, e.g. who owns social media). Not all these dimensions will be explored with each person or family, but they will all be kept in mind by systemic therapists. Systemic therapists generally adopt a social constructionist approach (McNamee and Gergen 1992), that is, that meanings are developed and agreed or contested between people, that there is no external truth/objectivity/reality. This puts a big emphasis on language and communication, and also draws therapists into a more humble position as they cannot assume they are right (about anything!).

Another core principle within family and systemic work is that people are much more likely to change 'under a positive connotation', that people are assumed to be trying their best and have good intentions even if currently the results of their actions or beliefs are negative. This illustrates the strengths-based nature of most systemic approaches, and can be particularly important when working with whole systems, when criticizing one person risks alienating them from therapy. On the other hand, therapists must be sensitive to and act to reduce abuses of power.

Family and systemic psychotherapy is an umbrella term for a range of models and approaches. What follows is a brief listing of some of the major schools under that umbrella, and the theme or process that they tend to focus on.

Satir (Virginia Satir; 1964, 1972). Virginia Satir is sometimes called the 'mother of family therapy' as she was instrumental in setting up the Mental Research Institute (MRI) in Palo Alto, California, and was the training director of the family therapy course there, which was the first anywhere. Satir highlighted that the presenting problem that families initially complain of may not be the most significant one going on; it may be the family's attempt to cope with issues that creates the problem.

Strategic (Jay Douglas Haley and Cloé Madanes; see Madanes 1981). While all therapy aims to facilitate change, strategic family therapists take this very seriously, and by holding responsibility for that will consider using methods that other schools would hesitate at. For instance, the therapist is not always transparent about what their goal is, so they might encourage someone to carry on with a problem behaviour in the belief that the person will do the opposite; a paradoxical intervention. The ethics of this has, of course, been questioned. This approach also relied on therapists being charismatic figures, which not all therapists wanted to be or were able to be.

Structural (Salvador Minuchin; 1974). As the name would suggest, this model focuses on the structure of families, in particular the roles and responsibilities of each person, boundaries around the sub-systems (e.g. the children and the adults) and transitions between life cycle stages. Minuchin developed techniques to elicit and effect difficulties in the therapy room – he wanted to see the problem in action and help people do things differently with his help, rather than 'just talking about what happens elsewhere'. The structural model has been criticized for making normative assumptions, for example about the closeness of a relationship between a parent and a child, but the ideas and techniques have been culturally contextualized by Nancy Boyd-Franklin and Brenna Hafer Bry (2000), among others. A related contemporary approach that also focuses on the power between parents and child is the Non Violent Resistance (NVR) model, taking the principles from the sociopolitical movement of the same name and applying them to families.

Milan (Mara Selvini Palazzoli, Gianfranco Cecchin, Luigi Boscolo and Giuliana Prata). The Milan four picked up the ideas of Gregory Bateson and reconsidered how these ideas translated into therapy (Selvini Palazzoli *et al.* 1980). They developed guidelines for conducting family therapy sessions (hypothesizing, circularity and neutrality), a five-stage structure for sessions, and a focus on communication between family members (following Bateson's cybernetics tradition). This model was very popular when therapy in general, including family therapy, was criticized, particularly by feminist writers and therapists, as using power over people without considering why and how these power differences came about. This led to 'second-order' practice in which therapists needed to consider their own position, subjectivity and privilege in the therapy encounter, and also aimed to help families not only change what they were doing or believing but how these patterns became established in the first place. So therapists helped families become observers to themselves, but also therapists observing and contextually placing themselves in this process. The Milan model evolved the guideline of neutrality to one of curiosity, and is sometimes now called post-Milan therapy.

Narrative therapy (Michael White and David Epston; 1990). Narrative therapy is one of the approaches that was used more within Building Bridges, so is described in more detail in this chapter, with an example of how it was applied.

Collaborative language systems (Harlene Anderson). Previously Harlene Anderson and Harold Goolishian proposed what they called the 'not knowing position', probably one of the most misunderstood and misused terms in systemic practice. It did not mean that therapists knew nothing; rather that their expertise was in the process of conducting therapy. What they didn't know was the content of the solution for each family. Anderson later started using the term 'collaborative language systems' (Anderson and Gehart 2007) to highlight the importance of the therapist's conversational expertise. The emphasis on the mutually influencing dialogue between therapist and client(s) has been picked up by Jaakko Seikkula (Seikkula and Olson 2003) in the Open Dialogue approach (used particularly with communities in relation to people experiencing psychosis) and also the systemic-dialogical approach developed by Paolo Bertrando (2007).

Multifamily therapy (Eia Asen). Family therapy is usually conducted with one 'family' (or a closely connected group of people) at a time. Multifamily therapy combines the opportunity to learn about the people you live with, as well as learning from and sharing with other families who may be experiencing similar things to yourself. This model has been used mostly with families where a young person is showing signs of an eating disorder, but is not restricted to that presentation (Asen and Scholz 2010).

The Family Resilience Framework, developed by Froma Walsh, emphasizes the family's capacity to adapt and grow through adversity by focusing on relational and systemic processes. In her foundational work *Strengthening Family Resilience* (published in 1996 and 2003, and revised in 2016), Walsh outlines a framework centred around three core pillars for building resilience in families. *Family belief systems* play a central role, as shared beliefs and values enable families to make meaning of their experiences. Through a foundation of optimism, spirituality and purpose, family members can view crises as shared challenges that are manageable together. *Organizational patterns* reflect the flexibility, connectedness and mutual support that strong families often display, allowing them to adjust roles and responsibilities to meet changing needs and to foster cohesion under stress. *Communication and problem-solving processes* also enhance adaptability by promoting open, clear communication and collaborative problem solving. Through honest, empathetic exchanges, families navigate both emotional and practical challenges more effectively. Widely applied in family therapy and social work, Walsh's framework helps practitioners guide families in leveraging their strengths to meet life's challenges with resilience and unity.

Case example of a systemic way of working

As an example of systemic work in a pioneering initiative, Hasan, one of the authors of this chapter, successfully adapted the Family Resilience Framework.

Hasan used the Family Resilience Framework while working at the Child Development Centre (CDC) in Qatar, catering to children with physical, intellectual and social communication disabilities and their families. As the lead of the psychology service, Hasan tailored interventions to address the unique multicultural aspects of the CDC clients' population, which is mostly composed of Arabic and Asian families. A needs assessment revealed significant impacts of disability on various facets of lives of the families referred to the CDC, including finances, emotional wellbeing and marital relationships, further complicated by cultural stigmas and caregiving burdens typically shouldered by mothers and older sisters. The findings of the needs assessment were supported by research that highlights the importance of familial responsibility and collective support in many Asian cultures, where the stigma associated with disability can challenge acceptance and integration (Naeem 2015). Similarly, in Arabic cultures, the significance of familial honour and collectivism plays a pivotal role in shaping the family's response to disability (Habib and Sayed 2019). Thus, the intervention's design was informed by the understanding that disability's impact in Arabic and Asian families involves a complex interplay of cultural, social and individual factors.

Given these insights, the chosen approach was deeply rooted in Froma Walsh's Family Resilience Framework, aiming to empower families to face challenges collaboratively and enhance their functioning and support for their disabled children. This framework guided the implementation of structured interventions focusing on strengthening belief systems, communication and organizational adaptability within families.

The interventions led to several positive outcomes. By fostering a shared understanding of disability through psychoeducation and normalizing emotional responses, families began to view their experiences as part of a broader human journey. Some families were inspired to volunteer with organizations that support others facing similar challenges, building connections within a larger community and finding value in their experiences. Integrating spiritual beliefs and practices also provided additional relief and strength. For example, some families engaged in prayer together, drawing on their spirituality for resilience, while others participated in faith-based support groups that offered both emotional and spiritual support.

A significant aspect of the intervention involved the strategic reorganization of family dynamics to distribute caregiving responsibilities more equitably. This reorganization frequently entailed engaging fathers more actively in caregiving roles, an approach that proved essential, particularly in contexts where traditional extended family support networks were absent, such as in expatriate communities. Additionally, the lack of formal support systems, such as respite care services commonly provided by social services in Western countries, further underscored the necessity of this equitable distribution of caregiving tasks. This adaptive strategy was vital in ensuring all family members shared the caregiving burden, mitigating the stress on any single individual and fostering a more supportive family environment.

When we worked with families where different members held varying explanations for a child's disability, the emphasis on open communication and collaborative problem solving proved invaluable. For example, one family member might have viewed the child's condition as a medical issue, while another interpreted it as a spiritual test or influenced by cultural beliefs about fate or destiny. In such cases, differing perspectives sometimes led to misunderstandings or tensions, especially when these beliefs affected attitudes toward treatment or support options.

A practitioner facilitated a family session where each member was encouraged to share their understanding of the child's disability in a non-judgmental space. For instance, a grandmother shared her belief that the child's condition was 'God's will', while a parent explained it through medical or developmental terms. By validating each perspective, the practitioner helped family members feel heard and respected, which opened the door to empathetic communication. The practitioner then guided the family in finding common ground, perhaps by discussing how each explanation reflected their shared values of care, protection and love for the child.

Additionally, by focusing on practical problem solving, the practitioner helped bridge these different perspectives. For example, if the family was open to it, they incorporated spiritual practices alongside medical treatments, respecting both traditional beliefs and evidence-based care. The practitioner suggested creating a family care plan that accommodated each member's beliefs, such as scheduling regular prayers or including extended family members in treatment decisions, fostering unity despite differing viewpoints. This approach respected cultural diversity within the family, promoting resilience and unity as they worked together to support the child's wellbeing.

The creation of a support group facilitated a safe space for parents to share experiences and coping strategies, enhancing community ties and emotional support among families dealing with similar challenges. This initiative not only alleviated the isolation associated with caring for children with disabilities but also fostered a robust support network extending beyond the immediate family.

The integration of Froma Walsh's Family Resilience Framework in Qatar's CDC illustrates the potential of culturally adapted systemic interventions in enhancing the resilience and wellbeing of families dealing with disabilities. By acknowledging and addressing the unique cultural and social dynamics of Qatari society, the intervention not only supported individual families but also contributed to broader community resilience.

This model serves as a testament to the viability and effectiveness of applying culturally sensitive frameworks in diverse settings, highlighting the importance of tailored interventions that respect and utilize cultural values to foster stronger, more resilient families. Through these efforts, the service has set a benchmark for future initiatives aiming to integrate cultural sensitivity into therapeutic practices, ensuring that interventions are both effective and respectful of the diverse cultural settings they operate within.

The evaluation of the work revealed several positive impacts. For instance, parents shared their feelings of empowerment in managing their children's disabilities. One parent expressed, 'I know how to engage with society and I feel proud of my child. I focus on the positives and am optimistic about our journey together.' Another remarked, 'This meeting made me trust myself more in my role as a parent.' Additionally, a mother noted, 'Seeing the videos and witnessing another parent with a child similar to mine improved my confidence as a mother of a child with Down syndrome.'

Narrative therapy

Narrative therapy, developed by Michael White and David Epston in the 1980s, is a collaborative and empowering approach to psychotherapy that combines the ideas that people have a narrative drive (they naturally tell stories about their life), social constructionist processes (how we describe things affects the meaning they have for us) and an appreciation of social power (what is said by different people has different power). Put together this leads narrative therapists to want to deconstruct the 'problem-saturated' descriptions that people often have about themselves, descriptions often embedded in the 'thin' but dominant terms of diagnoses that have been applied by powerful professionals. In place of this narrative therapists aim to draw out 'richer' and often subjugated stories of resilience, strength and success in people's lives, the sparkling moments in a cloudy view, the unique and preferred outcomes when everything seems to be going wrong. In the context of a trusting therapeutic relationship these processes inspire hope and change. One offshoot of this approach is attachment narrative therapy developed by Arlene Vetere and Rudi Dallos (Dallos 2004), which helps family members to articulate and connect with their emotional vulnerability needs.

Core principles of narrative therapy

- *Deconstruction:* Narrative therapy encourages the examination and breakdown of dominant stories that negatively influence clients' lives. By deconstructing these narratives, clients can challenge limiting beliefs and open up new possibilities for their lives (Epston and White 1992).

- *Re-authoring:* This process involves helping clients to create new, empowering stories that emphasize their strengths, values and abilities. By focusing on times when clients have successfully managed challenges, therapists assist them in building a more positive self-narrative (White and Epston 1990).

- *Externalization:* This principle involves separating the person from the problem, allowing clients to view issues as external to themselves. This helps to reduce self-blame and enables clients to tackle the problem more effectively (White 2007).

- *Unique outcomes:* Identifying and highlighting moments when the client was able to resist or overcome their problems. These instances serve as the foundation for building new, empowering narratives (Morgan 2000).

- *Collaborative relationship:* The therapist and client work together as co-authors of the client's new narrative. The therapist's role is to facilitate the exploration and articulation of the client's stories without imposing their own interpretations (Monk, Winslade, Crocket and Epston 1997).

Narrative therapy is inherently culturally sensitive because it respects and incorporates clients' cultural stories and values. It is effective in diverse cultural contexts as it allows clients to draw on their cultural narratives and strengths to address their problems (Denborough 2008). For instance, integrating traditional storytelling practices within narrative therapy can be particularly powerful in Indigenous communities, honouring cultural heritage and supporting healing processes.

Case example of a narrative way of working

One notable example of applying a narrative approach to community work is the Building Bridges Fathers and Sons Project, part of the broader Building Bridges service in Liverpool. This service focused on the psychological and emotional wellbeing of Black and Global Majority children and their families (Fatimilehin 2007). The Fathers and Sons Project was a preventative initiative aimed at fostering intergenerational understanding between African and Muslim fathers and sons, including refugees and asylum seekers, in particular Yemeni, Somali and Black British fathers and sons. Its primary goals were to enhance family functioning in the context of migration and to facilitate opportunities for dialogue, thereby improving relationships strained by migration, discrimination, dual cultural existence and cross-generational differences, and ultimately preventing family breakdown (Hassan *et al.* 2018).

The project utilized a narrative and participative approach similar to that employed by the Dulwich Centre for Narrative Therapy and Community Work with the Narrandera Koori community in Australia, as documented by David Denborough (2002). This approach was chosen for its respectful, non-blaming stance, positioning people as the experts in their own lives. It views problems as separate from individuals and assumes that people possess many skills, competencies, beliefs, values, commitments and abilities that can help them change their relationship with the problems in their lives (Morgan 2000).

The Building Bridges service believed it was crucial to work from a strengths perspective, as communities are often approached from a pathology-based understanding of their difficulties. This deficit-focused perspective can limit their ability to enact positive changes. Instead, we planned and developed the project with full community participation, engaging communities in their natural settings. Narratives containing fathers and sons' issues and concerns, as well as solution narratives, were developed and shared during meal-based events.

We employed the outsider witness framework, inviting individuals not directly involved, such as a family therapist, fathers from the Irish community and a social worker, who acted as an audience to the work. The role of these outsider witnesses was to bear witness to the fathers' and sons' experiences and offer their reflections on the narratives. This process aimed to validate the experiences of the fathers and sons, challenge dominant or problematic narratives, and provide alternative perspectives.

Subsequently, we developed initiatives based on the generated solutions, including traditional board games, DVDs and booklets, which were left as resources for the communities. These initiatives aimed to sustain the positive changes and support ongoing dialogue and relationship building within the community.

After the meal event, six sons who had participated in the consultation and narrative development stage formed a working group to identify and implement an initiative. Meeting weekly over a three-month period at the Merseyside Somali and Community Association, they decided to produce a magazine. This magazine aimed to inform their fathers about their lives in Liverpool, including the challenges they faced as young Somalis. It also sought to document Somali history and culture for other young Somalis in the community, enhance their understanding of their fathers' lives in Somalia, and strengthen their sense of identity and belonging. The project was facilitated by community workers and an art therapist.

The working group generated various themes for the magazine. These encompassed factual information about Somali history, culture and people, as well as traditional games from Somalia alongside contemporary games played in Liverpool. They included success stories of the local Somali football team and notable Somali figures, along with Somali and English jokes. Additionally, the magazine featured personal, traditional and modern stories and poems that highlighted successes related to migration. The sons divided the themes among themselves, conducting literature searches and gathering information outside of their meetings. They brought materials to the sessions for discussion and decision making, and they created drawings and photographs to include in the magazine.

To allow fathers to share their experiences in Somalia, a storytelling session was organized. The sons expressed a desire to learn about their fathers' childhoods, how they spent their time and the games they played. They were also interested in understanding their fathers' relationships with their own parents and mentors, including who they sought for advice and how they learned about life. Furthermore, they wanted to know about their fathers' experiences with marriage, such as how they met their partners and details about wedding ceremonies. With assistance from the project workers, the sons prepared a set of questions. Each son was assigned a father to interview, and all interviews were conducted in Somali. The interviews were recorded, transcribed and translated by the sons. Following this, a storytelling day was organized where fathers and sons shared a meal together. The stories from the interviews were edited and prepared for inclusion in the magazine. The sons, together with the art therapist, worked on the magazine's layout and design before sending it to a printing firm. They actively participated in the printing process by reviewing and commenting on all drafts.

The production of the magazine was a significant outcome of the project. Fathers who contributed to the storytelling session expressed feeling valued by the younger generation and were proud of their interest in their history and heritage. The sons reported initial anxiety about discussing topics of love and marriage with their fathers, but discovered that their fathers were open to these conversations. This experience fostered a sense of closeness, as fathers treated them with respect, boosting their confidence in approaching the older generation.

Solution-focused therapy

Solution-focused therapy (SFT) is a short-term, goal-oriented approach that emphasizes solutions rather than problems, by focusing on what clients want to achieve through therapy rather than on the problems that made them seek help in the first place. Developed by Steve de Shazer and Insoo Kim Berg at the Milwaukee Brief Family Therapy Center in the 1980s, this method operates on the belief that all clients have some knowledge of what would make their life better, despite facing numerous obstacles (de Shazer *et al.* 1986).

Core principles of solution-focused therapy

SFT proposes that every individual has the skills and abilities to solve their challenges, focusing therapy on identifying and utilizing these existing resources. Unlike traditional psychotherapies that delve into past traumas, SFT centres on the future, helping clients articulate their desired outcomes and the steps necessary to achieve these goals. The miracle question involves asking clients to envision a future where their problem is solved overnight, exploring what specific changes they would notice, enabling the therapist and client to construct concrete steps towards achieving that future (de Shazer 1988).

SFT's client-centred and goal-oriented nature makes it a valuable approach in multicultural counselling settings. By focusing on culturally aligned goals and respecting each client's unique cultural identity, SFT not only facilitates effective solutions but also strengthens the therapeutic relationship. This adaptability to diverse cultural backgrounds highlights SFT's role as a versatile tool in the repertoire of mental health professionals (de Shazer 1985; Gone and Alcántara 2007; Kim and Franklin 2009; Sue and Sue 2013).

SFT respects cultural values and beliefs by focusing on the client's perspective, utilizing their own cultural resources and strengths to construct meaningful solutions. For example, in working with clients from collectivist cultures, where community and family are emphasized over the individual, SFT can help clients articulate goals that are culturally coherent and socially integrated. This approach not only respects the cultural emphasis on family and community but also leverages these as resources in the therapeutic process (Gone and Alcántara 2007).

When working with clients from Asian and Arabic backgrounds, where societal expectations and familial obligations often influence personal choices, the focus is on how individual goals align with familial duties. SFT explores how personal achievements can contribute to family honour or how individual wellbeing supports collective harmony. This consideration of familial and societal expectations within goal setting can significantly enhance the therapy's relevance and effectiveness.

When working with Somali clients, where storytelling and communal values are integral, we aim to integrate these cultural elements into the therapy sessions. We encourage clients to narrate personal stories of times when they successfully overcame difficulties through community support or personal resilience. This method not only aligns with the cultural practice of storytelling but also helps in identifying strengths and solutions that are culturally resonant, thereby enhancing the therapeutic process and outcome.

Additionally, SFT's emphasis on asking 'miracle questions' can be tailored to fit the cultural narratives that most resonate with the client's worldview. For instance, in cultures where spiritual beliefs are predominant, these questions might explore scenarios where spiritual support plays a crucial role in overcoming difficulties (see Chapter 3). This not only personalizes the therapy but also embeds it deeply in the client's cultural fabric.

Conclusion

Strengths-based approaches in psychology emphasize recognizing and utilizing individual and communal strengths to effectively navigate life's challenges. This is much more likely to be culturally coherent for the people involved as it involves amplifying what they are already doing (or what they would prefer to be doing more of) rather than imposing a type of solution derived from monocultural, or supposedly culturally blind, theories.

Systemic approaches highlight that people exist in contexts that drive how they think, feel and behave. This wider lens makes it much more likely and possible to take cultural (racial, ethnic, religious, faith, community and family) differences and assets into account and into action. To not do so is not neutral; it is to take the side of a system that locates pathology within individuals rather than the social systems that are harming them. In Western psychology the phrase 'fundamental attributional bias' refers to the general tendency to blame others' mistakes for inherent failings while we understand our own mistakes as connected with situational factors. There is a danger that individual psychotherapy does the former; systemic approaches lean more to the latter. This is good for everyone, but it is especially important for those who have the least power and are the most marginalized as they are constrained and harmed by the social context the most. Taking a more culturally attuned and inclusive approach that respects and works with people's 'natural' healing systems might mean including senior family members, community elders, spiritual leaders, whole person healers and time in nature.

For therapists and counsellors working in the UK and in other Western contexts, systemic and strengths-based approaches can act as a bridge between typically reductionistic service structures (e.g. referral criteria, pathways, allocation meetings and case management) and the wonderfully diverse people and communities they are working with. Not only is this a more interesting approach, but it is ethically appropriate and more likely to be effective.

PART 2

CULTURALLY COMPETENT PRACTICE

CHAPTER 5

Multicultural Psychological Assessments in the Family Courts

EMCEE CHEKWAS, KATE HELLIN AND ANEELA PILKINGTON

Introduction

This chapter explores approaches to psychological assessments of Global Majority families within the UK family courts – in particular, in England and Wales. Family courts have the power to make decisions that have an enormous impact on children and families, even to place children for adoption against their parents' wishes. It is common that the courts are making such decisions about families from countries and cultures that legal professionals have little or no knowledge or understanding of. This risks the courts making ethnocentric decisions, wrongly assuming that parenting practices and manifestations of psychological distress are common across all cultures; they are blind to cultural differences. Just Psychology helps family courts to make decisions about the families before taking account of ethnic and cultural influences. It does so by providing specialist, culturally sensitive and informed psychological assessments of Global Majority families for the family court.

In the UK, the family courts become involved where there are issues facing parents and children they cannot resolve themselves. The UK child safeguarding legal system operates a two-track approach: private and public law. In private law proceedings, a parent or other family member applies to the court to resolve disputed matters relating to family breakdown and divorce – for example, with whom a child should live and arrangements for them to spend time with each parent. In public law, application to the court is made by social services when there are serious enough concerns about a child's safety and welfare. Social services are public services funded directly by the government to provide an array of social assistance and support. They are also responsible for helping families to care adequately for their children if those families need their assistance. Family courts may remove, temporarily or permanently, children from the care of their parents while assessments take place and while parents try to make the changes deemed necessary to enable them to look after their children safely.

Family courts will often face situations in which they believe that they cannot reach their decisions without the help of expert information and opinion. They can then instruct an *expert witness*. The term 'expert witness' can be confusing. An expert witness is not someone who has literally witnessed an event; rather, an expert witness is someone who, by dint of their knowledge, training, skills and experience, can provide independent, impartial assistance to the court. A vast array of expert witnesses may be instructed to assist the court depending on the issues. For example, if a child has been injured, medical professionals help the court to decide if those injuries have been accidentally or intentionally caused, when and how.

Whether private or public law, family courts and all professionals involved are focused on the child's welfare and not on what the parents might want or need. This also applies to the expert witness whose duty is to the court and not to the person who communicates with them about the assessment or to any member of the family.

Psychologists acting as expert witnesses must be impartial in their evidence. Psychologists[6] provide the court with an understanding of how or why the difficulties in the family before them may have arisen and what might help the family to address those difficulties. Some expert witnesses assess the *capacity* of family members and children to engage in the legal process. The word 'capacity' in this context

6   Chartered status for qualified psychologists is awarded by the British Psychological Society (BPS) and regulated by the Health and Care Professions Council (HCPC) that issues practising certificates only to suitably qualified psychologists who can then refer to themselves as practitioners or registered psychologists.

refers to a person's ability to understand the issues, weigh them up and communicate them. The purpose of a psychological assessment is to properly understand family members' feelings, thoughts and beliefs, their social and interpersonal behaviour, and developmental and neuropsychological issues, in the context of psychological theory.

The psychologist who agrees to undertake the assessment must be clear that they possess relevant competencies and expertise for the case in proceedings. This must include their cultural competence to assess parents and children from different ethnic and cultural backgrounds. As multiculturalism is a common feature of UK society, family proceedings inevitably involve individuals and groups from diverse cultural backgrounds, encompassing differences in ethnicity, religious beliefs, gender orientation, language, gender roles and honour-based beliefs and systems.

The underpinning legal framework for family proceedings in the UK (England and Wales) is the Children Act 1989. This sets out the structure for the protection and welfare of children. It also outlines the responsibilities of local authorities, courts and other agencies involved in safeguarding and promoting the wellbeing of children. The main legislation governing children's proceedings in Scotland is the Children (Scotland) Act 1995.

The application of the Children Act in England and Wales varies in some distinct ways to the application in Scotland. For instance, in England and Wales proceedings happen in family (civil) courts, while in Scotland it is in the sheriff court. The two court systems differ with respect to cultural competence. In England and Wales, the Children Act *encourages* professionals (social workers, barristers, solicitors, judges, guardians, medical practitioners, etc.) to undertake training to improve their cultural competence; the Children (Scotland) Act *expects* professionals to *demonstrate* cultural competence. This distinction matters because *encouragement* and *expectations* imply varying emphasis or obligations of actions. For example, encouraging professionals to have awareness of cultural factors is positive but not binding, while expecting them to demonstrate cultural competence is a stronger demand of professionals, one that suggests there may be consequences for not meeting the expectation. An expectation to demonstrate cultural competence helps family courts receive detailed evidence about a family in proceedings in ways not ordinarily pre-scribed in the England, Wales or Scotland Children Acts. Such information can be crucial in helping the courts to make their decisions.

There are often marked difficulties for professionals and for the courts in understanding the cultural practices, family structures and ethnic norms that operate in different Global Majority cultures and countries. Without a good, nuanced appreciation of cultural differences, the courts cannot meet their primary objective of acting in the child's best interests. To assist the court helpfully, the expert witness must understand the cultural needs, demands, practices and norms of those they are assessing.

Key cultural issues within the family courts

Just Psychology's particular expertise is in providing balanced culturally informed assessments that recognize and understand the dynamic interplay between heritage and adaptation dimensions of culture, which, in turn, shape behaviour that is of concern to the courts. As such, our reports focus on parenting practices that may be acceptable, albeit different to those in the UK, alongside parenting practices that may breach criminal law in the UK.

The litigating parties to child family proceedings must agree on what kind of expert witness they want and then apply to the family court for an order to instruct one. Just Psychology has an array of culturally competent expert psychologists from different disciplines of psychology. Culture is at the heart of Just Psychology's work. Just Psychology's experts understand culture as a framework of beliefs and values that are shared by a group. Culture is not a static construct; it is fluid and constantly changing. Culturally determined beliefs and values influence the perception and interpretation of experiences by individuals within that group and how the individual behaves.

There are many theoretical frameworks that underpin culturally competent family court assessments. A review of all of them would be beyond the scope of this chapter, but one that informs Just Psychology's experts' assessments is from Falicov (1995), who uses a multidimensional framework to understand culture. First, Falicov refers to the ecological context a family lives in, including multisystems within the family, institutions that a family or an individual may be in touch with, and communities the family is part of.

Falicov's framework also examines key issues of migration and acculturation – the extent and ways in which an individual has adopted and adapted the values of the UK while retaining the values from their country of origin. These are critical in forming a psychological formulation of individuals and the family. Falicov also looks at the importance of assessing families and how they are organized – for example, dominant dyads and generational effects – and the concept of nuclear vs. extended families. Finally, the family life cycle is a key part of Falicov's framework. This looks at additions and losses within families as well as disruptions and distortions, and the potential change of status in families because of migration or poverty.

A helpful construct in understanding families from the Global Majority is that of individualist/collectivist cultures and parenting (Cheng, Rizkallah and Narizhnaya 2020). Collectivist cultures emphasize values of social obligations, social responsibilities, obedience and helpfulness. Individualist societies, as in the Western world, assume values such as personal choice, individual rights, assertiveness and autonomy. These create fundamental differences in what are assumed and believed to be good parenting practices. For example, children may be raised by a number of adults in a collectivist family culture, something seen as an abrogation of parenting responsibility by those in individualist societies.

Collectivist cultures prioritize social intelligence, whereas individualist cultures focus on scientific and technical intelligence. This also has an impact on learning styles. For example, in collectivist cultures, there is a focus on keen observation, attentiveness and focused listening. Within individualist cultures, questioning, scepticism and curiosity are emphasized.

A number of safeguarding issues often arise when assessing families from different cultures within UK family courts: physical chastisement, sibling caregiving, children left unsupervised, levels of religiosity, enforced religion, extremist beliefs, concerns around spirit possession, honour-based violence, forced marriages, female genital mutilation and modern slavery.

Physical chastisement is a parenting practice that permeates most cultures and is not just the preserve of Global Majority communities. Notwithstanding its illegality in most countries, physical chastisement was, and continues to be, an accepted and promoted method of managing difficult behaviour in some collectivist cultures. Just Psychology experts have found, from working within UK (England and Wales) family courts, that physical chastisement practice may become prevalent within some communities following increased migration into such areas. The increase in physical chastisement may be caused by pressures and challenges that families face in their new environments, particularly when there may be various levels of acculturation within such family systems. This can, for example, result in different cultural values between parents and children, which increases the risk of familial conflict. Culturally informed expert witnesses help courts understand the conflicts parents face in understanding and using physical forms of chastisement. Research (Chan *et al.* 2023; Mrug *et al.* 2022; Sudo *et al.* 2023) shows that how physical chastisement is experienced may differ depending on the context in which it is practised. For instance, if a child is chastised in a country where physical chastisement is customary practice, the child may not internalize that experience as negatively as a child who is chastised in a country or a culture where physical chastisement is uncommon and is viewed as abusive.

Sibling caregiving is another issue of contention before the family courts. There are sometimes concerns that children are given tasks that they are not developmentally ready for, assumed often to be due to neglect and to be emotionally abusive. In fact, within some collectivist cultures, sibling caregiving is a central facet of the family system, key in promoting values that a parent may want to see in a child (Klassen *et al.* 2022). There are also associated economic pressures (e.g. childcare costs) facing some of these families that are ameliorated through sibling caregiving.

The courts are also commonly concerned about children being left unsupervised. It may be customary practice in some collectivist cultures to leave underage but capable children home alone. However, there may be different parameters within their country of origin. For example, the community may have offered children some level of informal supervision. It may be that the child is left alone in the family home, but there is an arrangement for a family member or neighbour close by to check in on the child (Ruiz-Casares *et al.* 2018). Practices in the UK differ. In an individualist society, practices that may have been considered safe in the parents' country of origin may be considered unsafe when in the UK.

Other key issues that we commonly see in the family courts are around levels of religiosity, and particularly concerns around enforced religion (the adoption of a religion under duress) and extremist religious beliefs that are not in accordance with the norms of the state (this is context-specific and therefore definitions will vary in different countries).

Concerns around spirit possession are also raised (Briggs and Whittaker 2018). This can be related to spiritual beliefs about the reasons for difficulties (an example may be health difficulties in a child), and subsequent parenting practices based on those beliefs (such as refusing treatment for the child). The aim of a culturally competent assessment would be to understand the nature of the spiritual beliefs and ascertain whether there are any concerns around parenting practices associated with those beliefs.

Other topics that can also arise in family court assessments include practices that may be more common or accepted in a family's country of origin but are safeguarding issues in the UK, such as honour-based violence, forced marriages, female genital mutilation/circumcision and modern slavery.

Culturally sensitive expert psychological assessment requires a different approach to assessment. The court's wish for a psychological assessment is, usually, intrinsically based on Western notions of psychological or mental distress. This is shown in the nature of the questions that are asked of experts. For instance, 'In your professional opinion, is it fair to say that a parent who uses physical chastisement to discipline their child/ren is displaying signs of abuse and personality disorder problems? Please explore with the respondent parent if the use of physical chastisement is a manifestation of unresolved trauma or psychological problems.' These and related questions imply that parents who use physical chastisement may have mental health problems or consider physical chastisement itself an indication of unwellness and/or dysfunction. Questions framed like these can wittingly or unwittingly suggest that the decision to use physical chastisement relates directly to psychological problems or abnormal behaviours, instead of being influenced by cultural, situational or socioeconomic factors. The very notion of mental health and psychological difficulties is understood and expressed differently across diverse cultural groups. Psychologists working as expert witnesses must provide a culturally sensitive interpretation of fundamental notions of mental distress.

There are often language and communication barriers when completing these types of assessments. Working with trained interpreters is a complex process, and not only adds to the time that is taken to complete assessments but also to the understanding of the assessment itself. The interpreter becomes an active part of the assessment process, something the psychologist must be cognizant of in drawing their conclusions.

Psychometric assessment is usually precluded. Assessments of intelligence use Westernized constructs of intelligence and, as such, the measures of intelligence commonly used in expert psychological assessments in Western families do not apply to all cultures. Psychometric tests that have been developed within Westernized, individualist societies are often not appropriate for different cultural groups (Fatimilehin and Hunt 2013). There are issues around reliability and validity, they have not been researched and normed within different populations, tests may contain language biases and tests developed in the English language may not readily translate to other languages (Qureshi *et al.* 2009).

No expert psychologist can have detailed knowledge and understanding of every culture, and to inform themselves they will need local resources and skills and knowledge of individuals from different communities. Just Psychology has a group of Cultural Consultants from different cultural groups who inform the psychologist in broad terms about key cultural issues.

Case study 1: Effiong, Ekwang and Ekpong from Nigeria

This was a Nigerian family of nine consisting of the father, Ekpong, the mother, Ekwang, both in their early fifties, and their only son, Effiong (14), and six daughters (16, 12, 10, 8, 6 and 4).

The family were from the Ibibio ethnic community in South East Nigeria. The parents had studied at the University of Calabar and gained high-level qualifications in science and education respectively. All the children were born in Akwa Ibom before the family relocated to the UK in the 2010s to pursue the father's career.

The family came to the attention of a local authority in North East England following an allegation that Effiong had barricaded the family home and threatened to stab his parents with a knife. Neighbours called the police who removed Effiong under an Emergency Protection Order (EPO). He was accommodated with the local authority children services. An Interim Care Order subsequently followed, although the parents opposed Effiong's removal. The Children's Guardian disagreed with his parents' stance. Investigating the alleged incident revealed other problems within the family that caused concern about child abuse and neglect. There was evidence of an overly strict parenting style, use of force against the children, Ekpong exerting excessive control over the children and their mother, overcrowding and a sparsely furnished home, the children sleeping on the floor and in the kitchen, lack of privacy for the teenage and preteen daughters and broken furniture as well as marked financial difficulties. The local authority considered the home circumstances unsuitable for the children and their development, and made the entire family subject to safeguarding and care proceedings.

While investigating Effiong's threats to stab his parents, the police recorded poor home conditions. They found the father, Ekpong, obstructive and uncooperative. The police concluded that the mother, Ekwang, acquiesced to Ekpong and did not seem to have her own opinions on the incident.

The instructing parties listed a myriad of concerns they wished to be psychologically evaluated to help the local authority as well as the family court move the case forward. They asked for assessment of the psychological profiles of the parents and children and for examination of the family dynamics, parenting styles, the parents' relationship with each other and with the children, attitudes and beliefs, prioritizing the children's needs, the parents' emotionality and stability and financial status, as well as risks of harm to the children.

The presenting issues in this case were complex and not easily discernible at the time of drafting the letter of instruction. The family were generically identified as Nigerian without recognition or distinction that Nigeria is a vastly diverse country with markedly contrasting cultural influences, leanings and practices, including language, communication, religion, gender roles, attitudes to education, children, women and customs. Even Ekpong and Ekwang came from different South East Nigerian areas with different values that influenced their respective parenting styles. Some of their values ran contra to the provisions of the UK Children Acts.

Of relevance were the gender roles in Ekpong and Ekwang's household. Ekpong was quite clearly head of the family and set the tone for the family dynamics. While they worked in conjunction, husband and wife accepted that Ekpong had the final say on family decisions. He held the role of the family breadwinner and would not allow Ekwang to work outside the home. Although both held doctoral qualifications, Ekpong and his family as well as Ekwang's family perceived his doctorate in science superior to hers in education, thereby further affirming him as head of the household. In furtherance of the idea that the male is the head in their family, their teenage son, Effiong, occupied one of the two family bedrooms by himself. His parents occupied the other bedroom, leaving his older and younger sisters to sleep on the floor in the living room or kitchen. The family view was that the girls would eventually find husbands, marry and move away from home, and that Effiong would inherit the family property.

Effiong accepted that he had threatened his parents with a kitchen knife to get them to remain inside the house and that he had barricaded the doors to the house from the outside, with his parents and all his siblings inside. He accepted that they were frightened, but insisted that he did not intend to physically harm them.

Effiong was initially involved in both criminal and family (public) law proceedings because of the alleged knife incident. The prosecuting authority did not find sufficient evidence to prosecute and dropped the case. The family (public) law component of the case went ahead as more child safeguarding issues came to attention through investigation. As Effiong was a minor, child protection concerns were for him and his siblings and for the motivations of his threats to the family.

Effiong explained that he felt stifled at home because of overcrowding. He said that his father exercised rigid control over the family and would often shout at the children when overwhelmed by the noise and unable to concentrate on his work. He resented his parents and siblings because there was never peace at home. He was ashamed that he did not have modern items that his friends at school had. He said that he thought that if he threatened his parents or destroyed the house they lived in, that they would get a bigger and better house. He felt that his parents, his father especially, did not understand that children's expectations and experiences in the UK differed markedly to those back in their hometown in South East Nigeria.

In contrast, Effiong's parents did not consider themselves overly controlling of their children. They believed firmly in the adult setting the tone and the children following it without question, unless invited to speak. The parents did not consider their home as sparsely furnished and/or unsuitable for their children. They were both survivors of the Biafra-Nigerian civil war and had grown up with very little. They placed emphasis on hard work, academic achievements and employment over material things. The parents expected their children to read books instead of watching television or playing. They did not believe a big house was necessary if they were not homeless. Ekpong was clear that he should earn a living and support his family instead of accepting help from the state, that they would shame themselves and their family back in Nigeria if they accepted state help in the UK. Even after receiving an explanation about the child primacy principle, Ekpong insisted that he and he alone would decide how to manage their children, regardless of what the UK Children Acts said.

There were clear clashes of cultures in this case. Nigeria is generally a collectivist society. While people are expected to and do pursue individual success, the ultimate ambition is for the betterment of the wider family and society at large. The primacy of children's needs rests solely with the father and his family. A father would decide what is best for the child, including education, where to live and who to live with, and would set boundaries and values. This was Ekpong's experience, and he would not have the UK Children Acts dictate to him. Ekwang's part was to dutifully follow her husband, but to influence him behind the scenes. To the police officers who came to her home, she appeared to acquiesce to Ekpong in contrast to their stereotypical expectation that she should forcefully oppose him. Consequently, professionals considered her complicit in their children's neglect.

Of relevance here is the United Nations Convention on the Rights of the Child (UNCRC). This is a globally accepted comprehensive rights and principles framework about the protection and promotion of children's wellbeing. Nigeria is a ratified signatory to the UNCRC, incorporating the Convention into its legislative framework under the Child Rights Act (CRA) 2003. The CRA provides for a broad range of child protection rights, including the comprehensive protection of children, best interests of the child, rights to survival and development and child participation as well as the prohibition of harmful practices.

The UNCRC, CRA and UK Children's Acts are all legal constructs that often conflict with cultural practices and beliefs. As educated parents, Ekpong and Ekwang were presumed to have understood that their parenting approaches contravened many of the clauses of the UNCRC as well as the CRA legal provisions. In fact, they strongly believed that they were serving the best interests of their children by providing a home, promoting education and emphasizing social status with less focus on materialism. They seemed oblivious or less interested in issues about child participation, rights to development and prohibition of harmful practices if inconsistent with their perspectives.

The challenges for experts advising UK courts about cultural differences in cases like Ekpong and Ekwang's must balance the parents' strong beliefs in their parenting style even though the

UNCRC applies similarly in the UK as it does or should in Nigeria. For example, the legal framework defines what is or constitutes excessive force, but its interpretation is influenced by local practices. In communities where physical chastisement, sometimes referred to as corporal punishment, is an aspect of child discipline, it may not be regarded as excessive force, despite how the law defines it. Just Psychology expert psychologists separate out these complex issues and often assist UK family proceedings immensely.

There are other pertinent factors that influence attitudes towards prosecution or not of physical chastisement, focusing, for instance, on survival. Communities that experience high infant mortality rates may focus resources on infants' survival rates over prosecuting parents who physically chastise their children. According to World Bank data, Nigeria had 56 deaths per 1000 live births in 2023 as opposed to the UK's 3.6 (ONS 2023a). Psychosocial, education and health factors as well as economic factors are among other influences that can impact attitudes towards physical chastisement. Just Psychology expert psychologists work to separate out these complex issues and assist UK family proceedings to do so.

In this case, the question was whether Ekpong and Ekwang's parenting style contravened child protection laws, whether in the UK or in Nigeria. There was also the need to understand whether cultural differences were an influence on parenting style. By the conclusion of the case the litigating parties reached a negotiated settlement as the most culturally sensitive outcome. The local authority believed that it was in the best interests of the children for the family to stay together rather than separate them and place the children in foster care. The parents agreed to modify their parenting style to accommodate their children's needs. They also agreed to accept help from the local authority to find a suitable family home. In the interim, Effiong was to remain in foster care until the family had a home big enough to accommodate them all. The older daughter was 17 years old and could leave home if she wished.

Case study 2: Shazia and Tariq, Shabana, Farheen and Qasim from Pakistan

The parents, Shazia and Tariq, were born in Pakistan. Tariq migrated to the UK in 1990. After a few years, when he had legal status to remain in the UK, he returned to Pakistan and entered into an arranged marriage with Shazia. Shazia then moved to the UK two years later. Shazia and Tariq already had members of their wider family within the UK. Tariq had gained employment in the UK. He did not have a high level of education in Pakistan, and worked as a taxi driver, in local takeaways and restaurants. Shazia had never worked. Shazia and Tariq had three children: daughters Shabana (15) and Farheen (13), and a son, Qasim (8), who were all born in the UK.

There was no involvement with the local authority until Shabana was 14 and told staff at school that she had been physically chastised by her father. The local authority investigated but took no further action. A few months later, both Shabana and Farheen talked about their parents hitting them with a belt on a regular basis. They said that they were not allowed to leave the family home after school and at weekends. They had to do a lot of housework, and if they did not do this, they were at risk of being further chastised. They felt that they were being forced to engage in their religion and they had to pray five times a day and read the Quran daily. Shabana stated that she had overheard conversations that her parents had with family members in Pakistan, and she was concerned that there was a risk of forced marriage. Qasim denied that there were any issues in the family home.

The instruction was to complete a psychological assessment of all members of this family. At the point of receiving the instruction, the case was in proceedings within the family court. All three children had been placed together in a foster care placement that was not culturally matched. The parents denied all allegations with regards to physical chastisement and concerns around forced marriage. Qasim was having contact with his parents twice a week; both Shabana and Farheen were refusing to have contact with their parents.

Both girls had started to question their religious and cultural identities. They refused to wear headscarves and read the Quran. They were asking to eat non-halal food. Both Shabana and Farheen had asked their foster carers if they could go to a local high street shop and buy clothing that would not normally have been allowed within their religion. The foster carers and the social workers saw this as a positive development – the girls were now being allowed to express themselves.

The assessment was conducted through observation and speaking to other professionals and in-depth interviews with both parents using a trained interpreter. It was ensured that the interpreter was able to converse in the correct dialect as well as the correct language. The psychologist met the children individually on three separate occasions. Interviews were completed with their foster carers, contact supervisors and their schoolteachers. Views of other professionals who worked with the children were also sought, such as Child and Adolescent Mental Health Services (CAMHS) practitioners. A contact session between Qasim and his parents was observed. The psychologist had full access to medical records for all members of the family.

Both parents were born in a village in Pakistan. They did not have access to formal education. They lived within a collectivist culture. Tariq took on an authoritarian role within this family system. Decisions were made by him and accepted by Shabana and all the children. There was an inherent expectation that the children would be obedient and compliant. Challenges to Tariq's rules were seen as a sign of disrespect from the children. No obvious psychological difficulties were noted for either of the parents.

The psychological assessment revealed elevated levels of emotional difficulty for both girls, Shabana and Farheen. They appeared to have low levels of emotional intelligence and emotional literacy with difficulty in naming their emotions. They were engaging in dysfunctional coping strategies such as self-harm. Both presented with a complex relationship to both their parents. They expressed high levels of anger towards their mother and their father because of their experiences in their care. However, they also expressed love and talked about feelings of guilt and shame because of the complaints that they had made. They stated that they no longer wanted to be Muslim and did not identify as Pakistani.

Research (Perez, Wu, Murray and Bravo 2021) shows that a healthy approach to acculturation involves integrations of cultural values within family systems. The rejection of their parents' and wider family's culture could have a negative impact on identity and psychological wellbeing in the long term for Shabana and Farheen.

Furthermore, the psychologist formulated that the wider professional system was possibly colluding with Shabana and Farheen. As they were the more acculturated members of this family system, Shabana and Farheen's values aligned with the professionals in the system. Therefore, professionals viewed the rejection of Islamic values and practices as positive.

In a collectivist culture, the focus is on expressing positive emotion to maintain harmony within the wider group rather than expressing individual negative emotion. There was an acculturation gap between the parents and the children. As Shabana and Farheen entered adolescence and as they were exposed to cultural values within the UK, their own cultural value base changed significantly from their parents, creating intergenerational conflict. The parents misinterpreted the girls' feelings and behaviour as a sign of disrespect. They both said that, as children, physical chastisement was used to manage difficult behaviours. It was likely that they began to utilize this parenting strategy as they attempted to manage their increasing concerns about the children's behaviour.

With regards to Shabana's worry about forced marriage, the parents stated that they did not believe in forced marriage. However, they said that they would encourage their children to marry an individual from a family who had a good standing in their community. They believed in arranging marriages to support their children to make positive choices about their partners. Their attempts to make decisions for the children may have become coercive. At the same time, there was a lot of anxiety in the wider system around the concept of forced marriage, with poor differentiation between forced and arranged marriage. There was a disparity in cultural understanding from the parents and from the wider system.

There were no significant concerns in Qasim's psychological profile. Perhaps he had not reached an age at which he would present with behavioural challenges. Alternatively, as a boy, he had an elevated status within this family, and there were perhaps fewer restrictions on him and his freedom.

The psychological assessment made no recommendations for individual therapeutic support for Shazia and Tariq. Instead, there was attention to the cultural factors affecting their parenting. The recommendation was for specialist parenting work to help them to understand the psychological needs of their children so that they could maintain key cultural values from Pakistan and also understand why they needed to adopt Western cultural values and behaviour, for example around physical chastisement.

Supporting Shazia and Tariq to change such fundamental cultural values was not an easy process. They needed high levels of support and intervention. The psychologist identified individuals within their local community who could work alongside the parents. A further recommendation was for a family group conference (see Chapter 6) to engage with the wider family to support change. Ultimately, the formulations took account of the wider cultural, social contact and the family networks to help the parents to make changes.

Shabana and Farheen were to be offered a low-level intervention to help them to express their emotions in a functional way and to develop coping strategies.

Despite the significant concerns that had been noted, the key aspect of this assessment was around culture and cultural differences. There was a strength of connection in this family. The court thought that it was in the best interests for both the children and the parents to find a more integrative and shared model of acculturation with a view to reconciliation.

How to improve cultural sensitivity in the family courts

There are significant challenges to ensuring culturally competent psychological assessments within the family courts. There is a developing but not universal awareness on the part of legal professionals that assessment frameworks for White British families are not appropriate for the Global Majority. Even when that general awareness exists, there are often language barriers with obvious potential for misunderstanding and misinterpretation, and practitioners often have poor knowledge and understanding of the specific cultural sensitivities and customs in families from different countries. These are factors that can bear significantly on the issues with which the family courts are concerned, with a risk that the quality of the decisions made by the courts will be compromised.

The presumption that culture is central to all aspects of the work

A proper understanding of cultural factors, including those pertaining to White British people, is an integral part of multiculturalism and cultural competence when working within the family courts. It is essential for ensuring accurate, fair and respectful assessments. Despite the Equality Act 2010 and the standard requirement for diversity training, sometimes cultural issues are still perceived as outside core business. We have known of a judge who explicitly instructed an expert clinical psychologist that cultural factors were not of relevance to a psychological assessment, an assumption (or wish) that was ultimately untenable.

The impact of bias and collusion

A denial that cultural differences are of relevance leads to bias, conscious or unconscious. Biases are shifts away from fairness and objectivity that can occur intentionally or unintentionally. It is important to keep biases to a minimum and/or avoid them altogether to increase culturally competent assessments. Intentional biases are deliberate and wilful deviations from fair and balanced judgements, especially in the face of veritable evidence. Practitioners who notice and ignore wilful biases would be colluding with such biases and effectively undermining cultural competence. Unintentional biases often occur from mistakes that the assessor or other parties involved in assessment may not have spotted or could not avoid due to systemic challenges.

The use of language, for instance, could introduce unintended biases. Using inappropriate assessment tools could introduce unintended perspectives of the person being assessed. Ignorance of culture could lead to misunderstanding of an assessed person's presentations or even misdiagnosis. The problem is not limited to proceedings in family courts, and/or psychological assessments; it permeates physical and mental health generally. Patients are disadvantaged by language barriers and systemic disparities. Al Shamsi *et al.* (2020) stated that patients who do not speak the local language of where they reside tend to receive poorer healthcare services due to miscommunication. A language barrier was identified as a singular cause of such poorer outcomes – it was reported that 44 per cent of communication failures caused severe harm, including deaths in the care of Arab patients by non-Arab-speaking staff (Al-Yateem *et al.* 2023).

Training in cultural competence

All professionals working in the area of safeguarding and the family courts, including judges, interpreters, lawyers, court staff, social care professionals and expert witnesses, should be trained in cultural competence such that they have a good understanding of the impact of migration, acculturation, collectivist parenting cultures, beliefs about discipline and punishment, sibling caregiving, and so on. Best practices should include diverse perspectives, accessible communication styles and language, cultural sensitivity, understanding cultural norms specific to the clients under assessment as well as understanding cultural beliefs and values concerning family dynamics, gender roles, religiosity and spirituality.

An effective cultural competence training model would consist of clear definitions of cultural competence, well-framed policies and procedures and how to implement them. Training and policies would use assessment tools researched and validated for the population being assessed. Integral to such training would be the opportunity for self-reflection, for professionals to explore their predetermined cultural biases, the assumptions and stereotypes they may have and how these influence their work with those from the Global Majority, the advice and recommendations they make.

Training should attend to cross-cultural communication techniques, especially focusing on active listening, displaying empathy and asking culturally appropriate and relevant questions pertaining to the specific case in consideration. The goal is to try to understand and accept cultural differences alongside managing safeguarding issues.

Cultural consultants

In order to bridge the gap in knowledge and understanding between Western perspectives and those of people from multiple different ethnic/cultural and religious backgrounds, Just Psychology has a group of trained Cultural Consultants from a wide range of cultural backgrounds, including the Caribbean, North Africa, Eastern Europe, the Middle East, China, West Africa, East Africa and South Asia (see Chapter 7). The Cultural Consultants are a resource with whom professionals can consult about the culture of parents and children with whom they are working. They offer an understanding of the cultural background of families who are involved with social services and/or in proceedings; this understanding is based on their own cultural background and experiences.

Typically, cultural consultancy informs social care professionals working with families in pre-proceedings and in proceedings, and expert witnesses who are providing psychological, psychiatric or social work assessments of parents and children from the Global Majority in order to support the cultural sensitivity of their work.

Cultural influencers or advocates

Wide involvement of cultural influencers or advocates enhances the cultural competence at all levels of society, especially when drawn from diverse sources. Cultural influencers or advocates are active in advisory committees and working groups. These must guard against tokenism and relying on individuals whose expertise is not directly relevant to the client or families whose needs are being considered. For instance, drawing expertise from Nigeria instead of from the specific Nigerian community under assessment is highly likely to undermine cultural competence and trust in cultural consultation/ cultural influence.

Community partnerships involve collaboration with reputable community organizations and action groups with understanding of cultural barriers to assessments of people from Global Majority communities. Alternatively, focus groups, cultural liaisons and diverse assessment teams are ways of enhancing culturally competent assessments.

Culture-fair psychological tests and assessment tools

Traditionally, psychological assessments for the family courts tend to use psychological tests (psychometrics) and standard assessment tools. A culturally competent assessment would mean that such tests and tools have been established as relevant, reliable and valid to parents and children from the Global Majority who are being assessed, culture-fair or culture-free. They must be robustly researched, designed with cultural sensitivity, available in different languages and adaptable to those being assessed. In order to be valid for people from a particular cultural background, norms need to be established in the culture of those being assessed, and they must be adaptable for use with interpreters.

The fact is that there are few psychological tests that are properly validated for those from the Global Majority. Some of those that claim to be culture-free may not be so. Similarly, cognitive assessment tools almost always rely heavily on Western European and North American notions of intelligence. The cognitive tests are also standardized on native English speakers. Tests are unlikely to be valid for use with interpreters and produce distorted results for people whose native language is not English.

For an assessment of cognitive functioning and intellectual ability, it is essential to look beyond standardized assessment tools to dynamic assessment (Feuerstein, Feuerstein and Falik 2010; Poehner, Davin and Lantolf 2017). These can identify how an individual learns and responds to support/instructions through, for example, behavioural observations in the context of a social and development history; observations of learning style; how the person approaches tasks and learns from feedback; and their willingness to adapt strategies.

Use of competent and trained interpreters

Language is the basic form of human communication that allows people to share thoughts, feelings, ideas and information. Language can be expressed as gestures, sounds, symbols or written. It is imperative for cultural competence that individuals involved in assessments and proceedings communicate in language easily accessible to all and relevant to the assessment. Using culturally appropriate language is particularly essential for individuals (clients, lawyers, social workers, interpreters, etc.) with limited knowledge and understanding of assessment language. Working with interpreters requires specific considerations and skills (Tribe and Thompson 2021).

Conclusion

The aim of this chapter has been to highlight why cultural competence is a critical part of any aspect of family court work. Alongside this, the key cultural issues as well as the challenges to working this way have been addressed. Although there are significant gaps in our knowledge and understanding of working in a culturally competent way, organizations such as Just Psychology work to address and support professionals to understand these issues. There is, in our opinion, a desire to work in a culturally competent way. Disseminating information, working with wider professional teams to explore some of these issues and ongoing training, research and support are critical to what we believe is a developing field.

CHAPTER 6

Family Group Conferences

DEANNA EDWARDS AND NIC BONHAM

Introduction

Family group conferences (henceforth referred to as FGCs) are social care decision-making meetings that emerged from Aotearoan (New Zealand) social work practice in the 1980s. They developed in response to concerns about social work practice with Indigenous Aotearoans (Connolly 2004). These concerns included wider family not being consulted, lack of understanding of Māori culture, racist social work practice and proportionally more Māori children entering state care than non-Indigenous children. FGCs were then enshrined in legislation in the Children, Young Persons, and Their Families Act 1989. This means that in child welfare social work where there are child protection processes in place, families by law have to be offered an FGC (Connolly 1994).

From Aotearoa FGCs have developed worldwide and were first introduced to the UK in 1992, where they were piloted and evaluated (Edwards 2007). This early evaluation showed promising results in terms of FGCs keeping children out of the care system (Marsh and Crow 1998). Since 1992 FGCs have greatly expanded in the UK. According to Wood *et al.* (2022) 58.8 per cent of local authorities had an FGC service, and since organizations such as Just Psychology offer spot purchase arrangements, many more local authorities would potentially have access to FGCs. Indeed, we might argue that since organizations exist that offer spot purchasing options, all local authorities potentially have access to a service should they wish to.

In UK practice FGCs are offered in both children and families and adult social care, but they were first developed (and remain more prevalent) in children and families social work. Since currently Just Psychology only takes referrals from children and families social care, this chapter will largely focus on their application in this area.

There can be an FGC referral if a decision needs to be made about the welfare of a child or children. In traditional social work practice this decision would be made by social work services in consultation with the family. However, in an FGC this decision is made by the family in consultation with social work services. Figure 4 illustrates the FGC model.

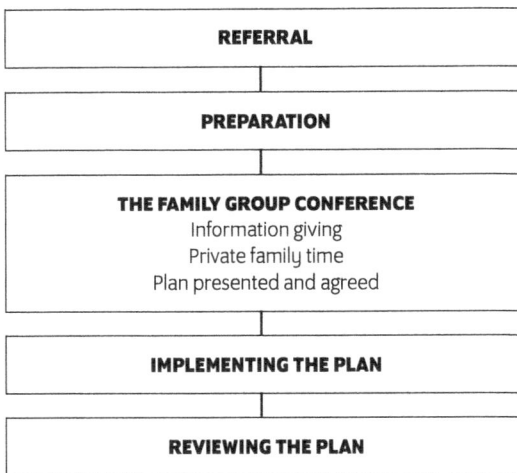

REFERRAL

PREPARATION

THE FAMILY GROUP CONFERENCE
Information giving
Private family time
Plan presented and agreed

IMPLEMENTING THE PLAN

REVIEWING THE PLAN

Figure 4: The family group conference model

The FGC process

The first step in the FGC process is the referral. Many FGC services will take referrals from multiagency sources, but the most common source is from a social worker (Ashley *et al.* 2006). Referrals need to be clear about what question/s need/s addressing at the FGC – in other words, what the family need to decide at the meeting and what boundaries there are to this decision making. Any 'bottom line' (i.e. the scope and limits of the decision, what is not permitted, etc.) needs clearly stating at this stage. Examples of bottom lines might include who the child is permitted to have contact with, where the child can live or the conditions under which the child can return home.

Once a referral is agreed, an 'independent' FGC coordinator is appointed to facilitate the referral. The coordinator will contact the family, starting with the person the referral is about and/or their main carer/s. They will help the family to decide who needs to be at the meeting. The family can choose whoever they think will be important in helping them to make decisions. This can be extended family members and friends, but may also include some people working with the family (such as education, health and social care workers). It is entirely up to the family who they wish to invite, and those considered to be 'family' may differ between cultures and indeed between different families. Once an invitation list is agreed, these people will be contacted by the coordinator who will help them to prepare for their FGC meeting.

Meetings take place in neutral venues, and apart from the referrer, those working with the family only attend if invited by the family. A neutral venue is a central part of the process. Meetings do not take place in family homes or social work offices as this would compromise that neutrality. The family all need to play an equal role in the meeting, and a neutral venue helps to facilitate this and to reduce power differentials. Food is provided at the meeting and is an important part of the process. It conveys respect for the family and means they can take their time at the meeting and not be rushed by having to get home to eat. Food is chosen by the family and is a good way of involving children in the process as they can help to design the menu. It also means the family can include cultural traditions and preferences in their food choices.

The meeting will start with a welcome and an introduction, setting ground rules and an overview of the current situation by the referrer. Referrers should offer a report that is clear and jargon-free, addresses strengths as well as concerns and asks the central question to be answered at the meeting. This report should also address any 'bottom line', that is, any decision that cannot be made and any limits to the decision making. Once the referrer and any other service provider have shared their information, the family will be invited to ask them any questions. After this, anyone there in a professional capacity is asked to leave the meeting and wait in an adjoining room and the family are left on their own for private family time.

During private family time the family will make a plan that can then be presented back to the family during the final stage of the meeting. In this final stage the family present their plan, the coordinator facilitates a discussion about the plan and adds any necessary additional details. The coordinator will check if the plan is acceptable to the family and then to the referrer. Referrers are asked to agree plans if they are safe and legal and address the concerns. The coordinator will then make arrangements for the plan to be written up, distributed and reviewed in due course.

WHAT IS AN 'INDEPENDENT' FGC COORDINATOR?

An 'independent' FGC coordinator is a person employed by the FGC service to facilitate an FGC. Their role is neutral and they do not 'assess' the family. Instead, they are trained and employed simply to help the family to plan and complete the FGC meeting. They do not have any decision-making responsibilities and are not part of any decisions made about the family.

The legal framework

The legal framework for FGCs varies between countries. In Aotearoa, parts of Australia, the Netherlands and Ireland, child welfare FGCs have a legislative mandate, which means that families must be offered them if they meet the criteria for an FGC (Parkinson 2018). No such mandate exists elsewhere, but in England and Wales FGCs are underpinned by the ethos and 'permissive legislative framework' (Ashley and Nixon 2007, p.14) of the Children Act 1989, which emphasizes the importance of partnership working and the central importance of the welfare of the child. For the first time, the Act also gives consideration to culture, race, disability, education and language.

The Public Law Outline (PLO) was introduced in 2008 and updated in 2014. This provides stages the local authority is required to follow to seek a Care or Supervision Order under Section 31 of the Children Act 1989. It states that the local authority has a duty to send a letter to those with parental responsibility before proceedings are issued. This letter outlines the concerns and invites carers to a pre-proceedings meeting. While FGCs are not mandatory, they are recommended as a useful tool in consulting and considering wider family at this stage. Further to this practice, Direction 36c states that a record of discussion with wider family must constitute part of the court's checklist documents, and FGCs are a recommended way of doing this. More recently the 2022 *Independent Review of Children's Social Care* recommended that legislation be introduced 'which makes family group decision making mandatory before a family reaches public law outline' (MacAlister 2022, p.99).

FGCs in Just Psychology

Just Psychology has been offering FGCs to families in the Greater Manchester area since 2015. When this work started, it was a small team consisting of two coordinators; it has now grown to a team of seven who come from a range of backgrounds and bring a wealth of experience and expertise.

Just Psychology currently offers FGCs to the Greater Manchester authorities of Trafford and Bury, having previously worked with Manchester as well as St Helens in Merseyside. In addition, they offer a range of training that includes FGC coordinator training and awareness sessions to teams within the local authorities. All FGCs offered by Just Psychology are children and families social care FGCs, and referrals come from social workers. Referrals are accepted across the range of social work involvement from Early Help, Child in Need, Child Protection, PLO, working with children and young people on the edge of care, Children Looked After and Reunification (making contact or reuniting with birth family).

Within Greater Manchester, Just Psychology is one of few organizations to offer an FGC on a contractual or spot purchase basis. There are some clear benefits of offering FGCs in this manner, including complete separation from the children's social work service. This enables FGC coordinators to maintain a completely independent status, which is perhaps more difficult to achieve when FGCs are an in-house service and closely linked to the social work teams.

In terms of perceptions from families, when you turn up at a home address wearing a local authority badge, it can be problematic for families to see you are any different to the social worker, and to trust that you are not closely linked. Families are used to information being shared by professionals with the social worker, who is usually the lead professional. In FGCs independent coordinators do not disclose what families have discussed with them unless there is a safeguarding concern. Families should be reassured that information they share with FGC coordinators is private and confidential. However, if the coordinator is an employee of the same local authority as the social worker, the family may not trust that this confidentiality exists. They may be seen as part of the social work 'system', and in this sense trusted less than an independent service that has distance from the local authority and is only involved to convene the FGC. In this respect, families may see the power balance differently in an independent service that is not part and parcel of their local authority involvement.

Some of the disadvantages of being a contracted service relate to difficulties building relationships with social work teams and having insider knowledge should the social worker change. Given that social work staff turnover is often high, with figures for 2021 suggesting an FTE (full-time equivalent) turnover rate of 15.4 per cent (Kulakiwicz *et al.* 2022), this can often be an issue. This has caused considerable delays at times when there has been a change of worker but the coordinator is not informed. Another issue can be in relation to updates in the status of cases; communication isn't as open, which can lead to coordinators walking into situations within a family home of which they were initially unaware.

Most FGC services have a non-recording policy that assists with maintaining independence. This means that unless there is a safeguarding concern, details of meetings and conversations between FGC staff and family members are not recorded. This is seen as important to enable families to speak freely with coordinators about their concerns. It also reinforces the neutrality of the coordinator, that they are not performing a similar role to a social worker and not assessing families. This can sometimes create tensions between social workers and FGC coordinators, with social workers sometimes seeing coordinators as other professionals who will share information about their work with families. To avoid this, FGC services must have a very clear non-recording policy that addresses exactly what information is recorded and shared.

Advocacy for children and vulnerable adults is standard practice in FGCs regardless of the means in which they are delivered, either in-house or on a contractual basis. It is how advocates are provided that can vary across services. Just Psychology offers advocates who are provided independently of the coordinator. Volunteers are used and their role is to simply work with the children or vulnerable adult and ensure their voice is heard clearly at the FGC. The advantage of this is two-fold – the advocate is truly independent, not speaking to other family members or professionals other than the coordinator, and there are two team members at the actual FGC, which can be helpful when the FGC is taking place in terms of helping to set up the venue or childcare if there are parts of the meeting family do not want children to be part of.

In some other FGC services, the coordinator also acts as the advocate for children. The benefits of this are that the coordinator gets to know all family members, and hearing the children's voice while preparations are taking place can help the coordinator to identify any issues and address them as part of preparing other family members. It could be argued that as the coordinator is independent, they are perfectly capable of being the independent advocate for children, but children's advocates can be useful when there are complex issues, when the child needs support over and above what the coordinator can offer, or where there are large families, particularly if the voice of the child is in danger of being lost.

Cultural consultants are a key part of FGCs at Just Psychology (see Chapter 7). All coordinators have access to a dedicated Cultural Consultant for any families they are working with who are from non-White British backgrounds. The reason this is so important in the FGCs is that unless we understand the culture of the family, how can we work with them effectively and ensure that their cultural needs are met? Without the use of Cultural Consultants, families may be misunderstood and the service perhaps less inclusive. As one of the key values at Just Psychology is promoting diversity, not to have this element to the FGC would be untenable.

Cultural consultants do not work directly with the family; rather, they are there for the coordinator as a point of reference and to ensure a full understanding of cultural issues is at the forefront of the coordinator's mind, even before they meet with the family. The consultants come from a range of backgrounds and Just Psychology is constantly recruiting new members to offer this unique service as the demographics of the communities in which we work transforms. Feedback from families is overwhelmingly positive and Just Psychology well respected within Greater Manchester for the unique and inclusive service offered to families within the locality.

Analysis of the Just Psychology model

Being a contracted service does bring some instability and there is an impact on the workforce. Just Psychology employs a part-time FGC lead along with two part-time coordinators. Alongside this are five FGC coordinators who are associates; this means that they complete FGC work on a self-employed basis. This model of delivery works well for Just Psychology in terms of allocation of work in a timely manner, and means the organization can be flexible in meeting the needs of the referrer. However, for associate coordinators, it is not work that can be relied on as a means of income, as the work may be sporadic. Despite this, Just Psychology enjoys a relatively stable and committed workforce; many of the coordinators have been involved in the FGC service since its creation in 2015, and as such, a wealth of experience and expertise is provided. In addition to this, the coordinators come from a range of backgrounds, including African Caribbean, West Indian, Black British, White British and Bangladeshi, which enables Just Psychology to meet the needs of the families who are referred, alongside the cultural consultation process; this ensures inclusivity. What is interesting is the level of commitment given by coordinators despite this uncertainty, and this goes back to the recruitment process where the values of each individual are seen as a key marker for whether they will be a good fit for Just Psychology, where values are at the centre of everything the organization undertakes.

The referrals received from local authorities within Greater Manchester between April 2017 and June 2023 totalled 538 and a total of

280 FGCs took place. This represents a completion rate of 52 per cent. What is far more difficult to measure for Just Psychology is the outcomes for families who have had an FGC. This is something that would need to be done in conjunction with local authorities, and is perhaps an area for future analysis.

The source of referrals over this time has varied, but overall local authorities have referred families at all stages of their involvement, from Early Help to Care Proceedings. However, the majority of the referrals do fall between Child in Need (Section 17, Children Act 1989) and Child Protection (Section 47, Children Act 1989), with each of these areas having a total of 157 and 185 referrals respectively over this time scale. It is interesting that there are less referrals overall at pre-proceedings and edge of care, 69 and 23 respectively. It can be argued that when families reach this stage, FGCs have the most impact in terms of children staying within their families as opposed to entering proceedings. There is a school of thought that early intervention is important, and preventing families moving to these stages is what is important. While this is ideal, experience shows us that families do not always want to engage their wider families when they are at the Early Help stage. Although FGCs have been shown to be effective at this point, gathering data as to whether this prevented escalation at a later stage is problematic.

Once in PLO, FGCs can be a useful tool in getting family united around the concerns and what they can do to ensure their children remain safe within the wider network. There is a clear need for FGCs at this stage, and there should perhaps be a mandatory requirement that FGC is at the very least discussed with family. The social and financial cost along with outcomes for children who enter the care system is unacceptable, so it is disappointing that Just Psychology has not been tasked with working at this stage in any meaningful way. Perhaps a targeted approach in the future could have profound and measurable benefits for both local authorities and the families who are in receipt of services.

Just Psychology commissioned a social impact report for 2018–19 that highlighted that 20.5 per cent of FGC service users were from a Global Majority background. Eighty-eight FGCs engaged 124 children and 278 adults. This equates to £729,672 fiscal savings and £109,150 social value delivered. Sixty-seven per cent of children and young people felt supported to engage with decisions about their care, 87 per cent of adults felt listened to and 61 per cent of families completed the FGC process. Feedback from families included:

> Making plans so I can have a more normal family relationship

> We were given plenty of support and time within the meeting to reach a mutual agreement that was best for our family

> Annette was helpful and I felt comfortable talking to her

> Being able to discuss everything without being judged

> It brought the family together and enabled them to talk in a neutral place.

The ages of the children referred to Just Psychology are spread across all age groups, although the majority are between the ages of 3 and 10 (291), closely followed by ages 11 and 16 (286) and 0 and 3 (184). Referrals for unborn children and those aged 17 are 17 referrals for each group, significantly less than other age groups. Gender seems to fluctuate, but overall is generally equally split. Just Psychology has no recorded statistics relating to gender identity.

Greater Manchester is a diverse area and the 10 local authorities that make up the region have a rich and diverse cultural mix. However, the local demographic data for one of the boroughs we work with at Just Psychology shows that the population is predominantly White (77.8 per cent), with non-White minorities representing the remaining 22.2 per cent of the population (2021 Census). This compares well with the data collected from Just Psychology, where White British families make up 78 per cent of referrals (see Table 1). Therefore, arguably Just Psychology is getting representative referrals, but as a whole FGCs are not capturing this diversity (Fatimilehin 2018). Considering the origins of the FGC model this is perhaps surprising. However, it could be that social workers make assumptions around what families from diverse cultures need, and it may be that there is a lack of understanding within social work teams that impacts on referrals. Just Psychology offers training around cultural competency, which would be beneficial if delivered to social work teams.

Table 1: 2022 data to reflect the ethnicity of referrals for one local authority

Ethnicity	Number of referrals	Percentage of total referrals
White British	90	80.3
Pakistani	2	1.8
Black British	8	7.1
White and Asian	4	3.6
Indian	4	3.6
Other	4	3.6
Total	112	100

Case study by Will Golden (Just Psychology FGC coordinator)

A referral was received following a strategy meeting and concerns that a six-year-old child was suffering or likely to suffer significant harm under Section 47 of the Children Act 1989. The child had been placed in emergency foster care as it was unsafe for him to remain at home. Historical concerns were around adult mental health difficulties and concerns regarding neglect and substance misuse. There had been a long history of involvement with social care as a result of the mother's poor mental health, self-harm and suicide attempts. The concerns were due to the potential impact of this on the child and the wider family. The FGC was requested to look at wider family support and alternative carers so the child could leave foster care. It also looked at support any potential carers would need to help the family with day-to-day care and possible respite. The family were of Mixed Asian/Eastern European heritage. The mother had lost contact with the father after the birth of the child and the social worker was trying to re-establish contact.

The family were asked to consider:

1. Who would consider themselves as alternative carers?
2. How can the wider family support the alternative carer?

3. How can contact be supported between the mother and child? What would this look like and what would the arrangements be?

The FGC was attended by six family members plus the FGC coordinator and social worker.

The plan agreed at the meeting was as follows:

1. The paternal grandparents would put themselves forward as alternative carers but the maternal aunt would also like to be considered should anything happen to the paternal grandparents, as she fully supported the arrangements being made because they worked best for the whole family right now. However, she could not afford to give up work at present.

2. The child's mother would have contact each weekend supported by the maternal aunt at her home. The mother would continue to work with professionals and undertake psychological assessments and work with the substance misuse team and housing to look at being able to move back and live together as a family.

3. The Interim Care Order (Section 31, Children Act 1989) and next steps in respect of the child would be discussed at the review. The family understood this and were in agreement.

The FGC addressed the cultural needs of the family by asking if they had a preference in terms of ethnicity and cultural background of the FGC coordinator. They expressed no preference and were allocated a White British male coordinator who worked with them throughout the process. The paternal grandmother requested a Hindi interpreter. The rest of the family members felt they had a good enough command of English to take part in the conference meeting, but chose to have South Asian food served. Some of the family were concerned about people from their community finding out about the mental health struggles of their relative, and were worried about shame being brought on the family. As a result of this the FGC was held outside their local area and the interpreter was not sourced locally. The FGC coordinator worked with the family, both in terms of assuring them of the confidential nature of the referral and offering to signpost to support services that work with the relatives of those receiving mental health support. A copy of the family plan was translated into Hindi so all family members could read it.

Reflections on current UK FGC practice

As stated earlier, a recent survey of current UK FGC practice by Wood *et al.* (2022) suggests that at least 58.8 per cent of local authorities had an FGC service, although we must recognize that response rates varied – from 86 per cent in Wales to just 62 per cent in England. Results suggest that FGCs are becoming more common. The vast majority of UK-based services are provided in-house. Hence, Just Psychology's social enterprise provision is a less common approach but one that arguably improves independence. Some local authorities had more than one provider, and this is indeed the case, with at least one of the local authorities that use Just Psychology's service having an in-house service and using Just Psychology to supplement this. Size also varied enormously, ranging from 5 FGCs per year to 800, with a median of 92.5. Data collected from one local authority supported by Just Psychology in 2022 recorded 90 referrals, which is slightly less than the average number of FGCs per authority. However, it must be noted that this local authority also has an in-house service for which we do not have data. This suggests that although Just Psychology provides slightly less than the average number of FGCs per year, the local authority's own in-house service may mean that the authority itself may well be above average. In terms of the overall output of Just Psychology, since we work with several local authorities providing FGC services overall, we will provide more FGCs than most in-house services. Organizations such as ours were not included in the Wood *et al.* (2022) research, making comparisons difficult.

Data is very limited as to who uses FGC services in terms of culture, ethnicity and social and economic status of the family. It is perhaps ironic that a service that developed in response to concerns about culturally sensitive and appropriate practice in Aotearoa remains poorly utilized in the UK by Global Majority groups (Haresnape 2009), despite the cultural competence of the model whose origins lie in working with Indigenous, disempowered communities. Fatimilehin (2018, p.146) argues that 'the family group conference model is widely agreed to be culturally competent because it takes account of the values, cultures and beliefs of the families'. However, she goes on to suggest that while its origins lie in a non-Western collective culture rather than a Western individualistic one, its practice is very much dependent on the skills of the FGC practitioners who facilitate the process. This will also be heavily dependent on who is referred for the service.

Barn and Das (2016) suggest that Global Majority families may be less likely to be referred to social work services for a number of reasons including distrust of services designed by and for White practitioners and families. It may also be that even when Global Majority families access social work services, they are not then referred on by social workers to FGC services. Fatimilehin (2018) argued that the reasons for this are unclear, but that it may relate to a lack of cultural understanding on the part of social workers and fewer Global Majority social work staff, similar to the concerns raised in the 1988 *Puao-te-ata-tu (Day Break)* (The Maori Perspective Advisory Committee 1988), which led to their introduction in Aotearoa in the first place. This lack of Global Majority referrals is mirrored by statistics presented by Just Psychology referrals, which, despite specializing in cultural competence work, still receives the majority of its FGC referrals about White British families. As we see from Table 1, 78 per cent of referrals from one local authority in 2022 were for White British families.

A recent randomized control trial of FGCs by Foundations (2023) found that FGCs reduced the likelihood of care proceedings from 72 per cent to 59 per cent, as well as the likelihood of children entering care and the amount of time spent in care. All reductions were statistically significant. This research based in UK practice is significant as it represents the first randomized control trial on FGC practice, and results are encouraging. It is therefore important that moving forward local authorities that commission FGC services develop robust methods of measuring FGC outcomes, which will hopefully reflect these FGC successes.

Case study by Annette Williams (Just Psychology FGC coordinator)

A referral was made for a family of South Asian heritage. The children were being cared for by the maternal grandparents as the mother's physical health (she had multiple sclerosis) was poor and it was considered that she could not safely care for them. The children were subject to an Early Help Plan.

The FGC was called to consider if, when and how the children could be safely returned to the care of their mother. This was the expressed wish of the mother, the children and the maternal grandparents. The meeting would also consider what support could be offered to the mother to enable her to care for the children.

The meeting was attended by the mother, and extended family members, a family friend, FGC coordinator, social worker and case worker.

The plan agreed at the meeting was as follows:

1. Contact between the children and the mother would gradually increase until it included overnight contact.

2. The support worker would be involved in supporting the mother to maintain and improve her physical health and support her with routines and parenting.

3. The aim was to return the children to their mother's care slowly until they were fully in her care.

4. The mother would continue with the routines imposed by the maternal grandparents, which included tea time at 5 pm.

5. The maternal grandparents would retain regular contact with the children.

6. The mother's close friend would be assessed as a suitable carer in the event that the mother and paternal aunt were unable to care for the children.

7. Stronger relationships would be established between the children and mother's close friend and paternal aunt, starting with short visits and progressing to overnight stays.

8. Paternal relatives would maintain regular contact with the mother and children including visits and telephone contacts. Since the mother became unwell contact largely ceased, and so it needed re-establishing.

9. Emergency plan – if the mother's health deteriorates the eldest child (11 years old) would speak with the pastoral lead at school or the mother's close friend. Both numbers were on the child's phone. These would, in turn, contact children's services.

10. Maternal relatives would provide respite by taking the children to their home in school holidays. This included ensuring that the children continued to attend the same church, whichever family member was caring for them.

The plan worked well and the children gradually spent more and more time with their mother over the last few months. This was progressing well. Children's services and health services were providing an intensive package of support every day to help with routines, boundaries and other practicalities concerning the care of the children. The family members who supported the FGC were of the same cultural heritage. The grandparents who cared for the children before they were returned to their mother's care were able to meet their holistic needs including their identity, faith, food, care and language.

When the FGC referral was made the family were asked if they wished to choose a coordinator who reflected their cultural heritage. As they were keen on this, their coordinator was also of South

Asian heritage. The family were asked if there was anything they wished to include in the meeting that represented an important part of their identity. The family said the issues had already been addressed.

Improving practice

Barn and Das (2016) argue that in order to work with Global Majority families, FGC staff need cultural knowledge. With their experts in cultural competency and use of Cultural Consultants, Just Psychology is in an excellent position to offer both culturally competent FGCs and training to other FGC providers. Barn and Das also discussed the importance of an ethnically diverse coordinator pool so that families can have a choice of coordinator and choose a 'matched' coordinator if they so wish. They reported that some of the larger London-based services had achieved this and had coordinators who spoke a variety of languages too, offering choice for families and provision for an FGC in the preferred language of the family. While it might be argued that this is an ideal, in practice this may not be attainable for a small provider. In Manchester, for example, up to 200 different languages are spoken, and no local service is large enough to realistically accommodate this diversity. Nevertheless, services could aim for as much diversity as is practical given the size, budget and remit of the service, and use services such as those provided by Just Psychology to supplement this.

As already suggested, this issue runs deeper than the FGC service itself, and evidence from Just Psychology statistics suggests that while the service may well be adept at providing culturally sensitive FGCs, they are not receiving referrals from social workers regarding Global Majority families. This would suggest that the agency has a bigger role in offering cultural competency training and awareness raising to social work staff, prior both to starting to take FGC referrals and as an ongoing venture to account for new staff and staff turnover. Even wider than this it can be argued that social work educators need to do more to ensure that social workers are culturally competent on qualifying. This is a requirement of Social Work England (2019) professional standard 1.5, which requires social workers to 'recognize differences across diverse communities and challenge the impact of disadvantage and discrimination on people and their families and communities'. This needs to be done by threading cultural competency work throughout professional social work courses, including specialist FGC courses, and ensuring a diversity of staff and trainers. An aid to this would be to invite people with lived experience to be part of this training and education, which is also a requirement of Social Work England's validation process for educational establishments offering social work programmes.

Given their flexibility, FGCs are in a strong position to offer some cultural competency. Since the decision making from the outset is with the family, they can decide who to invite and to have the meeting in a culturally appropriate setting if desired, at a time and day to suit their needs. They can (within the budgetary constraints of the service) make culturally suitable food and drink choices. Families can also design a meeting that includes worship, prayer, music or any other cultural practices they might desire. Coordinators need training and awareness raising to ensure that they ask the right questions that will offer families this flexibility. This can help to ensure they are greeting and welcoming families in ways that are comfortable and culturally appropriate and sensitive.

Service managers have a role to play in ensuring that FGC information is accessible to those who do not use English as their first language as well as those who do not read or who read with difficulty. Similar arrangements also need to be made for family plans. Service managers also need to ensure that coordinators and other FGC staff know where to find resources such as venues, food, interpreters and other support staff. Just Psychology is in a unique position within UK FGC provision. The way Just Psychology uses advocates and Cultural Consultants is unique in many respects, and vitally important in meeting the diverse nature of the families we work with. Not only does Just Psychology offer Cultural Consultants to support its FGCs, but it also offers both the opportunity to spot purchase culturally appropriate FGCs and training in both FGC practice and cultural awareness.

In terms of the wider FGC issue, we must also work to maintain FGC standards within practice. In times of austerity important aspects of the FGC process are in danger of getting lost; with pressure to save money local authorities may remove food from FGCs, may cut preparation time, reduce choice of coordinator and impose their own plans on families. Projects must continue to lobby for minimum standards to avoid these issues.

Conclusion

FGCs offer a family-led, strengths-based approach to decision making that is gaining a growing reputation in the UK for offering an ethical and effective alternative to social care decision making. Just Psychology offers an independent and culturally sensitive service that local authorities are able to commission or spot purchase. Families can be offered a choice of coordinator from a range of backgrounds. Just Psychology offers a flexible approach and, like other services (Wood *et al.* 2022), has offered a flexible, hybrid approach developed during the Covid-19 pandemic.

FGCs in Just Psychology would benefit from a more robust analysis of outcomes, and a positive evaluation of this may result in a wider range of referrals. Nationally FGCs would benefit from more attention being paid to increasing the diversity of referrals, and Just Psychology is in a strong position to offer advice, guidance and support on this.

CHAPTER 7

Cultural Consultancy

CATHERINE O'NEILL AND FATEHA BEGUM

Overview

This chapter examines Just Psychology's Cultural Consultants service, developed by Dr Iyabo Fatimilehin and Amira Hassan, based on their earlier work in Liverpool in 2013. The project has since partnered with local healthcare providers and community groups to address cultural misunderstandings that could harm professional–client relationships and to provide training around the influence of culture in professional settings. The project also aimed to improve employability for those who were unemployed or underemployed, particularly Cultural Consultants facing employment barriers due to non-transferable qualifications from their countries of origin.

The chapter will explore how ecological models of human development illustrate the pervasive impact of culture on life, discussing the significance of cultural identity for both clients and practitioners, and advocating an intersectional approach to cultural experiences. It will then detail the project's practice-oriented aspects, such as the recruitment and training of Cultural Consultants, their roles and their integration into Just Psychology's broader work. Using a co-production model, the service design included community and professional training, peer mentoring, practitioner consultation and co-production activities. Key practice implications discussed include venue accessibility, language use and service publicity, emphasizing the concept of 'cultural humility' and the challenges of representing a diverse culture through individual consultants. The chapter will also cover engagement strategies like the role of food in cultural exchange, power dynamics among participants and overcoming socioeconomic attendance barriers.

Introduction

There are these two young fish swimming along, and they happen to meet an older fish swimming the other way, who nods at them and says: "Morning boys, how's the water?" And the two young fish swim on for a bit, and then eventually one of them looks over at the other and goes, "What the hell is water?"

DAVID FOSTER WALLACE[7]

This parable about water, made famous by the author David Foster Wallace, suggests that we are often unaware of some of the most important and fundamental aspects of life because we are constantly immersed in them. The older fish in this story has gained a new perspective on his environment, perhaps through life experience, which has changed the way he sees the world. It can be a similar story when we think about culture. Culture is all around us, shaping our behaviour, our values, the way we communicate. It's invisible, yet it influences many of our decisions – how we parent, how we connect with something greater than ourselves, how we celebrate, even what is considered polite. However, like the younger fish in the story, many people are not aware of culture or its influence. It is often only migration, travel or connecting with others from outside our culture that allows us to gain some perspective and understand that there are different ways of experiencing the world.

Researchers and community practitioners often employ ecological models to consider the influence of culture on individuals. These outline the networks and systems surrounding a person, from close relationships like family to more distant yet influential factors such as societal values or culture. Ecological systems theory (Bronfenbrenner 1992) is a widely accepted approach that explains how

---

7   Adapted from the commencement speech the author gave to a graduating class at Kenyon College, Ohio: Foster Wallace, D. (2008) 'Plain old untrendy troubles and emotions.' *The Guardian*, 20 September.

social environments impact human development by mapping out concentric layers of ecological systems (see Figure 6).

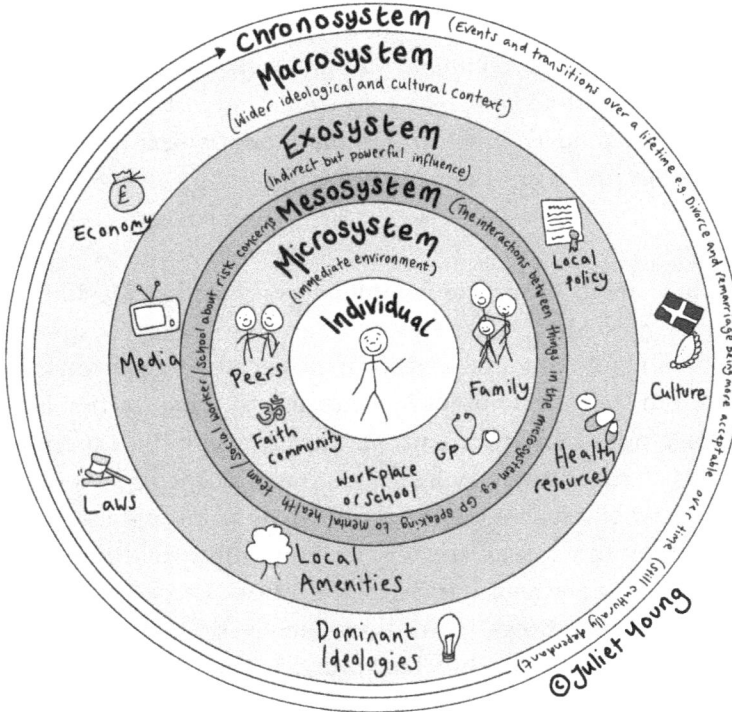

Figure 6: Ecological systems theory

Ecological systems

Microsystem

The microsystem encompasses direct relationships experienced in daily life, including with family, peers, school or workplace, faith community or services accessed. The culture, values and attitudes of these groups significantly impact an individual's development, which is supported by extensive research (Arias and Punyanunt-Carter 2017; Bukowski and Adams 2005; Mitic *et al.* 2021; Quintana *et al.* 2006). Disparities among cultural groups in the UK across education, health, deprivation, employment, policing and criminal justice highlight the influence of cultural factors on developmental outcomes (Cabinet Office 2018).

Mesosystem

The mesosystem illustrates how interactions within the microsystem affect individuals. For instance, strong cultural values within a family regarding education can positively influence a young person's academic achievements, while negative attitudes within a school toward Global Majority families can hinder a student's progress (Smith, Atkins and Connell 2003). Family perceptions of services can also affect whether they seek help – for example there can be a fear of authorities in some communities, sometimes based on hearsay or past experience (Bernard 2020). This can impact on a child or individual indirectly, in terms of their attitude to accessing support. This was seen during the Covid-19 pandemic, where Global Majority communities placed greater importance on the advice of people from their own family or community than public health medical officials (Eberhardt *et al.* 2022).

Exosystem

The exosystem encompasses broader social systems indirectly impacting an individual's development. Local policies, healthcare practices, workplace environments and mass media all play roles. In the UK, disparities in housing quality and access to social housing disproportionately affect Global Majority populations. Some examples include within the housing system, where individuals and families from Global Majority populations living in the UK are more likely to live in crowded or poor quality housing (Gulliver 2016; Haque, Becares and Treloar 2020; Kowalewska 2018; McFarlane 2014). Healthcare disparities, influenced by culture, language barriers and service decisions, further highlight the exosystem's impact (Ajayi 2021; Lehane and Campion 2018). There are additional barriers to accessing social housing for some Global Majority populations, heightened since the Localism Act 2011, which gave local authorities the power to limit access to social housing. Thus, many find themselves having to rely on an expensive and insecure private housing sector for accommodation (Bristow 2021).

There are also inequalities with regards to health within UK communities, and while poverty and deprivation has been suggested as an underpinning factor (Otu 2020), others have suggested a role of culture, language barriers and local decisions about whether to fund interpreters within services as a potential barrier to accessing support (Ajayi 2021; Lehane and Campion 2018). Initiatives promoting cultural understanding among healthcare professionals have shown moderate success in improving health outcomes (Horvat *et al.* 2014).

The mass media, a crucial exosystem component, often shapes societal attitudes and perceptions of sections of the populations. In the case of Global Majority communities, who are generally underrepresented in the UK mass media, there is an overrepresentation in relation to stories about immigration, crime and terrorism (Firmstone *et al.* 2009). Negative portrayals can therefore indirectly influence interactions within an individual's microsystem by impacting on social attitudes and values (Bjornstrom *et al.* 2010; Frost 2008; Hargreaves 2013).

Macrosystem

The macrosystem encompasses a society's cultural, ideological and political landscape, indirectly impacting individuals (Bronfenbrenner 1992). One example of macrosystemic influences includes the UK government's approach to Global Majority populations, which reveals contradictions between inclusivity and restrictive migration policies. Government documents advocate for trust, fairness and increased agency to integrate these communities (HM Government 2022). Yet the contentious 'Stop the Boats' Bill (2023) proposed harsh measures for migrants, including the use of detention centres and/or deportation to Rwanda, raising concerns by critics over human rights violations (Arnell *et al.* 2023; Home Office 2023; Stevens, Kingdon and Devakumar 2023).

Contrastingly, surveys by Ipsos MORI (Kaur-Ballagan 2020) and the British Social Attitudes Survey (National Centre for Social Research 2022) show a liberal shift in UK public opinion towards cultural diversity and immigration. Despite this, there are, however, significant differences in attitudes between those with socially conservative vs. liberal perspectives, and this has been reflected in much of the mass media 'culture wars' debate in recent years (Cammaerts 2022; Fernández-Reino 2020; Krzyżanowski and Ekström 2022; Zavattaro and Bearfield 2022). This may be a contributing factor towards the 19 per cent of non-EU migrants in 2018 who described themselves as members of a group who have experienced discrimination due to their ethnicity, race, religion or nationality, with 13 per cent stating they had been insulted due to their group membership (Fernández-Reino 2020). Yet a majority still find the UK welcoming, particularly those born outside it, although generational differences in stigma persist, with second-generation members more likely to feel treated as 'outsiders' despite being born in the UK (Giuliani *et al.* 2018). These dynamics suggest complex social attitudes impacting communities both positively and negatively.

The role of intersectionality and barriers to accessing support

When considering intersecting social identities, it's important to recognize how belonging to multiple groups can lead to diverse experiences. For example, women of different ethnicities or religious backgrounds may have varying experiences, which policies often overlook if they lack an intersectional perspective (Hankivsky and Cormier 2019). National policies promoting workplace equality for women may not equally benefit all, particularly Global Majority women, whose needs and voices are frequently absent from such discussions (Branscombe and Ryan 2013).

Additionally, a lack of cultural awareness in service provision can deter access and negatively affect user experiences (see Figure 7). Research identifies barriers at individual, practitioner and systemic levels, such as a lack of cultural awareness and communication style of practitioners, service referral processes, opening hours, consultation times and accessibility of printed materials (Scheppers *et al.* 2006). Similar findings around barriers to accessing mental health services suggest that language barriers, power imbalance and poor recognition and response to mental health need and cultural insensitivity impact service uptake and use (Memon *et al.* 2016). Proactive policies are necessary to improve engagement and service utilization, especially in mental healthcare.

Figure 7: Hard to reach groups vs. services

As many services struggle to effectively engage with Global Majority populations, strategies are needed to enhance access and cultivate cultural awareness among staff. Co-production approaches, involving service users or those with lived experience, show promise in increasing service uptake and retention (Hatzidimitriadou, Mantovani and Keating 2012; Lwembe *et al.* 2017; Vahdaninia *et al.* 2020). Overcoming participation barriers, reaching diverse communities, building trust and involving community leaders are crucial steps (Ocloo and Matthews 2016). Adequate resourcing is essential for meaningful co-production efforts, requiring time, resources and ongoing communication with those with lived experience (Oliver, Kothari and Mays 2019; O. Williams *et al.* 2020).

One way of involving individuals from Global Majority populations is through the use of cultural consultancy/interpreting/mediating. Guidance is emerging on the training of interpreters to include cultural information in their translations (Katan and Taibi 2021). The Cultural Consultants scheme was developed by Just Psychology in 2013, and four iterations of this service have now been delivered and evaluated.

The Cultural Consultants service

The Cultural Consultants service was developed in response to extensive professional and personal experience of inaccessible service provision in the NHS. This was supported by research literature that suggested that Global Majority communities encounter negative experiences with statutory services and have a lack of confidence in services and practitioners to understand and meet their cultural and religious needs.

Cultural consultants act as bridges between professionals in health, education and social care services and Global Majority communities. They provide consultations to foster understanding, assisting practitioners in exploring the cultural identity of service users to inform assessments and offering training or peer mentoring.

It's crucial to distinguish Cultural Consultants from interpreters. While interpreters focus solely on language, Cultural Consultants delve into cultural nuances, providing context and meaning to service users' voices and facilitating an understanding of culture (and sub-culture). The Just Psychology Cultural Consultant service is available to anyone working with culturally diverse communities, offering training to enhance professionals' cultural competence and ensure services meet the specific needs of each community.

Recruitment of consultants: understanding communities and co-production of the project

During the initial Cultural Consultants Project, 24 individuals were recruited from a range of communities. An important aspect of the project was using creative ways to work with and involve people from these communities, with a range of strategies.

One Cultural Consultant reflects on her motives for being involved in the project:

> My journey to becoming a Cultural Consultant at Just Psychology was profoundly influenced by my personal experience of resettling in the UK as a refugee, and having to navigate the complex and daunting system, a process fraught with challenges. Fortunate to have had family support, and most importantly being proficient in English language, I was able to overcome several hurdles, although the journey was far from easy and the emotional strain quite significant. It was therefore a logical progression for me to cultivate a deep-seated sense of duty and commitment to enhance and promote cultural understanding and inclusivity among organizations and service providers working with diverse communities. I draw from my personal experience in understanding and supporting these communities especially my own, and I am strongly motivated to guide and support them in their process of adopting to life in the UK.

TOP TIPS FOR RECRUITING FROM GLOBAL MAJORITY COMMUNITIES

– Contact organizations that work with the target population to find out more about them. For example, Just Psychology contacted CHIC (Chinese Health Information Centre), the Somali Adult Social Care Agency (SASCA) and Europia (a European migrant-specific organization) to gain knowledge and contacts within communities.

– Make sure any leaflet campaigns are targeted in areas and shops/ local businesses frequented by the population you want to recruit. One important lesson learned was that certain communities were more densely populated in certain areas, and posters/informal conversations in those areas helped recruitment.

- Do provide in-person information sessions where the community is located, so that people have a low-stakes setting to ask questions and decide about their involvement prior to signing up.

- Do demonstrate that you value the work and time of Cultural Consultants – the cultural knowledge that people have has a value, so look to budget in payment for your participants or Cultural Consultants, even if many would do so voluntarily. The Cultural Consultants role was pitched as an opportunity to gain accredited training and would be paid.

- Always consider childcare arrangements when arranging sessions – hosting sessions between 10 am and 2 pm can be helpful as they are within school hours. Consider budgeting and paying for a creche to facilitate attendance of people from Global Majority communities, who may have less availability of childcare.

- Consider the location of your sessions – ensure they are held in an accessible place that is on major public transport routes.

- Provide an overview of training, dates, times and venues to potential participants to check they can commit to it.

- Be transparent about what will happen after the training, e.g. what the likely level of uptake of their professional input is.

- Pay attendees for travel and parking to ensure finances are not a barrier to participating.

Training Cultural Consultants

In subsequent iterations of the Cultural Consultants Project, a key enhancement was accrediting the training through an external provider, the AQA (Assessment and Qualifications Alliance). This accreditation, implemented from the second iteration onwards, transformed the six-module training into accredited courses offering ten credits across various topics. Participants received official certificates, enhancing their future employability – a core objective of the project. Just Psychology prioritizes not just the outcomes but also the process of projects, aiming to support underemployed or unemployed individuals in communities through valuable training opportunities. However, it is crucial to acknowledge that migrants to the UK often face challenges due to their professional qualifications not being recognized, leading to unemployment, rather than a lack of skills or training. Many individuals join the Cultural Consultants training out of a desire to empower and support their communities despite their personal challenges.

The development of training materials and selection of guest speakers for the modules were collaborative efforts involving Cultural Consultants from previous projects. Sessions were co-delivered with Cultural Consultants where appropriate. The six-week training course covered modules such as Professionalism and professional boundaries, Working with health, education and social care systems, Counselling skills, Working with interpreters and Working across cultures, and specialized topics like Working with survivors of sexual violence and Peer mentoring.

Participants from all courses reflected on the profound experience of training with individuals from diverse backgrounds. The rich discussions and varied perspectives highlighted the importance of cultural considerations in various aspects of life, including physical contact, childrearing norms, familial and community dynamics, and views on healthcare and mental health. Despite the diversity, participants also noted remarkable similarities in experiences alongside differences in customs and values.

TOP TIPS ON TRAINING CULTURAL CONSULTANTS

- Food is a great way to share culture. The projects included a budget to provide a range of foods related to the background of attendees. Sharing this food at lunchtime offered an opportunity for people to discuss and share their heritage in a positive way.

- Be aware of the influence of more confident and dominant group members vs. quieter ones. Evaluation of the initial Cultural Consultants Project suggested that it is important to check in with quieter members to ensure they understand fully what has been covered in the material.

- However, more outspoken group members can have a positive modelling impact on the overall group and encourage others to speak out.

- Leave extra time for discussion throughout the training; the richness of the discussion is understanding all the different perspectives on the material, rather than 'broadcasting' your slides and content. For example, the session on cultural norms was particularly interesting and involved a wide range of perspectives on e.g. physical contact, treatment of elders and childrearing practices.

- Similar to your engagement and information sessions, take into consideration the childcare commitments of attendees. Sessions were held between 10 am and 2 pm to facilitate attendance.

- Consider socioeconomic barriers to attendance at workshops, paid sessions and ensure consultants are paid in a timely manner. Transport can be a challenge as can out-of-pocket expenses in advance, so ensure that there is provision to allow people to participate – perhaps through petty cash or providing bus tickets in advance.

- Make sure there is time out for a check-in after training sessions, particularly if distressing content has been discussed. Some Cultural Consultants may have direct experiences of trauma, which may be triggered.

- Make time for extra support and questions around assessments for accreditation or understanding content.

Feedback on the Cultural Consultants training included the following, which highlights the impact on attendees, as well as knowledge gained:

> And this is the biggest advantage of the training and the whole project, meeting all those amazing people (students but also Just Psychology people like you, Survivors Manchester people, previous Cultural Consultants, experts/speakers), learning from them, be inspired by them... I also never felt so welcome and listened and understood like during the training and later on during the project. Being surrounded by people who share the same beliefs, often have different opinions, but the core values are the same, which is equality, respect for other cultures, for each other; that special sensitivity we share made me believe in people but also in myself and in my community again or stronger than before.

Another Cultural Consultant reflected on her experiences of the project after her loss of professional status impacted her identity and self-esteem:

> Prior to arriving to the UK, I studied Linguistics in Asmara, Eritrea and worked for the Ministry of Information and Italian Embassy. One of the challenges arriving to the UK is my qualifications and experience are not recognized and when arriving to a new country your previous professional identity no longer exists, causing low confidence and self-esteem. Arriving in a new country you mourn the loss of identity and to carve out a new identity is complex within UK education systems. However, Just Psychology, through the enriching Cultural Consultant training, I have gained deeper understanding into the intricacies of diverse cultures and the dynamics of communicating effectively with immigrant communities. This organization has equipped me with essential expertise to enhance my advocacy and support for the individuals and families I serve, thereby fostering trust and building strong relationships in my role as a Cultural Consultant to help communities.

The initial Cultural Consultants service began in 2013 after securing

National Lottery Awards for All England funding. A pilot project was launched to develop and train Cultural Consultants from local communities in Greater Manchester. The aim of the project was to make services more accessible to culturally and linguistically diverse communities by facilitating understanding and communication between Global Majority service users and professionals. The projects were also delivered in 2017 and 2022–23.

Table 2: Project summaries

Project/date	Number recruited	Ethnic background of Cultural Consultants	Focus and activities
Project 1: Original Cultural Consultants service (2013)	24	Caribbean, African (Congolese, Zambian, Nigerian), Arab, Pakistani, Mixed, White (Other), Asian (Malaysian), Bangladeshi, Black British, Black (Other)	To increase understanding of health and social care professionals of diverse communities To increase access to services for those from Global Majority communities
Project 2: Survivors Manchester Project (now We Are Survivors) (2017)	13	Chinese, Eastern European, Somali, Iranian, African	The project was working with Survivors Manchester in order to increase awareness of and help seeking around male sexual abuse and sexual violence in key excluded communities (Chinese, Somali and Eastern European), and to increase the accessibility of Survivors Manchester
Project 3: Family Reunion and Parenting Project (2021–22)	13	Eritrean, Pakistani, Bangladeshi, Sudanese, Yemeni, Congolese and Nigerian	Cultural consultants provided support and peer mentoring to families and professionals around reunification and support with accessing services after serial migration. This project was undertaken in partnership with Rainbow Haven

Project/date	Number recruited	Ethnic background of Cultural Consultants	Focus and activities
Project 4: Sexual Violence Harm Reduction Project (2022–23)	13	Sudanese, Eritrean, Ethiopian, Nigerian, Pakistani and Bengali	The aim of this one-year project was to raise awareness of sexual violence in Black, Asian and minority ethnic communities and to increase accessibility of existing services

Stories from the projects

Project 2: Survivors Manchester (now We Are Survivors) (2017)

Survivors Manchester, now We Are Survivors, is a Manchester-based charity supporting males who have experienced sexual violence. It identified low engagement from Somali, Eastern European and Chinese communities in its services. To address this, Just Psychology recruited and trained Cultural Consultants from these groups to improve outreach and understanding. These consultants were selected through targeted advertising and information sessions that explained the role and provided a platform for inquiries. Two such sessions attracted 15 attendees from varied backgrounds.

Post-recruitment, 13 individuals underwent training on topics including professional issues, working with health and social care systems, with survivors of male sexual abuse and rape, and across cultures and with interpreters. They also covered basic counselling skills, with input from external experts. The training, which lasted 5.5 hours daily, was accredited by the AQA.

Over six months, these consultants participated in 10 community events, engaging 137 people to raise awareness of male sexual abuse. A notable aspect of this initiative was the co-production of training materials, particularly for the Chinese community, where a Cultural Consultant acted as a cultural and language interpreter. One example of the benefit of a culturally informed translation included changing the literal translation of 'survivor', which means 'victim' in Mandarin. This did not have the implication of 'someone who has endured great hardship and come through it' that it does in the UK. So, through discussion, a more neutral word was used. Similarly, examples from Chinese television programmes that would be familiar to the audience were suggested to help the attendees understand the concept of trauma and abuse.

One Cultural Consultant fed back their experience of the awareness-raising events:

> I appreciate "F's" [another Cultural Consultants] company. It was a pleasure to observe her talking to Somalian people, her understanding of the culture, and respectful way of talking to elders. I must say we spent three hours together, and campaigning for Survivors Manchester and cultural consultancy was a great experience but also just talking to "F" about her Somalian culture, politics and civil war in Somalia...racism in our countries and many more issues has been very inspirational and educational for me.

As part of their partnership with Survivors Manchester, the organization provided training for Cultural Consultants on supporting men from Chinese and Eastern European backgrounds who had experienced sexual abuse. One consultant attended bi-weekly drop-in sessions from January to May, offering culturally sensitive support to attendees from these communities. In May 2018, nine Cultural Consultants also trained Survivors Manchester staff in cultural awareness, covering key topics such as relevant aspects of their communities related to male sexual abuse, barriers to accessing services and the impact of racialized language. Additionally, they helped translate and culturally adapt key messages of the services. Feedback from these sessions included:

> The training was informative and accessible. It has given time for me to reflect on my practice and the responsibility of Survivors Manchester to do more for men and boys from Black and minority ethnic communities who have been victims of sexual violence.

> The Cultural Consultants helped to raise awareness of the importance of "cultural confidentiality".

Cultural consultancy case study by Steven Lau

Just Psychology was contacted by a social worker due to their concerns about a family from Hong Kong. The family had arrived in the UK four years earlier. They had three children: a boy aged 12, a girl aged 9 and a 5-year-old girl. There were concerns about the mental health and wellbeing of the 12-year-old boy. The mother worked as a kitchen porter and the father had been a doctor in Hong Kong but currently practised herbal medicine. Both parents worked long hours. The 12-year-old boy was being seen by Child and Adolescent Mental Health Services (CAMHS) due to concerns about anxiety, emotional regulation and attention deficit hyperactivity disorder (ADHD). The parents had attended a parenting programme, but little improvement had been seen, and they did not trust most of the practitioners. Both parents appeared anxious about the situation and were in regular contact with school seeking help for their son. They talked about suicidal ideation within the family and asked if the boy could be taken into care. There were no significant concerns about their daughters, but it was noted that the five-year-old was very quiet.

Just Psychology's Cultural Consultant met with the case workers and practitioners and helped to provide some context. He also accompanied the practitioner to a meeting with the parents. During these meetings, he provided context and clarity.

He observed that the family appeared to be from a traditional Chinese background. Their priority was the children's education and earning enough money to send them to private schools/ tutors. They were also experiencing shame regarding the involvement of health and social care services.

It was clear that the parents did not understand the roles of the professionals and had become upset as a result, believing that they were only interested in the viewpoint of the mother and had excluded the father from discussions. They believed that the aim of services was to break up the relationship between the parents.

The sessions led to a greater understanding of the roles of the professionals and an improved working relationship. The parents also became clear that the suggestions for changes in parenting did not mean they were being blamed for the difficulties their son was experiencing. The mother attended and engaged with an ESOL (English for speakers of other languages) class in which she improved her communication in English and also made friends with other families from Hong Kong, thus reducing her feelings of loneliness and improving her mental wellbeing.

Project 3: Family Reunion and Parenting Project (2021–22)

In 2021 Just Psychology started to set up the Family Reunion and Parenting Project (see Chapter 9 for a detailed discussion of this work). This four-year project was delivered by Just Psychology in collaboration with Rainbow Haven, an organization that works with refugees and asylum seekers. The aim was to enable families to overcome the challenges arising from family reunion following serial migration.

The Family Reunion and Parenting Project offered preventative and early intervention through family reunion groups, parenting groups and cultural consultancy. In 2022, Cultural Consultants were recruited from various countries including Eritrea, Pakistan, Bangladesh, Sudan, Yemen, Democratic Republic of the Congo and Nigeria, targeting unemployed and underemployed individuals from local Black and minority ethnic communities. These consultants underwent training to deliver cultural consultancy and peer mentoring, enhancing community resilience and social inclusion. They supported families transitioning out of the project, and facilitated access to other services, employment and volunteering.

Just Psychology's Cultural Consultants also co-facilitated parenting groups, adding a cultural perspective to discussions and aiding in the development of culturally appropriate project resources. This involved tailoring language and content to ensure accessibility and comprehension within the communities served. Their existing roles within these communities helped maintain trust and effectively engage families in the project – for example, is the language used accessible to this particular community? Does the content make sense? Do there need to be changes in facilitation to ensure the community understands and engages with the contents of the sessions?

The following quote is illustrative of the feedback received from parents about the project:

> I found this session so helpful because I learnt so much from (other attendees). These women are so strong and I feel like they are the best teachers. I am happy to have met them and I admire them.

During the first group with Eritrean families, the Cultural Consultant and facilitator explained that sharing coffee was a way of grounding and connecting in the community, opening up a space to talk. The Cultural Consultant brought freshly roasted, ground and cooked Eritrean coffee with kitcha, an Eritrean bread, allowing the parents to feel comfortable and make connections between themselves and the facilitators. The facilitators wanted to show the parents they wanted to learn about their culture and respected their traditions. This was one of the ways facilitators reflected on the dynamics in the room, as well as the way they delivered the content in the room:

> We also learnt that sitting down whilst delivering the content helped parents feel at ease because, within the Eritrean culture, standing up and pacing added pressure and stress within the group dynamics, so we all sat down while facilitating.

One Cultural Consultant reflected on her experiences with the Family Reunion and Parenting Project and the bidirectional understanding that the project facilitated between families and the Cultural Consultant:

> The Family Reunion process is yet another aspect of our work which is entrenched in cultural nuances, and challenges, adjusting to reunification after long separations and addressing family dynamics, which creates the opportunity to use my expertise to facilitate smoother transitions and promote healthy family relationships by providing interpretation to help break the language barrier. Through my involvement in parenting workshops and support groups tailored to the Eritrean community I can help address cultural-specific parenting challenges, promote positive parenting practices and strengthen family bonds. My expertise and interpreting skill has helped empower parents to navigate the intersection of Eritrean cultural values and parenting in the UK context.

Project 4: Sexual Violence Harm Reduction Project (2022–23)

The aim of this one-year project was to raise awareness of sexual violence in Black, Asian and minority ethnic communities and to increase accessibility of existing services. The project ran from January 2022 to February 2023. Just Psychology initiated the project by consulting with key organizations working with survivors of sexual violence in Greater Manchester in order to identify which Black, Asian and minority ethnic communities would be the focus of the project. They also wanted to understand which communities across Greater Manchester were underrepresented when accessing therapeutic support and consulting with services working with survivors of sexual violence across Greater Manchester.

Following successful completion of the training, the Cultural Consultants delivered eight awareness raising sessions within Global Majority communities and provided cultural consultancy to partner organizations to improve access to their services.

One Cultural Consultant reflected:

> I appreciated also the opportunity for personal and professional growth, through being involved in delivering training, raising awareness and sharing knowledge within the communities and families, on various topics, including the sensitive topic of sexual violence with organizations such as Survivors Manchester, the NHS and addressing the sexual violence issues within specific communities. Through my understanding of cultural nuances, I was able to softly approach and help break down barriers preventing discussing sensitive topics, promote prevention strategies, and improve access to support services for survivors.

Sexual violence harm reduction training: working across cultures with survivors of sexual violence

Just Psychology delivered two training sessions for staff working with sexual violence and abuse. This training was delivered by the project lead and six Cultural Consultants, three of whom represented South Asian perspectives and three of whom represented East and West African perspectives towards sexual violence. Two preparation days were attended by the Cultural Consultants. This time was used to develop a presentation by focusing on the following questions:

1. What is important to know about your cultural background in relation to sexual abuse/rape?
2. What would be the barriers to a person from your community accessing sexual violence services?
3. How can services improve access for your specific community?

The training was attended by 17 staff from a range of organizations across Greater Manchester. Feedback from attendees highlighted the important role the Cultural Consultants played in sharing their personal and in-depth experiences, exploring barriers to services and the cultural nuances of issues such as consent. One of the participants commented at the conclusion of the training:

> One size does not fit all. We need to do more to reach out to people of different cultures. Not all interpreters are suitable for this.

Implications for practice

As discussed, there are clear messages from the Cultural Consultants Project about the value of including people from diverse cultural backgrounds in mainstream services. Cultural consultants bring additional knowledge and expertise around cultural aspects of service provision and the nuances that help facilitate understanding. There are examples that highlight the diverse roles that this group may undertake, from staff training, one-to-one consultancy, peer mentoring and in the development of targeted marketing materials. Furthermore, the project itself appeared to have a beneficial impact on those attending training and working as Cultural Consultants, not only through improving their employability, but also through the shared connection, self-efficacy and understanding and deepening of knowledge about culture that they gained through participation. The included top tips demonstrate how services can engage with diverse and Global Majority communities, if they are willing to step outside their traditional engagement strategies.

Some of the challenges of the project lie in a philosophical question: how can any one person reflect an entire culture? Given what is known about intersectionality, it is important that recruits are ideally taken from across class/educational boundaries within diverse communities. There will be louder and quieter voices, and it is important to ensure that services are listening to those most able to step forward, but also those who may not be as forthcoming. This may necessitate one-to-one discussions outside of group settings, or understanding cultural nuances around politeness and speaking out, which may be reflected differently in cultures, particularly those that prioritize social harmony rather than challenge.

One of the Cultural Consultants summed up her experience of the project:

> Overall, my role as a Cultural Consultant and specifically being part of the Just Psychology team allows me to bridge cultural gaps, advocate for the needs of the Eritrean community, and empower individuals and families to thrive in their new environment. It is deeply rewarding as I get to contribute to the wellbeing and empowerment of my community and other communities, while also fostering personal growth, cultural understanding, and resilience in the face of challenges.

Conclusion

Reflecting personally, I (Catherine) found the project transformative, both as a participant and facilitator. The unity and connection within the group was inspiring, enhanced by sharing our cultures through food, stories and discussions. A powerful lesson was recognizing the diverse ways of approaching universal challenges – like family support and celebrations. It is through contact and human connection that we are able to discover where we differ, but, more importantly, where we are similar, and the shared values that underpinned this work formed a concrete basis for us to build our relationships as a group, and go on to make the project a success. Hopefully this is something the reader of this chapter will consider doing in their own service or lives:

If you don't know who I am how are you going to provide a particular package of care for me to deliver something? When you do not know how important my religion is to me, what language I speak, where I am coming from. How are you going to help me cope? The first step is about identity...it's absolutely fundamental. (Kamlesh Patel, Chair of the Mental Health Commission, in Mulholland 2005)

CHAPTER 8

Emotional Health and Wellbeing Services for Children and Families

IYABO FATIMILEHIN

Overview

The achievement of significant improvements in the psychological health and mental wellbeing of children and their families is at the core of Just Psychology's vision along with the prevention of problems with mental health. Therefore, Just Psychology has developed and delivered early intervention and preventative emotional health and wellbeing services for children and families. These have included short-term projects as well as services commissioned by the public sector. The focus of this chapter is on an early intervention service that was commissioned in 2017 in Greater Manchester to provide an emotional health and wellbeing service for 5- to 12-year-olds (Trafford Sunrise), and a funded service that aimed to address the emotional health needs of primary school-aged children from Global Majority communities during and after the Covid-19 pandemic (The Ark Project). The chapter will describe the issues that the service and project were designed to address and the outcomes that were achieved.

Introduction

The research literature has evidenced significant increases in the incidence of mental health and emotional wellbeing difficulties in children and young people over the past 20 years. Longitudinal studies and surveys in the UK and in other countries described increases in anxiety disorders, depression, autistic spectrum disorders (ASD), self-harm, eating disorders and attention deficit hyperactivity disorder (ADHD) (Cybulski *et al.* 2021; Deighton *et al.* 2019; Haidt 2024; NHS Digital 2023). Cybulski *et al.* (2021) reported a substantial increase in psychiatric disorders and self-harm for boys and girls aged 1–19 between 2003 and 2018. National surveys in England reported that 20.3 per cent of children aged 8–16 had a 'probable' mental disorder, and that this was similar for boys and girls. The incidence had risen from 12.5 per cent in 2017 (NHS Digital 2023).

A range of factors has been implicated in the rise in mental health difficulties for children and young people. These include social and economic deprivation, parental mental health, social media use, educational stressors, climate change and the impact of the Covid-19 pandemic. These factors are linked and not isolated. For example, there is evidence that children who spent more time engaging in adventurous play during the Covid-19 lockdown had fewer internalizing problems and more positive affects (Dodd *et al.* 2023), and that this was more evident in lower income families. Furthermore, a study reviewing the mental health of 3- to 24-year-olds across 11 countries before and during the Covid-19 pandemic described increased negative affect and loneliness (Kauhanen *et al.* 2023).

Parlatini *et al.* (2024) also reported that increases in emotional deterioration for children and young people with ASD and ADHD were higher than those of other children with emotional difficulties. They suggest that these findings may be linked to housing inadequacy, financial concerns, lack of family support, difficulties with social distancing, lower engagement with and enjoyment of remote education and parental mental health. Ethnicity and the experience of being racially minoritized can impact children and young people's development and experiences of mental health difficulties due to a strong association with socioeconomic deprivation (see Chapter 2). Climate change is also contributing to children and young people's experiences of increased anxiety (Hickman *et al.* 2021), and there are ongoing concerns about the heightened use of social media and smartphones by children and young people and the possible negative impact on cognitive and social development, including social interaction, sleep deprivation, addiction and attention fragmentation (Haidt 2024; Maza *et al.* 2023).

It is indisputable that the mental health and wellbeing of children and young people has deteriorated in recent years and there are a number of social and economic factors that have contributed to this. The demand on NHS services in the UK has risen and services are struggling to provide treatment and support; this has led to prioritizing those who are in crisis with less focus on prevention and early intervention. The services we have delivered have embodied Just Psychology's values, including acknowledgement of the economic and social factors that affect mental health, principles of equality and social justice and ways of working that prevent a deterioration in mental health. We always seek feedback from the children and families we work with, and, where possible, we adapt and co-produce our service delivery.

Trafford Sunrise

In 2017, Just Psychology was commissioned by the public sector to provide an early intervention service for children aged 5–12, offering emotional health and wellbeing support for mild to moderate emotional difficulties. These were children who did not meet the threshold for the local Child and Adolescent Mental Health Services (CAMHS) as they did not have a 'significant' mental health need. The service was commissioned to align with *The NHS Long Term Plan* (NHS England 2019) to expand access to community-based mental health services and to address the finding that half of all mental health problems were established by the age of 14. The main aims of the service were to increase emotional resilience, develop positive coping mechanisms, build strong relationships and increase protective factors.

We developed a systemic approach (see Chapter 4) to the service from the start. While we were commissioned to work with children in groups, we introduced their parents to these groups in order to strengthen their relationships and their understanding of their child's difficulties. This approach builds resilience and increases the sustainability of change. In addition, we ensured that our work was delivered in local venues that were accessible, non-pathologizing and familiar to the families (e.g. schools and community centres). We regularly reviewed the postcodes that families lived in and moved delivery venues to improve access for families from lower socioeconomic backgrounds. Trafford Sunrise initially provided four main offers, including parent workshops, working together groups, individual work and staff consultations.

Parent workshops: These were one-off sessions (usually lasting 1.5 to 2 hours) that were open to all parents of 5- to 12-year-olds in the borough. They did not need to be referred by a professional and each session had a theme. Each was facilitated by a qualified psychological/mental health practitioner and co-facilitated by an assistant psychologist (psychology graduate). Over the years, the themes covered included anxiety, bullying, behavioural difficulties, sleep problems, digital wellbeing, parental separation and divorce, and neurodiversity. Sessions included sharing psychoeducational information about the issues, exploring coping strategies and signposting to local services and resources. There was also an opportunity for parents to ask questions and contribute to each other's experiences. Parent workshops were promoted throughout the area via schools, community venues and mental health professionals. In the first year of the service, 104 parents attended parent workshops with 44 per cent attending the anxiety workshops and 28 per cent attending the behavioural difficulties workshops. This pattern remained consistent over the years. We collected written feedback from all parents at the end of each workshop, and this quote reflects the most common themes:

> Attended two parent drop-in sessions by Just Psychology at school on two diff topics. Immensely useful intro level guidance that was sensitively and appropriately delivered and gave me some really helpful practical reassurance. Delivery in a peer environment felt supportive and appropriate too.

Working together groups: These were offered to children and parents who had been referred to the service by a range of professionals including general practitioners (GPs), school nurses and community paediatricians, etc. The sessions were attended by children and their parents with the aim of increasing emotional wellbeing and learning coping strategies through different approaches, such as narrative, cognitive behavioural, compassion-focused, psychoeducation and creative/art therapy. While we had standard plans for each group session (e.g. introductions in the first session), approaches used were tailored to the different age groups and the presenting emotional health difficulties being experienced by the children. Each group provided six sessions lasting one-and-a-half hours, and was attended by the child with at least one parent. All sessions were facilitated by a qualified psychological/mental health practitioner and co-facilitated by an assistant psychologist. Groups were delivered by age in order to tailor them to the children's developmental stages: 5- to 7-year-olds, 8- to 10-year-olds and 11- to 12-year-olds. In the first year of the service, 120 children and parents attended group sessions. We collected written feedback in the final session of each group. For example:

> My daughter really enjoyed her sessions with Sunrise, she was very upset when they came to an end. They definitely made a difference to her emotional wellbeing at the time and for several months after, and although it was nearly a year ago, she still refers to stuff they discussed. Communication was good, keeping me informed of days and times of sessions.

The fact that our staff were 'knowledgeable' was also appreciated by the parents.

The outcomes for Trafford Sunrise were always good. We used standardized outcome measures as well as written feedback to review the effectiveness of the service. In the year April 2023 to March 2024, using the Outcome Rating Scale (ORS) (Miller et al. 2003), 69 per cent of parents who attended a working together group reported an improvement in the wellbeing of their child, and 53 per cent reported a significant improvement in emotional resilience. Children who completed the Child Outcome Rating Scale (CORS) (Duncan et al. 2006) reported a 72 per cent improvement in wellbeing, and 63 per cent reported an improvement in wellbeing at school.

Individual work: This was provided for referred children who would not benefit from a group intervention due to the nature of their difficulties (e.g. aggression towards peers, ASD) or more complex systemic issues (e.g. bereavement, adoption). They were provided with six to eight sessions and this usually included sessions with the child and parent and liaison with school staff where needed. Psychologists and mental health practitioners delivered this work using CBT, solution-focused and compassion-focused therapy approaches. Individual work was delivered to 10 referrals in the first year of the service and this had increased to 95 in 2023/24:

> We have seen a huge improvement since the sessions. He will now go upstairs on his own and play up there alone, which he hasn't done for at least two years because of his fears. I can just tell as a mum that he is a lot less anxious.

In 2023–24 80 per cent of parents completing the Strengths and Difficulties Questionnaire (SDQ) (Stone *et al.* 2010) reported that the problem had improved, and 100 per cent that the intervention was helpful in other ways (e.g. reduced impact of difficulties on home life, friendships, classroom learning and leisure activities). For children completing the CORS, 60 per cent reported improvements in wellbeing, 80 per cent improvements in wellbeing at school and 60 per cent improvements in relationships and social engagement.

Staff consultation: Initially, the service included the delivery of consultation sessions with staff in other organizations in order to build capacity in meeting the needs of specific children. For example, we worked with a weight management service to enable them to include psychological perspectives in their work with children, and also with child and family mentors in schools. However, the increasing demand for referrals of children to Trafford Sunrise and the limited capacity to respond to this resulted in consultations being an aspect of the service that was suspended at the end of the first year.

The largest changes in the delivery of the service occurred during the Covid-19 pandemic. Monitoring reports compiled on a quarterly basis show that, in October–December 2017, the service received 80 referrals, and in the same period in 2019, it received 66 referrals with an additional 68 parents attending the parent workshops. However, by April–June 2021 (when Covid-19 lockdown restrictions had started to ease), referrals had risen to 107, with an additional 84 parents attending the parent workshops. Furthermore, in 2023–24 a total of 404 referrals were received by the service, with 111 parents attending the parent workshops.

This increase in referrals and level of need for children and young people was evident across the region and nationally, and a range of government initiatives was launched to address the issues. There was recognition that parents of primary school-aged children were experiencing the additional pressures of preparing their children for starting school, home-schooling, periods of isolation and financial insecurity. This was beginning to impact on cognitive and social development, and the mental health of the children and parents. Parents were recognizing these issues, and this was represented in the huge increases in demand for support.

We worked with our commissioners and with voluntary, community, faith and social enterprise (VCFSE) organizations across Greater Manchester to provide more timely support, and membership of the Greater Manchester VCFSE Mental Health Leadership Group enabled us to access Covid-19-related funding (the Covid Surge Fund). It was through this funding that we designed and delivered the early support groups.

Early support groups: These were delivered in 2021 as a response to the increased need generated by the Covid-19 pandemic and lockdown. We implemented online provision of two sessions for parents who were on our waiting list for group or individual work so that they received psychoeducation and support while awaiting the more substantive service provision. This approach was successful and enabled us to understand more about the needs of the children/families, and it was also an opportunity to introduce them to the service offer. Therefore, we incorporated it into the core service delivery in 2022 and the early support groups became the first offer for all new referrals. Examples of feedback that we received from parents include:

Reassurance, great advice and knowing we are not on our own. Very casual/relaxed and welcoming. Thank you!

Lovely positive information, well put across. I felt able to bring up any questions or concerns, which can be difficult on Zoom.

I really enjoyed the information given, it has really helped already. I'm looking forward to working together.

This service is so important and I really hope it continues to be funded.

One of the challenges we faced in delivering the Trafford Sunrise service was ensuring that it was consistent with Just Psychology's values, mission and vision. It was an early intervention and prevention service, and the parent workshops meant that parents could receive support without having to contend with the barriers inherent in referral processes or other impediments to access such as pre-registration. They could turn up in the location and engage with our practitioners immediately.

Another value important to Just Psychology is that of systemic working – acknowledging that children are members of families and communities, and that there is a strong connection across the system. Parents, carers and siblings are the closest connections that young children have, and their understanding of the issues that affect their child's mental wellbeing and ways of supporting them has a significant impact. There is a strong evidence base for the importance of systemic approaches (see Chapter 4), and our service ensured that parents were directly involved in group work as well as any individual work that we did with the children.

Havighurst *et al.* (2015) evaluated a multisystemic early intervention for primary school-aged children that included parents and the children's schools. Results showed improvements in children's emotional understanding and behaviour and that parents were also less emotionally dismissive and more empathetic following interventions. The evidence suggests long-lasting preventative changes and positive impact can be made by engaging support systems around the child in early systemic intervention (Faulconbridge, Hunt and Laffan 2019; Harway *et al.* 2012). Our practitioners were experienced in delivering family interventions that ensured the sustainability of improved outcomes by embedding change in the micro- and mesosystems around the child (Bronfenbrenner 1992).

Case study of James (working together group) by Iyabo Fatimilehin (clinical psychologist)

James was an eight-year-old White British boy who was referred to Trafford Sunrise by a speech and language therapist. He lived with his parents and two-year-old sister. James' mother Abigail was concerned about his emotional wellbeing and requested support with managing his anxiety and emotional resilience. She said that James was becoming increasingly anxious and reluctant to go to school. He was struggling to make friends and worried a lot about minor issues that had happened at home or school. He had stopped going out to meet his friends and had become very clingy to his mother. Protective factors included having a supportive family and the good working relationship between his parents and his school.

James and his parents were offered a working together group and attended all six sessions. They engaged well with all the activities and reported that an understanding of the thoughts, feelings, behaviour cycle was very helpful. It helped them to identify techniques that would work well (e.g. relaxation) and when to use them. James' scores on the SDQ improved as a result of attending the working together group. In the first session, he scored within the 'High' range (6) for emotional problems, and this had fallen to 'Close to average' (2) in the final session. The impact of difficulties had also decreased, moving from a 'High' score to 'Close to average' at the end of the group. This indicates that James' difficulties were no longer impacting on his home life, friendships, classroom learning and leisure activities.

At the end of the group sessions, children complete feedback forms, and James wrote:

> I want more sessions... I like being able to speak about my emotions.

On the Experience of Service Questionnaire (ESQ) (Brown *et al.* 2014), James' parents rated the service 10/12 overall. They commented that:

> In the last month James has been more settled, seems less anxious about situations and able to discuss his emotions with clarity. Uses helpful thoughts when feeling anxious.
>
> [The group facilitators] were attentive and took time with each child in the group. Parents and children all involved and made to feel welcome.

Ensuring the accessibility of Trafford Sunrise to children from diverse ethnic backgrounds was a priority from the beginning as well as ensuring that it was available in the more socioeconomically deprived areas of the borough. In order to achieve this, we developed strong working relationships with schools in more deprived areas and delivered our parent workshops in them. This meant that parents were aware of the service and how to seek a referral if needed. We also reviewed the cultural appropriateness of our interventions and adapted some narrative and strengths-based approaches, such as the Tree of Life (Ncube 2006), to ensure that they were accessible for families from diverse ethnic backgrounds. This was in addition to using interpreters where needed and seeking assistance from Cultural Consultants or other Just Psychology team members from similar cultural backgrounds in order to engage and support specific families. We reviewed data relating to postcodes and ethnicity on a quarterly basis with the commissioners, and implemented any changes that would address discrepancies. In 2023, 30.5 per cent of the children seen in Trafford Sunrise were from diverse ethnic backgrounds compared to 22 per cent of the general population in the borough.

Case study of Maria (individual work) by Iyabo Fatimilehin (clinical psychologist)

Maria was an 11-year-old mixed race girl who was referred to Trafford Sunrise by a community paediatrician due to concerns about her feelings and expression of anger. Her mother was White British and her father was Black British of Caribbean descent. Maria wanted help with feeling less angry and her parents were keen to understand how best to support her. Maria had an autistic spectrum condition (ASC). Her father had a positive experience of being parented in a collectivist culture that included the extended family, and an understanding that children would be involved in household tasks and looking after each other. The family's religious faith also had a strong influence on their approach to coping with life's challenges. Maria valued her extended family (aunts, uncles and grandparents) and had daily interactions with them. She was saddened that she was unable to visit them during the Covid-19 pandemic lockdown.

Maria and her parents were offered individual/family work due to the combination of emotional difficulties and neurodiversity. This included six sessions that combined both behavioural- and solution-focused approaches. The aim was to implement findings of any assessments in a culturally competent manner that respected the family's parenting approach and strong faith. A functional analysis of Maria's distress indicated that she was experiencing sensory overload due to the increased activity in the home during lockdown. Therefore, it was agreed that she would have specific times away from the family in her bedroom in order to manage this. Alternative ways of communicating her emotions were also explored and agreed (e.g. through text). She also identified different ways of managing her feelings and activities that helped with soothing (e.g. reading specific psalms in the Bible, breathing exercises). The family was supported to identify their strengths and what was working well and to build on this. At the end of the sessions, Maria's SDQ score for emotional problems had reduced from 9 ('Very high') to 4 ('Slightly raised'). She said that the help she had received was 'good!', and that she was experiencing less distress: 'Before I was angry and things but I learnt the breathing exercises and things that help so I don't get so angry.' Her parents said: 'Thanks very much; the focus we had on using her voice was positive. We were pleasantly surprised that it uplifted and bettered her life skills. It's clear that the values and work of Just Psychology include cultural awareness in the service.'

The numbers of referred children who have been diagnosed with or thought to have a neurodiverse condition (e.g. ADHD, ASD) have increased since the beginning of the service. As mentioned earlier, the research shows that this is in line with the increase in mental health difficulties in children and young people. In 2023, 30.1 per cent of the children referred had either been diagnosed or were in the process of seeking a diagnosis for ASD or ADHD. This was similar across other child mental health services in the borough. We customized our delivery and the ways in which we interacted with children to respond appropriately to neurodiversity. This included using tools and resources (e.g. fidget toys) and introducing the service to children by sending them personalized letters that included photographs of the staff they would be working with as well as the venue where the group would be taking place.

Case study of Adam by Jawahir Mohamed (mental health practitioner)

Adam was a 10-year-old Polish boy who was referred to Trafford Sunrise by his GP for support with his emotional wellbeing, challenging behaviours and toilet training. He had been diagnosed with ADHD, ASC and sensory processing difficulties. Adam often masked his difficulties at school to fit in with his peers and expectations, resulting in emotional meltdowns when at home. Adam was also struggling with interacting with his siblings (Maja and Jakub), often becoming angry and frustrated. He had difficulty sharing and taking turns, and any play or interaction with his siblings typically ended in fighting and shouting.

His parents attended an early support group and followed this with a working together group. The working together group sessions were adapted to enable Adam to engage with the content.

He had access to fidget toys for managing his feelings in the sessions and was provided with visual cards to support his understanding of concepts discussed in the group. Behaviour activation approaches were used and soothing exercises (e.g. breathing) were introduced. An emotional toolkit was developed during the sessions so that Adam could use it when needed. Sessions were attended by both parents, and they were supportive and attuned to his needs. We explained that challenges with social skills and interactions are common for children on the autism spectrum and provided psychoeducation to help them understand and view the situation through an autistic lens. We supported the family by coaching them on how to facilitate play and interactions, using descriptive commenting and modelling. We also encouraged the parents to use praise and rewards to reinforce positive behaviours. By the end of these sessions, we observed that Adam had started to wait for his turn and was learning to share more.

Adam had been referred to an occupational therapist for support with toilet training. The therapist identified delays in his physical motor skills and significant sensory modulation difficulties. At the end of the working together group, we provided three sessions of individual work in which we collaborated with the occupational therapist to address his toilet training through a combination of emotional regulation, challenging negative thoughts, increasing his awareness of physical/body sensations and using a reward scheme. By the end of the sessions Adam and his parents were very happy with the progress that had been achieved. He reported being more aware of his physical sensations, had been dry for three weeks and was more able to manage his levels of energy. He said he felt proud of himself and in control of his body.

The Ark Project

In 2020 it was becoming clear that the Covid-19 pandemic was having a disproportionate impact on people from ethnically and racially minoritized communities in the UK. The Office for National Statistics (ONS) (2020) reported that when taking account of age and population size, Black males were 3.3 times more likely to die from a Covid-19-related death than White males, and Black females were 2.4 times more likely to die than White females. Males of Bangladeshi, Pakistani and Indian ethnicities also had a statistically significant increased risk of death involving Covid-19 and were 1.5 times more likely to die than White males.

While the reasons for these disparities were not yet fully understood, it was clear that socioeconomic disadvantage played a significant part. People from these groups were more likely to be unemployed, on low income or experiencing child poverty. As many people from Global Majority communities come from disadvantaged backgrounds, they were more at risk of the issues that were facing society at large during the coronavirus pandemic, such as financial difficulties, underlying health conditions, difficulties with supporting their children with education, poor housing, living in overcrowded homes and English as a second language (ESL). These factors undermine the ability of parents to provide effective support for their children.

Many families from Global Majority backgrounds also experience difficulties with accessing mainstream support due to the inability of services to respond appropriately to their cultural and religious belief systems. Research has shown that children and young people from Black, mixed race and Asian backgrounds are more likely to be referred to mental health services through social care, youth justice and other compulsory routes and less likely to be referred through primary care or voluntary routes (Chui *et al.* 2021; Edbrooke-Childs and Patalay 2019; Edbrooke-Childs *et al.* 2015). Issues of culture, race and religion can result in significant barriers to accessing a range of support for mental health. Arogundade *et al.* (2023) reported that Black and Asian children and young people were markedly underrepresented in referrals to CAMHS when compared to White British children and young people, and that those of 'mixed' ethnicity were overrepresented. Children and young people from Asian backgrounds were underrepresented in referrals but also more likely not to be accepted.

National and local evidence showed that the pandemic was making a significant contribution to poor mental health (e.g. Young

Manchester Partnership 2020), and that there were considerable vulnerabilities for children and young people from Black, Asian and minority ethnic communities. Reports from Black community organizations were also raising concerns about the impact of Covid-19 on mental health, and the fact that it was exacerbating a situation in which people from some Global Majority communities were already overrepresented in mental health services. There was evidence that the disparities that already existed were being exacerbated by the pandemic.

A Mind survey (2020) of factors contributing to poor mental health showed that children and young people with anxiety-based difficulties (e.g. eating disorders, obsessive-compulsive disorder (OCD) and post-traumatic stress disorder (PTSD)) were struggling the most. Poor mental health was impacted by not being able to go outside, not being able to go to school or college, not seeing friends and concern that someone in their family would be infected by coronavirus, and difficulties getting help. For Global Majority communities, there was the added anxiety caused by the overrepresentation of ethnically minoritized people in the cases and deaths from coronavirus, and the emotional impact of losing loved ones. Accessing culturally appropriate and effective mental health support was crucial for reducing the long-term impact of the pandemic on Global Majority communities.

Therefore, during the pandemic, we applied for funding from the Social Enterprise Support Fund to address its impact on the emotional health and wellbeing of children and families from Global Majority communities. Our experience in delivering culturally competent and appropriate services and the resources that we had already developed (e.g. Cultural Consultants), and our existing collaborations with communities and services across Greater Manchester, meant that we were in a good position to do this. For example, we collaborated with Making Education a Priority (MEaP), the Caribbean & African Health Network (CAHN) and Rainbow Haven (a charity that provides support for refugees, asylum seekers and vulnerable migrants) to co-produce the project with their beneficiaries and ensure that the content and modes of delivery were accessible and appropriate. Our Cultural Consultants (see Chapter 7) supported this process and also contributed to decisions about the name of the project in order to ensure that it was non-stigmatizing and appropriate for a range of communities.

We aimed to provide high-quality, evidence-based interventions and culturally competent interventions at the time of need. There was no other organization providing a systemic family-based culturally competent offer to ethnically and racially minoritized children and families in Greater Manchester at that time.

Project objectives included:

- To reduce the impact of the coronavirus pandemic on the mental wellbeing of Global Majority children and young people
- To support children and families with the emotional impact of the transition back to school
- To provide culturally and linguistically appropriate emotional health and wellbeing support.

The Ark Project was funded for 18 months by the Social Enterprise Support Fund, Awards for All and Greater Manchester NHS Commissioning to work with primary school-aged children in areas where there were high Global Majority populations. We built on the learning from Trafford Sunrise to provide emotional health and wellbeing support to children and their families through group work, parent workshops and individual sessions. Throughout the project, we worked collaboratively with community organizations (e.g. Longsight Children's Centre, Wai Yin, Unity Community Primary School, Big Life group) to review the content and delivery locations for the project (e.g. children's centres, mosques).

Our Cultural Consultants co-facilitated sessions with the project lead (a practitioner psychologist) to ensure that specific cultural needs were addressed. The Ark Project also linked in with our Family Reunion and Parenting Project (see Chapter 9), which provided relationship support to children/young people and parents who have experienced separation and reunification following serial migration. The Family Reunion and Parenting Project referred families to the Ark Project in order to address specific mental health needs (e.g. strategies for emotional regulation, online safety and autism).

We delivered 12 parent workshops (in online and face-to-face formats), all of which were co-produced with children/parents and partner organizations. Key topics identified by families were: Helping your child with strong feelings, Understanding and managing behaviour, Strategies for your child's behaviour, Bullying, and Online screen use. We adapted the number and frequency of workshops to meet the needs of each group. One parent described the project as 'professional' and 'accepting' of her culture. Written feedback showed that 92 per cent rated the workshops as very useful, and 83 per cent stated that the content was relevant to their child's needs. Parents reported that they liked group discussions, strategies, tips and the use of real-life examples.

We also delivered multifamily groups for parents and children with two to three families in each group and individual support for families. Two parents/families receiving one-to-one support rated their progress through their sessions starting at 4/10 before their first session, 7/10 after their second session and 9/10 at the end of the final session. The project supported a total of 73 families (children and parents) from a broad range of cultural and racial backgrounds including those who self-identified as Arab, Bangladeshi, Hong Kongese, Pakistani, Black British, Indian, Libyan and British Asian.

Parents informed us that our ability to provide interpreters and a creche improved the accessibility of the project.

Case study on parent workshops in a local mosque by Dr Hasan Waheed (clinical psychologist)

We delivered two workshops for parents at Cheadle Masjid. The structure and content of the workshops was based on consultations with the chairman and Imam of the mosque, and discussions with one of our Cultural Consultants – a Muslim woman who had attended female-only groups within the mosque. The Imam stated that mothers were particularly concerned about the mental health of their children, and that it would be important to deliver the workshop in the mosque as this was a safe and familiar environment that was close to where they lived. Both the Imam and Cultural Consultant reflected that it was important to create a space for discussion and to include visuals and reflective/practical activities.

Therefore, both workshops were delivered in the mosque and we tailored them accordingly, for example using the green space outside the mosque to facilitate a playful activity focusing on parental self-care and the importance of this when managing children's emotional needs. There was also a Q&A space at the end of each workshop for parents to ask questions that focused on the intersection between Islam and mental health. The workshops were co-facilitated with the Cultural Consultant and an Urdu-speaking interpreter. The Cultural Consultant provided support with addressing cultural issues around gender (e.g. a male facilitating a session with a group of women) and incorporating an understanding of mental health within an Islamic framework.

We delivered two workshops, one focused on understanding challenging behaviours and one on understanding anxiety. A total of 30 mothers attended the sessions. They signed up for the workshops using the mosque's booking system, and 100 per cent of those who booked attended the workshop. No one dropped out!

The workshop on understanding challenging behaviours focused on understanding the reason and functions of behaviours that challenge, how behaviours are maintained and what we can do as parents. The session was delivered using both didactic styles and reflective exercises. Mothers who attended self-identified as: Pakistani (44 per cent), Arab (21 per cent), Indian (14 per cent), Mixed: Pakistani/Italian (14 per cent) and Bangladeshi (7 per cent). Most of their children were aged 5–11 (49 per cent), with 27 per cent aged 12–18. Most of the mothers (75 per cent) described the session as 'very interesting', with 25 per cent saying it was 'interesting'. Fifty per cent of mothers reported that the session was 'Very useful' or 'Useful'. Qualitative feedback showed that the mothers valued:

Room for discussion and sharing.

The stress/relaxed bucket activity.

Strategies to manage stress.

Understanding how to manage behaviours.

Sharing personal life examples.

Illustrating activity, techniques taught and allowing questions and interactions.

They would have liked the session to be longer, more frequent and for fathers to be involved.

Conclusion

Just Psychology's commitment to systemic practices and early intervention is ongoing, and this chapter provides clear evidence of the impact that this can have for children and their families. In 2018, I had a trainee clinical psychologist on placement and allocated a child who was on our waiting list for individual work to her. The child and his parent had attended a working together group several months earlier but had asked for further support when that ended. The trainee and I visited the family at home for our first appointment. The child's mother explained that they were still using the techniques and resources that they had learned in the group and this had been very effective. Therefore, she only wanted a couple of 'top-up' sessions.

Collaboration and co-production are also essential when working with children and families. We cannot make assumptions about what will or will not work. We might be experts in the mental health field but the children and parents are experts on their own lives. We need to bring our expertise together to get the best outcomes, and this is even more important when working across cultures. It is essential that we prioritize an awareness of the Eurocentric nature of many of our approaches (Fatimilehin and Hassan 2016; Watters 2011) and values, and ensure that cultural competency is embedded in the delivery of our services.

One of the themes throughout our journey with Trafford Sunrise was that demand always outstripped our capacity. The service was initially funded to be delivered by 0.6 qualified psychological practitioner and 0.8 assistant psychologist. In 2019–20 this was increased to 1.4 qualified psychological practitioners and 1.0 graduate psychologist, and a further increase occurred in 2022 due to the impact of the pandemic, with the service delivered by 2.0 qualified psychological practitioners and 2.0 graduate psychologists. However, this was not sufficient to address the increased demand for the service, and the waiting times continued to grow rapidly.

Our experience is backed by the research evidence that clearly demonstrates that the impact of systemic factors on people's mental health cannot be underestimated, whether this includes poverty, parental mental health, educational stressors, social media, technology, climate change, pandemics, war or displacement. It is imperative that approaches to mental health difficulties focus on the systems around the individual/family/community, and that we do not focus solely on providing interventions. Community psychology and human rights-based approaches (Casale *et al.* 2019; Kagan *et al.* 2020) incorporate interventions at wider systemic levels (e.g. exosystem, macrosystem), and directly address policy, practice and commissioning across health, education and social care as core aspects of prevention (Community Psychology Section 2022). To quote a saying often attributed to Desmond Tutu: 'There comes a point where we need to stop just pulling people out of the river. We need to go upstream and find out why they're falling in.'

CHAPTER 9

Beyond Borders

Family Separation and Reunification in the Migrant Journey

HASAN WAHEED AND FATEHA BEGUM

Overview

This chapter will introduce the concept of family separation and reunification following serial migration while placing a lens on parenting practices and family functioning. It will highlight key issues that arise within the contemporary political and sociocultural contexts in which families are parenting and raising their children. The chapter outlines how the Family Reunion and Parenting project addresses these issues by using strengths-based and narrative therapeutic approaches across three work streams: (1) parenting groups, (2) family reunion groups and (3) peer mentoring. The chapter will also examine the implications for families who have migrated to the UK, and the challenges they face as they adjust to a new cultural context.

Understanding migration in the UK

The UK's Nationality and Borders Act 2022 has generated significant controversy for introducing measures that criminalize attempts by individuals to enter the UK without a visa or through irregular routes. Initially introduced as the Nationality and Borders Bill, it was described by the government as the 'cornerstone' of its immigration strategy (UK Parliament 2021). However, the legislation has drawn sharp criticism from human rights advocates and civil society organizations, who argue that it undermines core protections enshrined in the European Convention on Human Rights (ECHR). Critics contend that the Act disproportionately targets asylum seekers and may breach international obligations, particularly those related to the right to seek asylum and protection from refoulement.

The process of migration, adaptation and adjustment is complex and multidimensional (Bhugra 2004), and has been described as the most radical transition and life-changing experience that a person can experience in their lifetime (Greeff and Holtzkamp 2007).

The migration journey, in and of itself, consists of different stages, which start from families leaving their country of origin (pre-migration), travelling across international borders (migration) and adjusting to a new host country (resettlement). It is sensible at this stage to introduce terminology for clarity and transparency before we continue with this chapter. Understanding the terminology is important because of its legal consequences and implications for families.

The UK has a legal obligation to offer protection under the Refugee Convention. By the end of June 2023, out of 81,130 asylum applications in the UK, only 7 per cent received an initial decision, while the majority, equivalent to 67,095 cases, were still awaiting an initial decision. From an international perspective, the term 'asylum seeker' refers to those who have moved across international borders, while the meaning in the UK offers a different definition, as a person who has applied for protection under Article 2 of the European Convention on Human Rights (UNHCR 2022). Furthermore, it refers to the 'prohibition of torture or inhuman or degrading treatment or punishment and prohibits the return of a person to a country where the person may suffer a violation of their rights'.

The UK and its previous government (the Conservative Party, in power until mid-2024) were under scrutiny as their proposal to potentially relocate asylum seekers to Rwanda as part of their efforts to deter increased migration rates was considered to be a violation of international refugee law, human rights law and domestic legislation. In November 2023, the UK Supreme Court ruled the plan unlawful, citing that Rwanda was not a safe third country to send asylum seekers. Despite this, the UK government pressed forward, with plans to implement the Safety of Rwanda (Asylum and Immigration) Act in 2024, which would effectively force UK courts to treat Rwanda as a safe destination for asylum seekers. This legislative move was met with international criticism, including from the United Nations and human rights organizations, arguing that the policy violated refugee and human rights laws, and undermined the UK's responsibilities for protecting those seeking asylum.

With respects to the term 'refugee', the United Nations Convention on the Status of Refugees (1951) uses this terminology to describe a person who,

> owing to a well-founded fear of being prosecuted for reasons of race, religion, nationality, membership of a particular social group or political opinion, is outside the country of his nationality and is unable, or owing to a such fear, is unwilling to avail himself of the protection of that country; or who, not having a nationality and being outside the country of his former habitual residence, as a result of such events, is unable to or, owing to such fear, unwilling to return to it.

In the UK, refugee status is given to those people who have been recognized by the Home Office.

It is important to understand these terms as it provides practitioners context to what is happening politically in the UK and internationally. Throughout this chapter, we will offer food for thought and guidance to practitioners who aspire to work with this population. We find it helpful to familiarize ourselves with what is going on in the family's country of origin, whether that be through conversations with personnel who are embedded in the asylum application process or by conducting a detailed search on the Human Rights Watch website.

In our experience, practitioners cannot truly know what the experiences are of those who are seeking asylum or migrating to another country unless they have been through it themselves. Typically, most practitioners will be understanding these life experiences from a position of power and privilege. However, they can start to try and understand their experiences and become more attuned to what may or may not come up in their interactions with these populations. By doing this, we can start to unravel the turmoil that may exist in the mind and inner psyche. Without any understanding, practitioners put themselves, and the person they are working with, at risk of re-enacting past traumas and, in turn, precipitating psychological symptoms.

The migration journey will be experienced differently in response to the context in which the migration has occurred. Families that have decided to migrate from one place to another by their own choice will often do so to search for better living conditions, employment and education opportunities, while those that are forced or displaced due to war, persecution or environmental disasters are typically in a context that is beyond their control. Either way, one of the narratives that often emerges is 'at least they are safe now'.

This brings us to the first, and arguably most important, theme that epitomizes the refugee experience – *home*. Together, we have close to 30 years' experience of working either directly or indirectly with children, adults and families from asylum-seeking and refugee communities. One recurring theme in our collective experiences of working with these populations is the pervasive challenge of housing instability. We will often receive a call on the morning of a parenting group from a family member, after several weeks of preparation, saying 'I am going to get evicted, and I do not know where to go', 'We have an appointment with our social worker/housing officer' or 'They are going to move us to a different area'.

Abraham Maslow, a renowned psychologist and developer of the hierarchy of needs model (1943), proposed that individuals must fulfil basic physiological needs (e.g. shelter/home) before they are able to self-actualize and experience a profound sense of fulfilment and inner peace in their life. However, the 'home' transcends its physical attributes. It encompasses tangible elements, but its essence lies in the intangible qualities that create a sense of belonging, safety and comfort. It should be a sanctuary where individuals find solace and forge emotional connections where they can cultivate a sense of identity in their new beginning. It embodies memories, traditions and experiences that shape personal narratives and family bonds, and serves as a symbolic representation of stability, rootedness and familiarity in an ever-changing ecological context.

The current state of affairs sees this population continuously pushed from pillar to post, grappling with instability and periods of destitution through the refusal of an asylum application. These conditions are further amplified when we bring into consideration the term 'serial migration'. This is when parents migrate to a new country first and settle before sending for their children, or when one spouse arrives and settles before the other joins with or without their children. Put simply, families will experience multiple separations at different timepoints before they are able to meet the immigration requirements of the host country to be reunited with everyone in the family system – the achievement of reunification can take place after one year or after over a decade. Those children who are left behind, usually in the care of trusted extended family members (e.g. aunts, uncles or grandparents), will experience a disruption in attachment relationships to, what is defined by Western academics and practitioners, their primary caregivers, and in some cases be left to experience neglect or abuse. When parents are in a position to bring their children to the new host country, the children will experience a second disruption of familial attachments, which are those relationships forged with extended family members.

This now leads us on to our next theme within this chapter – *connection*. The constant changes to the family system lead to an 'uprooting of meaning' where life-long relationships and environments are disrupted (Falicov 1995). Family reunification after migration offers a beacon of hope, amid the challenges of displacement, to the extent where it is often only interpreted as a positive experience. In some cases, this can be true. However, a growing literature illustrates feelings of resentment, abandonment, confusion, rejection and being estranged when children are left behind in their country of origin. The care received from extended family members can impact on children's relationships with their parents at the point of reunification, which tends to present as insecure anxious or avoidant attachment relationships. This typically surfaces at the resettlement stage of migration and can lead to many issues, such as difficulties with knowing what to call their parents, the shifting roles and responsibilities within the family system, lack of physical or emotional connection, feelings of being exploited, conflict with younger siblings who did not experience separation, unrealized expectations, intergenerational gaps, disciplinary issues and experience of loss (of country, identity and relationships).

In our collective experience, we often observe the shift in roles and responsibilities within family systems. Traditionally, and still in many parts of the world today, societal expectations often assign specific roles to family members based on gender norms, with fathers typically fulfilling the role of the primary breadwinner, mothers being responsible for caregiving and housing duties while children often follow the lead of their parents in these roles. There are many themes, but we routinely see fathers not being able to work or mothers having to work and, in turn, not being able to be as present at home. How can practitioners start to make sense of the relational dynamics that unfold when children are reunited with their parents? First, we must start by exploring the work of three prominent contributors to the field of cross-cultural psychology: Diana Baumrind (1967), Geert Hofstede (1980) and John Berry (1992).

The culture–parenting nexus

In a recent review of parenting articles, Lansford (2021) found that 64 per cent of studies were conducted in the US, with a further 11 per cent across European countries. This raises longstanding concerns from many in the field of cross-cultural psychology that our understanding of parenting is culturally niched and biased. This does not mean that the issues parents bring to us are any different in nature; we still have parents saying to us 'We need help in managing our children's behaviour' or 'How do we help our children with their feelings?' These questions are not exclusive to a particular population. In fact, our experiences tell us that this is a growing concern across most of UK society. However, the expression and the way families deal with matters will be different.

Diana Baumrind (1967), a German psychologist, developed a model that describes three parenting styles – authoritative, authoritarian and permissive – which were later elaborated on by Maccoby and Martin (1983) through the incorporation of two dimensions: (a) the number and type of demands that parents make on children and (b) the level of responsiveness that parents display toward children. These produced four styles:

- Authoritative: High on demandingness and high on respon-siveness
- Authoritarian: High on demandingness and low on respon-siveness
- Indulgent: Low on demandingness and high on responsiveness
- Permissive: Low on demandingness and low on responsiveness.

What we know from the literature base is that collectivist groups have a tendency to adopt a more authoritarian parenting style (Bornstein 2012). While this may be true in some cases, it is important that we do not generalize, and understand that the conceptualization and expression of parenting does differ between and within communities. That being said, authoritarian parenting styles generally tend to be stricter and parent-led with less consideration of social, emotional and behavioural needs. This latter point can often raise eyebrows in the world of safeguarding, but it can be better understood by looking at the work of a Dutch cultural psychologist, Professor Batja Mesquita.

Mesquita explains in her book *Between Us: How Cultures Create Emotions* (2022) that emotions differ across cultures, and illustrated this through the development of the MINE (Mental, Inside, Essence) and OURS (Outside, Relational and Situated) model of emotions. In many parts of the world, emotions are not considered to be borne out of a mental act that results in an inward focus and outward expres-sion. Rather, emotions can also be understood as a relational act with an outward focus, suggesting that emotions are not solely internal experiences but acts that occur between people which unfold within a specific cultural context. It is also thought that emotions are situ-ated from the outwards in, meaning that they aim to meet the social norms and values of the host culture, and suppression can help to cultivate the appropriate feelings (Mesquita 2022).

Very quickly, we can now see two interesting dynamics at play. First, emotions are not typically shared or expressed in the way it is promoted across individualist societies. Contrary to the emphasis on expression of emotion in individualist communities, emotional sharing and expression in collectivist cultures is often guided by values of maintaining harmony and conformity within the group, and not prioritizing individual goals. This brings us to Gert Hofstede, another

Dutch social psychologist, who developed the individualist-collectivist framework that is borne out of his cultural dimension theory.

This dimension refers to the extent to which individuals in a particular culture prioritize their own interests over the group or community they belong to. It has long been suggested that individualist cultures, especially those from the Global North, have a tendency to prioritize their personal goals and individual achievements over group goals. Collectivist cultures, on the other hand, also referred to as the Global South or Indigenous communities, prioritize the goals and wellbeing of their family or community over their own personal goals. What we often observe when families migrate to the UK, especially when there has been prolonged separation followed by reunification, is a distance between shared attitudes, beliefs, expectations and values. The separation transcends spatial distance and plays out in social distancing between family members.

This brings us to our next concept – *acculturation*. John Berry (1992) proposed a model of acculturation that illustrates an individual's ability to adapt to a new environment along two dimensions: (a) Is it considered to be of value to maintain one's identity and characteristics? (b) Is it considered to be of value to maintain relationships with the larger society? The answer to these two questions leads to the development of a quadrant describing four acculturation strategies:

- Integration: Values identity and maintaining relationships with larger society
- Assimilation: Does not value identity at the expense of maintaining relationships with larger society
- Separation: Values identity at the expense of maintaining relationships with larger society
- Marginalization: Does not value identity or maintaining relationships with larger society.

What we typically find is families swaying into the separation or marginalization phase of the acculturation process, typically due to the conditions and environment they find themselves in. In fact, we should mention that the simple wording of these questions not only reinforces a 'them vs. us' narrative that has long existed in the UK, which has been inflamed under the more recent Conservative government (2019–24), but it also assumes that the responsibility is on families, and removes any accountability to those in power or in positions of influence in our health and social care systems. The families clearly go through many transformations throughout this process, but we often see how the reciprocal communication, the part that involves mutual adaptation, negotiation and exchanges between families from culturally diverse backgrounds and the host culture, is ignored and neglected. For us, as professionals from health and social care fields who have lived experience of cultural diversity, we aim to stand in a position where we accept what we may not know and try to tackle our own cultural biases in an attempt to respect any cultural differences.

Once this has been addressed through team reflections or individual clinical supervision, we then support families experiencing separation (post-migration) or marginalization. The families will often say 'There are no activities that our children can go to' or 'We do not want our children to forget who they are and where they come from'. Second, and closely overlapping with the former point, children and parents find it difficult to find a language to process their collective experiences in a non-problem-saturated way. As Ncazelo Ncube (co-developer of the Tree of Life methodology) aptly phrases it, 'life is multi-storied, not single-storied' (2006). Indeed, the collective experience of those who have migrated to the UK, and the hardships they experience in adjusting to a new cultural context, puts them in a position to become trapped in a problem story. Often, we find by simply helping families to remember their culture (e.g. 'What was your favourite thing to do in Eritrea?') brings a momentary happiness and sense of empowerment that is usually noticeable when they are sharing their stories within a group setting. In doing this, we are enabling the 'second story' in the family's life, one that does not sustain problems but rather seeks to find solutions.

What we see by asking families to reflect on their strengths, skills and resources (e.g. 'What is important to you and your family?') is an acknowledgement, a shift in cognition and affect, that results in an increase in awareness, allowing them to tackle current problems head on. While this may not address all the issues, we start to see the beginning of a change process, especially for those young people who have been in the UK far longer than one parent, leading to an acculturation gap, that is, a difference in attitudes, beliefs and values.

Now we will introduce the Family Reunion and Parenting Project and some of the lessons we have learned throughout the delivery of this project.

The Family Reunion and Parenting Project

The current landscape of mental health service provision often relies on individualized and reactive interventions, which may not adequately address the needs of this diverse population. Assessment tools and interventions designed for culturally and ethnically diverse populations are limited and often applied universally, despite their inadequacy in capturing the nuances of different communities' experiences. Meaningful and practical services are more likely to be effective when they take into account the social, cultural, economic and political realities of the communities they aim to serve. Early intervention across relevant systems during the resettlement phase has been shown to positively impact the psychological wellbeing of children and families. Projects like Geedka Shirka (Under the Tree), which provided narrative-based community support for Somali families, and strengths-based approaches, like the Child and Family Refugee Service at the Tavistock Centre in London, have demonstrated success in strengthening family relationships and improving mental health outcomes.

Within Just Psychology, our project aimed to support families facing challenges stemming from serial migration. Through the Family Reunion and Parenting Project, funded by the Reaching Communities National Lottery Community Fund and Trafford Housing Trust Social Investment, we sought to strengthen relationships within, and between, families and communities. The goal was to build networks of support where parenting strategies and relevant legislation in the UK could be shared. The project was developed through a collaborative process, with input from families who had lived experience of migration and separation, Cultural Consultants (see Chapter 7) and partnership agencies, aiming to serve and address identified priorities through preventative and early intervention approaches.

The project aimed to support families in overcoming the challenges arising from family reunion following serial migration by providing preventative and early intervention through three interlinked activities:

- *Family reunion groups* aimed at families that had recently been reunited following separation as a result of their migration journeys. This was aimed at both parents and children who had been separated with a focus on rebuilding relationships as well as developing new ones. In addition, the groups also aimed to address the expectations of both children and parents by providing resources that families could use to help negotiate their relationships in a new culture. The groups aimed to support children and parents to talk to each other about their experiences while separated, and their hopes and aspirations now that they were reunited. This was all informed by using a narrative therapy methodology known as the 'Tree of Life' approach (Ncube 2006). This approach is not based on Western models of mental health. It is non-stigmatizing and promotes a positive self-concept by focusing on the strengths and resources individuals possess, rather than on their problems or deficits. This work was delivered in multifamily groups in partnership with other community organizations.

- *Parenting groups* available to parents who had recently migrated to the UK, as well as Global Majority parents who had lived in the UK for some time. The group content and material consisted of understanding expectations around parenting, legislation, accessing community resources, leisure activities and services, and developing social networks, approaches to parenting, other families and school (more details can be found in Olabi *et al.* 2022). As alluded to in Chapter 5, a key issue that arises in the family courts is the dynamic interplay between the heritage and adaptation dimensions of culture that, in turn, shape behaviour.

- *Peer mentoring* aimed at developing community resilience and social inclusion (Fatimilehin *et al.* 2015). People who identified as underemployed from local ethnically and racially minoritized communities received training in delivering cultural consultancy work and peer mentoring with the aim of supporting families to transition out of the project and access other available services, volunteering and employment opportunities.

The challenges for parents who have migrated to the Western world can be best described through the use of a case study. This is a story of a mother whose story will enable us to grasp some of the specificities of the asylum seeker and refugee experience. This case, although poignant, is not uncommon and sheds light on the many challenges experienced by families who have migrated to the UK.

Luwan is awaiting two teenage children, Adham (17) and Rulia (14), to join her from Eritrea through family reunion. The children's father had passed away and the children were surviving unaccompanied in a refugee camp in Ethiopia – a harsh and dangerous living situation. Luwan was worried about how she would raise her children alone in the UK. After a long and complicated reunion process, they were reunited in Manchester in 2023. Rulia, the youngest son, quickly embraced life in the UK, doing well academically and securing a place with a local netball team. Adham, the oldest son, started exhibiting challenging behaviour soon after arrival. He estranged himself from his mother and school and became withdrawn. Throughout this the Rainbow Haven caseworker worked closely with Luwan to try and help her access the support she needed to help her son.

On referral to the Family Reunion and Parenting Project, Luwan found herself embraced by a team employing a holistic contextual model tailored to the intricate dynamics of the family. With an emphasis on the relational, community, cultural and sociopolitical context, the project team sought to provide comprehensive support. Luwan's journey began with her participation in the parenting group, a group designed to address the nuances of parenting in the UK and equip her with strategies to address Adham's emotional and behavioural challenges post-reunification. Delving into discussions about universal services, Luwan gleaned valuable insights into accessing assistance promptly, arming herself with knowledge crucial to her children's wellbeing.

She then accessed family reunion groups, which served as an outlet for her and her children, affording them the opportunity to unpack their shared experiences of separation and reunification. Encouraged to articulate their hopes and aspirations for the reunion, they found solace in the solidarity of shared struggles, fostering deeper connections with each other and other families in the group and, in turn, dispelling feelings of isolation. This communal exchange not only bolstered their familial bonds but also underscored the universality of their challenges, offering a sense of belonging amidst adversity.

Finally, the project provided a dedicated Cultural Consultant to support Luwan in accessing tailored services for Adham. The peer mentor accompanied Luwan to various appointments with health, social care and education services, facilitating a seamless reintegration into the community. This concerted effort to rebuild Luwan's community network highlighted the project's commitment in addressing the broader community context, recognizing the significance of social support in fostering resilience and empowerment. In essence, Luwan's engagement with the Family Reunion and Parenting Project exemplifies the transformative potential of a holistic, culturally sensitive approach in empowering migrant families to navigate the complexities of reunification and integration with confidence and resilience.

Insights and lessons learned

In the journey of developing and implementing a project aimed at supporting families navigating the complexities of migration and reunion, the process often unveils a plethora of reflections, some of which we have described earlier in this chapter. This final part of the chapter explores the insights gained from the development and delivery of the Family Reunion and Parenting Project.

The role of the advisory group: Central to the success of this project was the collaboration and input of key stakeholders. The formation of an advisory group, consisting of a parent representative with first-hand experience of family reunion and parenting issues, professionals deeply rooted in the local community and personnel from partner organizations such as Rainbow Haven (an organization offering support to refugees and asylum seekers in East Manchester), Greater Manchester Immigration Aid Unit (a charity organization offering free legal immigration advice to children and families from the asylum-seeking and refugee community) and the British Red Cross (an organization providing health and social care services across the UK) proved instrumental in shaping the project's trajectory. The project was developed in partnership with Rainbow Haven, which offered culturally and linguistically tailored spaces for families to meet, with appropriate childcare support and travel expenses provided. Together, these stakeholders identified referral criteria, established processes, ensuring a holistic and effective approach to supporting migrant families.

Utilizing Cultural Consultants: Harnessing the expertise and cultural insights of Cultural Consultants played a pivotal role in engaging families effectively. These consultants, deeply embedded within the community, served as invaluable bridges, facilitating communication, understanding cultural nuances and building trust. Their involvement not only enhanced the cultural competency of support services but also fostered a sense of cultural affirmation and belonging among families, thus addressing one of the core challenges of migration – the preservation of family and cultural identity. This, combined with their training in peer mentoring, allowed them to provide a meaningful contribution to the project.

Holistic approach: One of the cornerstones of our approach was recognizing the myriad factors impacting families' lives. This includes, but is not limited to, housing, education, health and social issues. By addressing not only their basic needs but facilitating access to community resources and expanding social networks, we aimed to create a comprehensive support system. This perspective allowed us to identify intervention opportunities and tailor our services to meet the diverse needs presented by each family.

Importance of co-production: In our endeavour to support culturally diverse communities, we recognized the importance of co-production and being culturally responsive. Each group, whether focused on parenting or family reunion, was co-produced in order to be more accessible to the different communities. This approach was not a one-time task but rather a continuous learning process, necessitating both in-the-moment reflection and ongoing consultation with Cultural Consultants from relevant communities. In order to build trust and rapport with the communities we served, we attempted to humanize our project by being visibly present and actively participating in community events, and establishing connections with existing organizations trusted by families. This was either through attending drop-in sessions to introduce our service or through invitations to coffee mornings. This laid the foundation for families to feel safe and comfortable sharing their challenges with us. Furthermore, we ensured that the venues for our groups were not only physically accessible but also meaningful to the communities we served. By choosing community venues with strong connections to the families, we fostered a sense of belonging and created an environment for building relationships. This was also supplemented by changing the structure of the family reunion groups, at the request of the families, from multiple sessions over the course of four weeks to one full day in the school holidays to improve attendance. We also took deliberate steps to acknowledge and celebrate cultural diversity within our groups. For example, in our parenting groups for Eritrean families, we incorporated cultural elements such as serving Eritrean coffee and kitcha bread during sessions and culminating with a celebration featuring Eritrean cuisine. Overall, our commitment to co-production, cultural responsiveness and celebrating diversity enhanced the effectiveness of our groups, and ensured that families felt valued, respected and understood throughout their journey with us.

The therapeutic approach adopted by our team was both strengths-based and culturally sensitive, acknowledging the importance of culture in parenting practices and the adaptation to new cultural contexts. Understanding that culture shapes parenting styles and practices and that parents possess inherent skills and strengths, we aimed to empower families by respecting their expertise and resources in overcoming challenges. Drawing from evidence-based practice suggesting diverse strategies for adapting to new environments, we implemented solution-focused and narrative approaches. These methodologies aimed to maintain a non-blaming and respectful stance while positioning individuals as experts in their own lives. By embracing solution-focused techniques, such as exploring strengths, skills, values and commitments, we facilitated a positive outlook on problem solving and resilience building.

Challenges

The impact of the Covid-19 pandemic and successive lockdowns presented significant challenges for our project to start when originally expected. Longstanding relationships with local communities were strained as people became less likely to gather in traditional community venues, necessitating a reliance on technology for remote engagement. However, this shift risked digitally excluding individuals with limited access to technology. The pandemic exacerbated demands on our resources, particularly in terms of the time required to attend drop-ins at community venues to complete referral forms with parents. Balancing these logistical challenges with the urgent needs of families transitioning to the UK, including reunification, housing, education and access to basic resources, proved to be a delicate endeavour.

Furthermore, in the face of rapidly changing migration policies, we recognized the importance of developing cultural and transnational competence. Informed by sociopolitical and economic contexts, this competence is integral to effectively supporting the population navigate evolving policy landscapes. For instance, changes to immigration rules, such as those effective from December 2020, highlighted the need for heightened awareness and adaptability to policy shifts impacting migrant families. Despite these challenges, our commitment to serving families remains unwavering. By acknowledging and addressing these obstacles, we strive to continually refine our approach and enhance our support to meet the evolving needs of those we serve. Through collaboration, resilience and a steadfast dedication to cultural competency, we aim to navigate these challenges and continue our goal of supporting families through their resettlement journey.

In the UK, practitioners working with this population may encounter additional challenges related to government legislation, policies and immigration regulations. Some of these challenges include:

- *Immigration status and access to services:* Families may face barriers in accessing mental health services due to their immigration status and need to prioritize other aspects of their life, for example the other challenges often presented within the health, education, housing or social settings. Changes in immigration laws and policies, such as restrictions on access to healthcare for certain groups, can further exacerbate these barriers and limit their ability to receive timely and appropriate psychological support. There is a lot of uncertainty and families are often awaiting decisions on their asylum applications, which can lead to heightened stress, anxiety and psychological distress. Practitioners may need to navigate complex legal frameworks and collaborate with legal professionals to support families through asylum procedures and appeals.

- *Access to specialist services:* Families with specific mental health needs, such as survivors of torture, trauma or other violence, may require specialist psychological support that is not readily available within mainstream services. Even if these specialist services do exist, they are often limited in their cultural sensitivity, and significant adaptations are needed including the use of trained interpreters. Families are often referred to as 'hard to reach', but our view is that professionals within teams could think more creatively in how they do more outreach work and consult with the communities in question. It is important that this is done in the spirit of collaboration, and, in the words of Carolyn Kagan, for practitioners to 'work on the edge of communities', by which we mean it is not about going into communities and colonizing them, but rather appreciating that there can be an abundance of resources when two ecological communities collaborate. We need to find the area of edge and maintain it so there is a mutual agenda. Practitioners may need to liaise with specialist organizations or community groups to ensure families receive appropriate and culturally sensitive care. In the quest for integration into British society, families will often face challenges in social isolation, discrimination and barriers to employment and education. Practitioners may play a key role in supporting social integration by addressing psychosocial needs, promoting community engagement and advocating for inclusive policies and practices.

Acknowledgements

We extend our heartfelt gratitude to the Cultural Consultants, administrators, assistant psychologists, trainee clinical psychologists, interpreters and parent representatives, past and present, for their unwavering support and dedication to this project. Their invaluable contributions have been instrumental in shaping the success of our endeavours.

We are deeply appreciative of our partner organization, Rainbow Haven, and advisory group members, the British Red Cross and Greater Manchester Immigration Aid Unit, for their generosity in sharing their knowledge and expertise. Their collaboration has enriched our project and enhanced our ability to serve migrant families effectively.

Last, we extend our sincerest thanks to the families who have placed their trust in us and shared their stories. Their resilience, courage and willingness to engage have inspired us and propelled our efforts to support more families in their journey of reunion and resettlement. Without their participation and collaboration, this endeavour would not have been possible.

CHAPTER 10

Capacity Building

CAROLYN KAGAN AND IYABO FATIMILEHIN

Introduction

From the outset, Just Psychology had 'capacity building' as a key objective, outlined in the business plan. Capacity building was necessary in order to increase the accessibility and appropriateness of mental health and family support services for Global Majority children and their families. We recognized that it would be essential to engage with statutory and public sector agencies to increase awareness and understanding – and thereby capacity of a wide range of individuals and organizations – to meet the needs of Black and minority ethnic children and families, and ultimately contribute towards changing the service system. At the same time, we knew that we would need to actively ensure that the capacity of Just Psychology and our staff continue to be effective. Thus, capacity building refers to the internal capacity of Just Psychology and the external capacity of services and communities to support Black and minority ethnic children and families.

A systematic review of capacity building in public health concluded that different capacity-building interventions can enhance knowledge, skill, self-efficacy (including confidence), changes in practice or policies, behaviour change, application or system-level capacity (DeCorby-Watson *et al.* 2018). We recognized that we would have to continually work at individual, organizational and institutional capacity building, and the linkages between the different levels, and to include:

- Hard capacities (technical knowhow, including explicit knowledge and methods, organizational functioning and organizational systems)

- Soft capacities (social relational aspects, including personal and organizational values, intercultural communication, ability to self-reflect and learn from experience, self-confidence, willingness to innovate and share experiences).

The main mechanisms we have used for capacity building include training (individual and organizational levels), consultation (organizational and institutional levels), work with commissioners (institutional), expert witness programme (institutional), board membership of other organizations (organizational and institutional) and staff recruitment and retention (organizational) (see Figure 8).

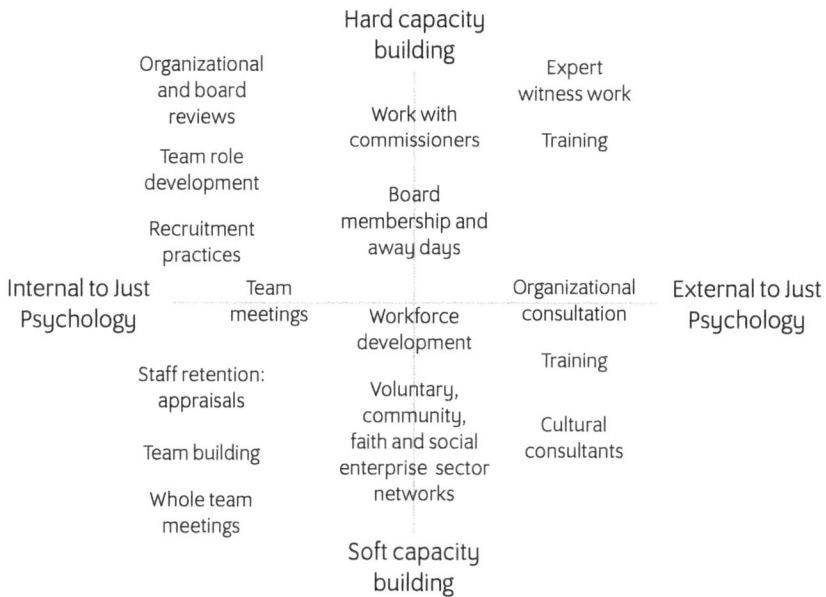

Hard capacity
building

Organizational
and board
reviews

Expert
witness work

Work with
commissioners

Training

Team role
development

Board
membership and
away days

Recruitment
practices

Internal to Just
Psychology

Team
meetings

Workforce
development

Organizational
consultation

External to Just
Psychology

Training

Staff retention:
appraisals

Voluntary,
community,
faith and social
enterprise sector
networks

Cultural
consultants

Team building

Whole team
meetings

Soft capacity
building

Figure 8: Different capacity-building strategies along two dimensions – internal and external

This chapter will focus mainly on external training, consultation and workforce development (employability and career development).

Training and consultation have been directed at professionals from a wide range of disciplines, with the aim of developing their awareness, knowledge, skills and confidence in working with children and families from ethnically and racially minoritized communities, and to innovate and share knowledge and expertise, thereby contributing to systems change.

When we talk of the 'system' we mean all those complex, interwoven elements that contribute to the experiences of Global Majority children and their families and the shape of the services that support them. Some of these elements are immediate and close by (such as the make-up and dynamics of the families or the staffing in services); others are more distant but have just as much impact, including, for example, commissioning strategies or legal requirements and the wider social context; still others are cross cutting, including the nature and operation of power – by ourselves, families, communities and services – and of culture. The system is a human (or soft) system, and elements interact through relationships and the actions of those involved.

When we talk of change, we mean change at individual, organizational, institutional and systems level. We recognize that not all change can be radical, transformative and systems changing. However, Kagan *et al.* (2019, p.323) suggest: 'In a complex system, chipping away at different parts of the system, bit by bit, whilst each individual change is incremental and ameliorative over the time the culmination of ameliorative changes can be transformational.'

We are not idealistic about achieving systems change. However, we recognize that the system(s) in which we are embroiled is a messy and complex one, and is infused with power. All our capacity-building work, in one way or another, explores how both power and resistance operate. Power mapping (Hagan and Smail 1997; Kagan *et al.* 2019) is a way of surfacing the hidden operation of power, in all aspects of day-to-day life, work and in society more generally, with direct and indirect impacts on practice. Sources of relevant power include information (how information, including the media, both frames experiences and influences life chances and wellbeing); politics (how current local, national and international policies influence life chances and wellbeing and frame ideological forces); economics (how the capitalist system and global economics have direct and indirect influence over life chances and wellbeing); and culture (how nationality, age, gender and religious culture influence life chances and wellbeing). Resistance can be understood in many different ways, but capacity building entails articulating those forces of resistance that balance or outweigh the enabling forces in any given set of circumstances. Kagan *et al.* (2019, p.174) argue that a force-field framework is helpful in thinking this through (see Figure 9).

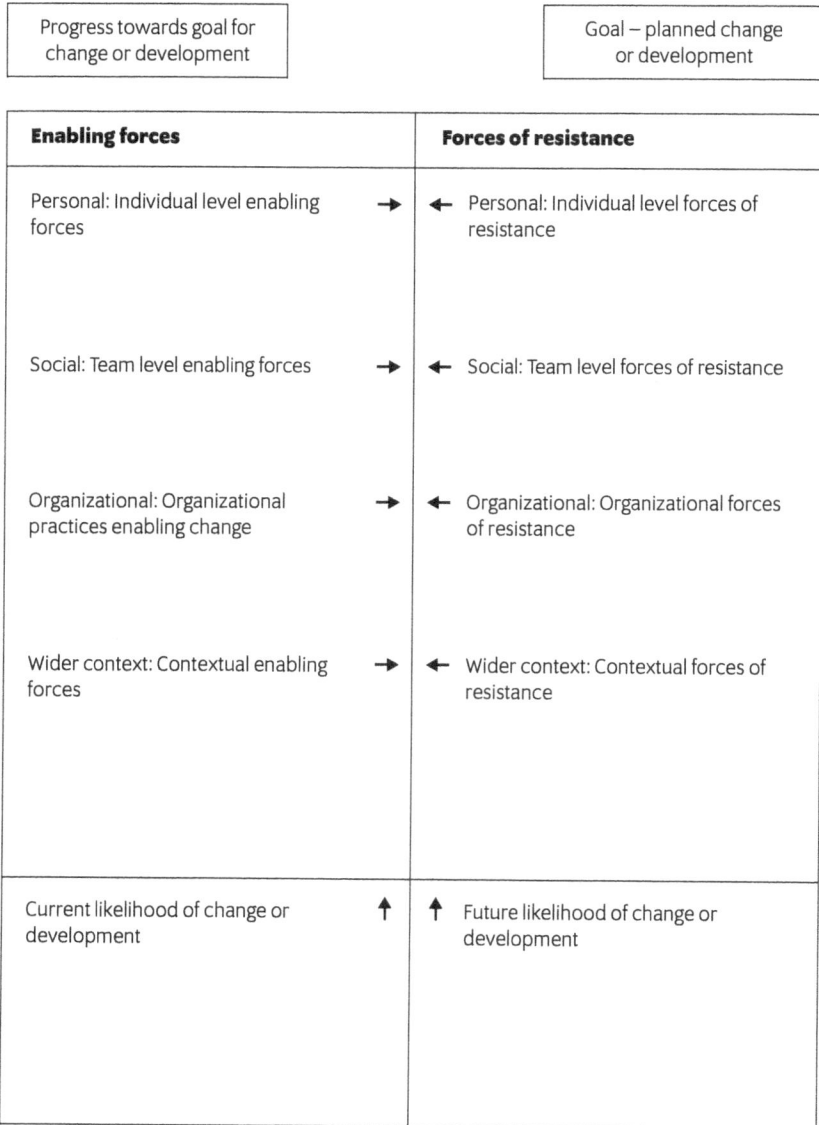

Progress towards goal for change or development			Goal – planned change or development	

Enabling forces		**Forces of resistance**	
Personal: Individual level enabling forces	➜	⬅	Personal: Individual level forces of resistance
Social: Team level enabling forces	➜	⬅	Social: Team level forces of resistance
Organizational: Organizational practices enabling change	➜	⬅	Organizational: Organizational forces of resistance
Wider context: Contextual enabling forces	➜	⬅	Wider context: Contextual forces of resistance
Current likelihood of change or development	↑	↑	Future likelihood of change or development

Figure 9: Force field analysis

These understandings of both systems and of change place personal and organizational development at the heart of Just Psychology's capacity building. Training, consultation and career development all involve growing self-awareness, explorations of identity, identifying the elements of the system and how they interact, constantly questioning assumptions, understanding the context in which action takes place, understanding different perspectives and embracing complexity and continual learning. These are all important aspects of systems change (Birney 2017; Green 2016). Critical self-awareness and reflection and a commitment to continued learning are core to capacity building (Kagan 2007).

External capacity building: approach to training and consultation

Participants in our training programmes, those on the receiving end of consultations and staff, are adult learners, intrinsically motivated to deepening their knowledge, building on their experiences and applying their understanding to their work. We draw on theory and practice in the field of adult education in both the design and delivery of programmes, taking an andragogical stance (Purwati *et al.* 2022). This means that we approach both training and consultation as a process of thought and discovery, critical reflection and action, and not as an opportunity to impart information through a one-way didactic process. Although consultation is focused more on an organizational level, it is still best thought of as a two-way process of learning.

We draw on a number of different perspectives and traditions. First is Vygotsky's (1978) notions of learners' active roles in the construction of knowledge through the interaction of thought and language, highlighting that learning cannot be separated from the societal context in which it occurs. Thus, our starting point is participants' own ideas and experiences, embedded as they are in their own social contexts.

These social contexts are particularly important for awareness raising and exploration of change as well as for taking action for change. Freire (for example, Freire, Freire and Barr 1999) argues against a one-way imparting of specialist knowledge (what he calls 'banking education') in favour of a process of awareness raising gained through dialogue and exchange of realities. He calls this process one of 'conscientization' (a translated term from the original Brazilian Portuguese – there is no word similar in meaning in English). Kagan *et al.* (2019, p.189) explain:

> Conscientization, then, is a process grounded firmly in people's lived experiences and starting with people's own levels of consciousness and ability to take action. As critical awareness develops over time, through dialogue and reflection, people's agency increases and their potential and ability to take action is enhanced. This process enables people to move from a passive, uncritical acceptance of how things are at the present time, to envision routes to change.

Next, we adopt humanistic ideas about the provision of enabling environments in which learners need to experience positive input to enhance their self-confidence (Rogers and Freiberg 1994), impacting on the creation of optimal learning.

Akhurst *et al.* (2016) argue that the learning environment is enabling when open communication is encouraged and relationships are based on mutual respect – relevant to both training and consultation. We think carefully about who is invited to particular training sessions and ensure that facilities are comfortable, with refreshment breaks. As some of the issues we address in training touch participants in unexpected ways, this means that our facilitators are always on the lookout for emotional reactions to the subject matter and can ensure 'emotional safety' in discussions. Consultations are by invitation, so there is already some kind of positive relationship between Just Psychology and the other organizations, even if this is only by reputation. Agreements are negotiated with the other organizations about the focus and anticipated outcome of the consultation, so it can be tailored to that organization; this co-creation of the consultation helps to build trust and increase the likelihood that actions for change will be taken.

We try to build communities of practice (Lawthom 2011; Wenger 1998) within and following training sessions. The learning community here comprises Just Psychology trainers or consultants alongside trainees and organizational teams, all bringing their experiences of practice. If communities of practice are seen as aggregates of people who share doing, talking, beliefs and values (i.e. practices), then participants learn through shared problem-centred learning, becoming and belonging. This perspective highlights the role of reflection and participation in sessions, leading towards more critical thinking, itself leading to more critical practice, and most of our training is action-focused – trainees leave with a clear idea of what they might do differently, via an action plan (Moore 2010). Indeed, a central plank of our training sessions is reflection – on the contexts in which we work, ourselves and on possibilities for change.

It has been known for a long time that reflective practice, where those taking part in training or in organizational consultation are supported to gain insight, is the route to a different kind of learning, one that is characterized by critical thinking and action (Brookfield 2010; Halpern 2013). We adopt a similar approach to consultation, encouraging and building on relationships within organizations, and between them and Just Psychology, in moving forward. Consultations that we undertake (or indeed that external facilitators undertake with Just Psychology, as in board reviews and organizational development processes) are approached as a meeting and sharing of knowledge and experiences. While consultation leads to change in the partnering organization, Just Psychology also benefits from the experiences through learning; both organizations become aware of new possibilities for change and development (see Figure 10, after Kagan *et al.* 2019, p.125).

We have stressed the role of collaboration, sharing and mutual exchange in our approach to capacity building, particularly external capacity building. We have often borrowed ecological systems thinking and the concept of the 'ecological edge' to understand why this approach is a useful one. Each partner (organization or trainers/trainees) can be understood as an ecological community, with its own set of resources. Where two or more communities come together, they can do so in a number of ways. They could come together maintaining strict boundaries and each continuing to operate without change; they could offer each other expert advice and tuition, still maintaining their own boundaries; or they could share their resources (knowledge, experiences, understanding) and create a permeated boundary, known as an 'ecological edge'. The task of capacity building is, then, to maximize and maintain that 'edge', each partner benefiting from the other and moving forward for change (Kagan *et al.* 2019).

> At each boundary is the possibility of an "edge" that maximizes ideas and practices. The "edge effect" is the phenomenon of enrichment through alliances and collaborations. When edge is actually created we notice an increase in energy, excitement and commitment. What characterizes all these boundary settings (whether edge is significantly created or not) is the problem of spanning social entities with greatly differing modes of operation, power structures, cultures, physical environments, practices values and ideologies. (Kagan and Duggan 2009, p.8, cited in Kagan *et al.* 2019, p.222)

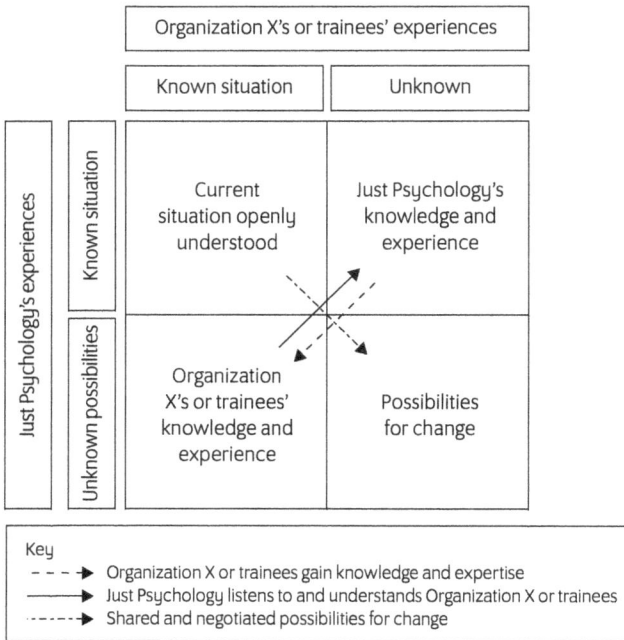

		Organization X's or trainees' experiences	
		Known situation	Unknown
Just Psychology's experiences	Known situation	Current situation openly understood	Just Psychology's knowledge and experience
	Unknown possibilities	Organization X's or trainees' knowledge and experience	Possibilities for change

Key
- - - ▶ Organization X or trainees gain knowledge and expertise
──────▶ Just Psychology listens to and understands Organization X or trainees
·····─▶ Shared and negotiated possibilities for change

Figure 10: Creating possibilities for change through consultation

Capacity building needs this energy, excitement and commitment. Having outlined our approach to training and consultation, we will now look at training in more detail.

Training

Our training focuses on both soft and hard capacity; it aims to help professionals to develop their awareness, knowledge, skills and confidence in working with children and families from Global Majority communities, and to innovate and share knowledge and expertise. This includes developing awareness, increasing knowledge and skills, gaining confidence in multicultural work, improving understanding and communication when working with children and families from Global Majority communities, and enhancing the skill of reflexivity (the process of thinking critically about the basis of our own knowledge claims) (Landy *et al.* 2016).

In the early years we designed and advertised open access training courses, aimed at health and social care staff, marketing them to relevant professionals and organizations. This entailed building a data base of contacts and spending considerable time ensuring information was widely communicated. This was not always successful and take-up was unpredictable. Similarly, marketing our expertise in consultation sometimes led to inappropriate requests for the service. As we shall see, we have moved to a more effective, less time-consuming, demand-led approach to both training and consultation. This is only possible because we now have a strong, positive reputation – partly due to the early years of training, consultation and delivery of services.

Commissioners of training have included NHS trusts, schools, local authorities and housing associations, as well as some voluntary, community and social enterprise (VCSE) providers. The demand for our training increased during the Black Lives Matters movement, and has remained high. Our focus is on the impact and importance of considering the racial and cultural heritages of service users and beneficiaries on the approaches that practitioners take. Although Iyabo has retained overall responsibility for the negotiation and design of training courses, all training is delivered by qualified staff, often associates, and sessions are co-facilitated. Those new to training spend some time as observers before moving on to co-facilitate.

In our training we incorporate research findings and also consider the wider service and systemic context and government legislation. We have delivered training on topics such as Attachment and safeguarding across cultures, Culturally competent assessment, Eating disorders and culture, and Parenting across cultures, among others.

Training aims and objectives might include the following:

- Define cultural competence and cultural humility and explore how to develop culturally competent practice.

- Draw on frameworks and examples showing how culture influences health beliefs, practices and communication, and how this affects our work with individuals.

- Identify some of our own biases and assumptions about others.

- Understand why cultural competence and humility is important in mental health services in our culturally diverse society.

- Feel more confident in being able to promote equality and challenge discrimination in the workplace.

Our approach to training is interactive, with ongoing discussion of case studies that illustrate the theories and frameworks we present. We address issues of confidentiality from the start and place people's lived experiences at the centre of our discussions. From our early experiences of delivering training to practitioners, we noted the conflict between the enthusiasm shown by participants at the end of the training and their subsequent ability to influence change in their workplace. Therefore, we introduced an action planning exercise that included an acknowledgement of the barriers they face and options for addressing them.

Most training is face-to-face. However, we have also delivered online training, which presents different kinds of challenges. Most of these challenges are to do with ways of monitoring participant engagement, but also on picking up on the psychological impact of the issues under consideration, particularly those concerned with growing understanding of racism. To mitigate some of these challenges, we ask participants to keep their cameras turned on, we do not use breakout rooms, and we endeavour to follow up anyone who leaves during the session. We have found that engagement is less with online training, and yet we know from feedback that it is the discussions and reflections that are shared during sessions that participants value the most. Consequently, we would prefer to run face-to-face training wherever possible.

We evaluate all our training courses and seek verbal feedback throughout so that we can adapt delivery where possible during the session. We also use pre- and post-training questionnaires to obtain information about changes in awareness, knowledge and confidence with regard to the learning objectives as well as the content, appropriateness and anticipated impact of the training course. We analyse evaluation sheets after each course to determine what worked well and what could be improved, and we use it to fine-tune subsequent training that we deliver. We share this feedback with the commissioner of training as relevant.

Training case study: Child and Adolescent Mental Health Services (CAMHS)

In 2021–22, Greater Manchester Health and Social Care Partnership commissioned Just Psychology to deliver training in cultural competence for staff in CAMHS over several days. Seventy-four staff attended the training including mental health practitioners, consultant psychiatrists, education mental health practitioners, clinical psychologists, service managers, children and young people counsellors, nurse specialists and systemic psychotherapists.

Our feedback forms showed increases in attendees' confidence in their ability to identify their own biases about culture and promoting equality in the workplace after the training. There were also significant improvements in their understanding of the factors that influence migration and family functioning in different cultures, and the impacts culture can have on health beliefs, parenting practices and communication. The participants were very positive about the content of the training – 78 per cent said it was 'Very interesting' and the presentation style was marked as 'Excellent' by 78 per cent of the participants. The length of the day was about right for most of the participants (94 per cent), and the level of difficulty was about right for everyone (100 per cent).

When participants were asked what they liked most about the training, their written feedback included:

> I felt that I learned a great deal without feeling overwhelmed. I really valued how much discussion the themes generated collectively but also personally. I thought the training was well formatted and delivered.

> Content – interactive discussions specific to CAMHS.

> Informative, covered a broad range; multidimensional framework was useful.

CAMHS conducted their own internal report once all the training sessions had been delivered. It showed that 100 per cent of the participants rated the training as 'Good' or 'Very good' and 100 per cent said they would recommend it to other professionals. One participant described:

> Feeling more able to be curious about others' cultural backgrounds; as well as being reminded of the idea that even if you are from one background your experience is unique, so asking curious questions is not a sign of not having taken the time to understand another person's culture. Cultural competency is not something that is ever complete.

Furthermore, 84 per cent stated they made changes to clinical practice following the training; for example:

> Increased use of interpreters and greater consideration to the impact of migration and the family journey.

> More thorough assessment process to gather information about family and cultural background.

> One client commented that they really appreciated an increase in their understanding of the issue that came from this training.

However, 50 per cent of staff reported barriers to making changes in practice, including reduced workforce and staff turnover, lack of diversity in the team, workload, and pressures undermining time to focus on implementing change. This challenges the sustainability of one-off training sessions and their ability to effect long-lasting change in the understanding and skills of staff.

Combined training and consultation

While our training has often been recommissioned so that new members of staff can also benefit and sustain the team's understanding and culture regarding race, ethnicity and culture and the impact on practice, we have also been commissioned to deliver both training and consultation to whole staff teams in order to embed cultural knowledge and understanding in the organization's culture – not seeing it as a one-off exercise, but one that needs to be embedded in the organization or team's policies, procedures and processes in order to introduce and sustain change.

Over the years, we found that a combination of both training and consultation is most effective in ensuring sustainable change in teams and organizations. Sometimes we focus on consultation.

Consultation

Consultation is about capacity building at an organizational level. Just Psychology has been involved in various forms of consultation, all of which involve us working with other organizations to identify and support actionable plans for both enabling those working within the organizations to better support the mental health and wellbeing of Global Majority children and their families and for helping organizations build cultural awareness into their own processes, thereby enhancing their relevance and accessibility for Global Majority children and families.

Our process of service consultation includes the following:

- Development of a working group and key responsibilities
- Creating a shared vision and ownership

- Identifying goals and objectives for the team and organization as a whole
- Identifying barriers and enablers
- Collecting, analysing and disseminating data on service mapping and accessibility, adaptations to delivery of services, engagement with service users, workforce and staffing
- Mapping the community/faith organizations in the locality and identifying key contacts
- Identifying opportunities for co-production and collaboration with local communities, and working with them to develop and pilot accessible and culturally appropriate interventions
- Development of resources that address cultural and racial diversity
- Development and implementation of a plan of action – benchmarking and assessing progress.

Training and consultation case study: Perinatal services

We were commissioned by Cheshire and Merseyside NHS Trust in 2022 to deliver training in parenting across cultures to staff in their specialist perinatal services. The positive impact of the training was similar to that of other training that we have delivered (e.g. 24 per cent of participants indicated they felt 'Fairly confident' pre-training compared to 95 per cent of participants who felt 'Fairly confident' or 'Very confident' post-training). However, we were also commissioned to provide ongoing consultation to address issues of system change over the course of two years. The consultations involved regular sessions (three times per year) with a small group of senior managers and practitioners with the aim of 'increasing access and developing culturally responsive psychological interventions in perinatal and maternal mental health'.

The consultations involved reviewing and supporting the implementation of systems change and addressed issues such as improving staff engagement, issues of ownership and leadership, project planning, staff training and supervision, reviewing resources, data collection and measuring change, sustainability and team cultures. The service also commissioned us to deliver the training in parenting across cultures on an annual basis to ensure that all new staff received it, thereby ensuring consistency and a shared understanding of the needs of families from Global Majority communities.

The team reported significant changes to the delivery of their services and to staff engagement with monitoring and increasing the ethnic diversity of their service users. They described the consultations as providing containment and scaffolding with implementing their plans. They shared their plans with us first, and felt more confident with proceeding to change their service models. Having a perspective from experienced consultants that were external to their organization was reassuring and enabled a clearer sense of direction – it helped to have someone else 'bearing witness to the process'. The shared goals and values with Just Psychology were critical to developing a trusted relationship.

Training and consultation case study: Counselling support for international new arrival pupils

Our largest capacity-building project was commissioned by Salford Council as part of their 0–25 Emotional Health and Wellbeing Strategy to provide counselling support for international new arrival (INA) pupils, including asylum and refugee children, EAL (English as an additional language) and Roma children. We were commissioned to provide training and consultation support to build capacity in schools and enable staff to effectively meet the holistic needs of INA children and families by training key staff in counselling skills and culturally competent practice. Commissioners were also seeking a better understanding of the needs of these children and their families. The pilot lasted two years, with the first year focusing on training and the second year focusing on implementation of changes in the system. It was delivered in half a day per week during term time and was attended by nine staff (including family wellbeing coordinators, one-to-one support workers, teaching assistants, learning mentors and an attendance coordinator) from four primary schools and one secondary school.

Topics covered in the training included: Basic counselling skills, Counselling children, Supervision, INA family context, Creative approaches, Impact of migration, Child development,

Biculturalism, Attachment and culture, Impact of parenting in conflict/war zones, Culturally sensitive safeguarding, Working with refugee children in schools, Bereavement and culture and Cultural consultancy. Throughout the course, participants also gained and developed key skills in self-awareness and reflection, and using supervision. We supported participants with developing and implementing case studies in which they each worked individually with a child in their school to put their new skills and understanding into practice.

The second year focused on systemic change with the same participants developing projects within their respective schools. These were designed to meet the needs of specific groups of children/families based on the learning from the project. For example, one participant implemented family music groups in their school as a way of engaging with Global Majority families in a non-pathologizing way. The participants were supported with supervision and practical skills for implementing and managing their projects. The second year also included visits to local organizations and services offering support to refugee families, vulnerable adults and children. This included The Broughton Trust, Salford Loaves & Fishes, Revive UK, Rainbow Haven and Mustard Tree. Participants reported gaining greater awareness of the support available in the local area for families in need, and saw this as 'invaluable information and advice' that could be passed on to parents. They also reported that visiting these organizations had given them ideas for future support sessions in schools. Some other organizations also delivered sessions to the participants (e.g. Greater Manchester Immigration Aid Unit on immigration and the legal processes and the Parental Engagement Network on engaging families in their children's education).

Participants gave anonymous written feedback on the impact of the learning on their work throughout the project:

I have definitely made a conscious effort to ask more open-ended questions.

I was able to implement some of the counselling strategies that I have acquired over the last few weeks. They really helped when supporting a Year 10 pupil with anger issues.

I'm more aware of how well I'm listening and responding to children's needs.

Taking time to talk to individual children about their home life and different cultures.

More aware of race and gender.

Know more about some of the services that are available throughout Salford and sharing these with schools.

Counselling skills – paraphrasing, reflecting.

Visiting other organizations has been really interesting and has given me some ideas for future sessions.

Our experience of the impact of our team consultations is that they are highly effective if they take place regularly over an agreed period of time. However, they are tailored specifically to each team/organization and require a significant amount of work investment in becoming familiar with the organization, teams, roles and organizational culture.

Internal capacity building: recruitment and whole team meetings

Internal capacity building has been embedded in our recruitment and induction processes and procedures. Interviews always include a focus on alignment with our vision and values, including examples of how candidates have demonstrated this in their work and personal experiences. We have bi-annual team events that are aimed at involving all staff (including volunteers, board members and advisory group members) in reviewing our values, their implications for our work and organizational development.

Recruitment and whole team meetings case study: Just Psychology team event

In June 2019, we held a half-day team event at a local community venue. It was attended by all our employees, as well as several Cultural Consultants, associate psychologists/therapists, advisory group members, non-executive directors and associate family group conference (FGC) coordinators. The event was co-facilitated by an advisory group member and a non-executive director, and included lunch and time to gather and connect over culturally diverse food. It began with team members from each service presenting 'Good news stories'. This was followed by small group discussions in which the question 'What makes Just Psychology special?' was explored. Responses were collated on flip charts and a thematic analysis was conducted following the event.

Five broad themes emerged from the analysis:

- *Service and standards:* Attendees described our work as 'innovative' and 'accessible', with 'preventative' interventions being offered by 'highly skilled staff'. Attendees also valued the flexibility and integrity of the team as well as the focus on 'respecting humanity'.

- *Professional development and team work:* Attendees stated that 'the whole team engages in continual learning, reflection and reconceptualization of issues affecting children and families as well as their own practice, and this contributes to the process of "changing the narrative" around challenges faced by children and families as well as agencies working with them'.

- *Cultural awareness:* Attendees described Just Psychology as having 'a great sense of cultural awareness' and 'community knowledge and presence' with 'huge potential to grow and make a difference in communities'.

- *Making connections:* Attendees reflected that everyone working at Just Psychology shares a common goal to ensure consistency in their practice and to engage with other services and communities – 'bit by bit they are developing new narratives for change: for systems change, not just individual change'.

- *Inclusivity:* Attendees described Just Psychology as 'collaborative', 'cooperative' and providing a 'sense of belonging'. The team and services were 'inclusive and welcoming'.

These team events are an opportunity to reiterate and embed Just Psychology's vision, mission and values on a regular basis, thus building capacity within the team to enact and develop them. Not only that, they are a reminder that, taken as a whole, Just Psychology makes a strong contribution to systems change.

Workforce development: employability and career development

Another approach that we have taken to increasing the capacity of the workforce to address and respond appropriately to the needs of Global Majority people has included the use of employability and career development programmes. Just Psychology is mainly staffed with psychological and social care professionals. This includes qualified practitioners as well as people who are at the beginning of their career journeys. We have always created psychology graduate positions (voluntary and paid) with a clear focus on developing skills and experience so they can access NHS roles and apply for training as practitioner psychologists (including clinical, counselling and health psychology). They are supported to develop skills in report writing, group facilitation, delivering training, etc. Within these programmes, we focus on the skills and knowledge of Global Majority and White British staff regarding the impact of race and culture on the mental health and wellbeing of children and families, as well as addressing the underrepresentation of people from Global Majority communities within the psychological professions.

We are aware of the concerns about voluntary graduate experiences being discriminatory as they require volunteers to have sufficient resources to enable them to live while taking up the voluntary experience, and the danger of using unpaid workers to replace full-time jobs (BPS 2024). Early in the development of Just Psychology's workforce, we consulted with trainee clinical psychologists on placement with us and psychology graduates to develop our voluntary work placements (honorary assistant psychologist) and to adhere to best practice, outlined by the British Psychological Society (BPS 2024). We addressed issues of privilege and accessibility in this programme by limiting it to a maximum of two days per week over a six-month period. This ensured that participants were able to access opportunities for paid work elsewhere, and those from lower-income backgrounds were not excluded by having to commit more hours to the placement.

All applicants had to demonstrate a clear interest in cultural diversity and psychology and show an interest in pursuing a career as a practitioner psychologist. The placements were structured to include relevant opportunities (e.g. group co-facilitation, service audit and evaluation), and assistance with navigating the pathway into the profession (e.g. assistance with writing job applications or training applications, job interview role-plays). Support and mentoring was provided by qualified psychological practitioners and trainee practitioner psychologists on placement with Just Psychology in their final year.

Employability and career development case study: From voluntary work to a professional training placement (by Clio Oliver, trainee clinical psychologist)

After completing my undergraduate degree, I was fortunate to apply for a part-time honorary assistant psychologist position at Just Psychology. With my retail job providing financial stability, I was able to accept this opportunity. However, I now realize the inherent privilege of being able to take on an unpaid role, particularly in light of the current cost of living crisis, which limits such opportunities for many psychology graduates (especially those of colour).

During my time at Just Psychology, I supported the family group conference (FGC) project, which heightened my awareness of health inequalities and enabled me to contribute to improving care for underrepresented children, young people and families. Under the supervision of Dr Iyabo Fatimilehin, I co-facilitated cultural awareness training, assisted in organizing team events and supported the evaluation of training sessions and FGCs. This experience not only enriched my clinical skills, but also broadened my understanding of the challenges faced by diverse populations, and was instrumental in securing my first full-time position as an assistant psychologist in the NHS.

Several years later, as I near the completion of my Clinical Psychology doctorate, I often reflect on how my early career experiences laid the groundwork for my professional development and instilled the confidence needed to pursue a career in clinical psychology. So, when the opportunity arose for me to complete my final placement at Just Psychology, it was a particularly meaningful full-circle moment. This experience has allowed me to reflect on my journey and appreciate the growth and learning that has shaped my career. While on placement, I have valued participating in the Trafford Sunrise and Family Reunion and Parenting Projects. By leading the facilitation of training sessions, group interventions and providing peer mentoring/supervision, my placement experiences have enhanced my confidence and made me feel better equipped for life as a qualified clinical psychologist. By returning to where it all began, I am reminded of the invaluable lessons and opportunities that have guided me towards becoming a clinical psychologist, and having that voluntary opportunity so early in my career is one I will always treasure.

The voluntary work placements have existed alongside paid assistant psychologist (psychology graduate) positions, with some volunteers moving into paid positions as they became available. An understanding and commitment to cultural and racial diversity continued to be essential criteria that were included in the recruitment process. For example: *Understanding of the experiences of minority ethnic groups in the mental health system and in society at large* is an 'Essential' not 'Desirable' criterion. All assistant psychologists were supervised by qualified clinical or counselling psychologists and actively supported with applying for doctoral training.

Many of these early career workers with Just Psychology have gone on to further training, some returning to work for Just Psychology as vacancies arise. We also provide placements for clinical and counselling psychology trainees and social work students, opening up experiences that would be difficult for them to obtain through other placements. We specifically seek to improve accessibility to health and social care careers for young people who are from racially and culturally minoritized communities, as well as ensuring that all those starting their careers have an improved understanding of the importance of addressing cultural diversity and cultural competence in practice.

We also have a commitment to increase employability skills for Global Majority communities, and the Cultural Consultants Project (see Chapter 7) is a good example of this. All Cultural Consultants undergo training in cultural diversity and safe cultural practice, in addition to counselling skills and professional skills. Some Cultural Consultants have remained in contact with Just Psychology over the years despite gaining employment elsewhere, and have continued to contribute to the development of our work, for example through being involved in development and delivering training and consultation to other organizations (such as neurodiversity and culture, working with families from Hong Kong).

Challenges faced by capacity building

While our approaches to capacity building and development both within and external to Just Psychology have resulted in positive outcomes overall, there have also been many challenges and dilemmas. Our training programmes have been developed by our team over the years and our personal experiences of working as psychologists and practitioners are embedded within them. As we have grown this work, we have encountered issues regarding the protection of our intellectual property. Some people who have attended our training have proceeded to use some of it in the delivery of their own training, and this has led us to question our openness in sharing our materials. On more than one occasion, managers and training leads have explained that they were not going to recommission us because their staff already had our training materials and could use them themselves.

This has led us to reconsider our charges, setting a realistic price not just for delivery but also for our materials, which at the moment we include in the price for the training – but not with the expectation that they will then be copied and used internally. It also means we are unable to monitor how people are responding to the training and change the pace of sessions, spend more time on some aspects than others, and ensure that everyone has positive, safe experiences. As we are helping people better meet the needs of racially and ethnically minoritized children and families, our training includes explorations of racism and power, which will sometimes raise profound emotional reactions. This is not an insignificant issue – we have a responsibility in both training and consultation to ensure that these are safe places for personal and group development.

Our assistant psychology programme has also presented us with dilemmas over the years. It has led to high staff turnover within our team as both the honorary and paid roles are designed to be fixed term in an attempt to encourage a strong focus on career development and making the best use of the opportunities available. However, this commitment to time-limited posts has also had some very positive outcomes. An audit of the career development of the voluntary and paid assistant psychologist roles shows that since we started the programme in 2014, a total of 27 graduates have engaged with it, 74 per cent of whom were from Global Majority backgrounds. Forty per cent of them have either completed training as clinical/counselling/ educational psychologists or are currently on the training courses. An additional 40 per cent moved on to employment in mental health practitioner or assistant psychologist roles in the NHS.

Providing these opportunities for young people from minoritized ethnic backgrounds who might not have the connections to enable them to engage with and be supported into psychological careers is a significant outcome of Just Psychology's work. It is not just about representation but also about the engagement with their lived experience and the development of their understanding of the impact of cultural diversity, cultural competence and social justice when working in health and social care settings with Global Majority communities.

Conclusion

We have implemented both hard and soft capacity building strategies at individual, organizational and system levels. We used our understanding of soft systems in designing and implementing collaborative external capacity building. We have endeavoured to employ best practice in supporting early career mental health practitioners, and to ensure that opportunities for employability and career development are integrated into the work of the organization.

Acknowledgements

We would like to acknowledge and thank current and past colleagues who have made significant contributions to Just Psychology's external capacity building approaches over the years. They include: Dr Hasan Waheed (now Just Psychology's training lead), Dr Aneela Pilkington, Amira Hasan, Annette Williams, Dr Ruth O'Shaughnessy, Georgina Hughes and Dr Cat O'Neill.

Conclusion

IYABO FATIMILEHIN AND HASAN WAHEED

This book has provided a reflective overview of the work that Just Psychology has delivered since it was constituted as a Community Interest Company (CIC) in 2011. We have explored the ways in which it has journeyed towards its vision of the full participation of all Black and minority ethnic children, adults and their families in an equal and fair society through the achievement of a significant improvement in psychological health and mental wellbeing, and the prevention of problems with mental health. This vision is at the heart of the development and delivery of services that acknowledge the cultural diversity within our society by embedding culturally competent interventions, and working towards social justice.

Just Psychology has delivered services that use systemic and narrative approaches, that support families through the process of migration and settlement, and that acknowledge the assets within our culturally diverse communities. We have emphasized the strengths and resources of local community members and supported employability and community engagement. Our services and projects are community-based to improve accessibility and also to enable us to understand the challenges that families are facing. We acknowledge and have lived experience of the impact of racism and discrimination, and this underpins our values. We have promoted the use of strengths/asset-based approaches that empower people from Global Majority communities and enable them to develop solutions to the problems they face.

Just Psychology also has a strong commitment to capacity building – both internally and externally. We address cultural competence within our organization and also support other organizations to continually improve their understanding and knowledge of working across cultures. Our understanding of cultural diversity incorporates diversity within cultures and over time. It is extremely important that we do not have a stance that assumes complete knowledge of a specific culture but includes intersectionality and changes over time. We encourage a posture of continuous learning and development.

Our work has taken place in a context of increased levels of connectivity across the world, both virtual and physical. Along with this there have been significant changes in the political, social and economic contexts within the UK and globally (e.g. Brexit, hostile immigration policies, Covid-19, wars in Sudan, Palestine and Ukraine, and the cost of living crisis). These contexts must be taken into account when delivering services, with an understanding of how globalization is affecting the beliefs and values of people from different cultural communities. While these local and global changes have been extremely challenging, they have also presented opportunities.

One of our consistent observations has been the ways in which people from different Global Majority communities have been able to connect and support each other within our services. Just Psychology does not work with a specific ethnic group; we work with a wide range of ethnicities, cultures and communities, and the connections and solidarity that people have built across cultures has been inspiring. However, this does not mean we have taken a 'one size fits all' approach. We have developed services and interventions in consultation and partnership with people from specific communities and ensured that they are accessible and appropriate. We are committed to co-production and creativity in the development and delivery of our services. We believe that it is the services that are 'hard to reach' and not the communities. Co-production leads to more accessible and non-stigmatizing services.

We believe that significant improvements in the delivery of health and social care services will require changes in government policies and priorities. Primary prevention needs to be prioritized above tertiary intervention in order to improve the health of the whole population. This is not just relevant for mental health but also essential for physical health (e.g. obesity), drugs and alcohol, social media and safeguarding. It is increasingly evident that the physical, emotional and social aspects of human beings are linked both individually and collectively, and interventions need to take this into account. Similarly, the commissioning of services would benefit considerably from a more collaborative approach across health, social care and education services. The inclusion of voluntary, community, faith and social enterprise (VCFSE) organizations has been a significant and positive development in recent years, but requires a commissioning approach that respects the commitment of local organizations and does not drain their resources. There is a stark difference between public sector and VCFSE providers regarding their ability to withstand changes in commissioning requirements and processes. The competitive approach to tendering for public sector contracts is also a drain on local organizations, and a partnership approach would enable a more stable and effective delivery of services to local communities.

We are strong advocates for systemic family approaches to intervention and prevention, and have witnessed shifts towards more individualized approaches in recent decades. One manifestation of this is the increase in practitioners who have only been trained to work with children and young people as individuals and not as members of families or communities. While this might be cheaper due to the lower levels of training required, it fails to address the issues within families that may be precipitating or perpetuating the child's difficulties. It also fails to leverage the strengths and resources of families and communities. A counsellor or practitioner is only in the child's life for a limited number of hours; engaging with the system around the child/young person has more effective and sustainable benefits, and can also impact positively on other children and young people in the family, thus preventing difficulties in the medium and long term. We would argue that systemic approaches are more cost effective as forms of both intervention and prevention.

We believe that everyone has the right to accessible and appropriate services, and that the development of culturally competent interventions should be mandatory. Despite the legislation that is in force in the UK (e.g. Race Relations (Amendment) Act 2000), most public sector services take a *voluntary* 'nice to have' approach to cultural competence unlike other aspects of service delivery (e.g. safeguarding, confidentiality). This is tantamount to discrimination as it maintains a position where certain communities are unable to access services due to their protected characteristics (see the Equality Act 2010).

We will continue to work towards our organizational vision and collaborate with a wide range of stakeholders in order to achieve it. We have not achieved this on our own and acknowledge the commitment and passion of those who have journeyed with us and helped to make a difference. This includes authors of the chapters in this book, our advisory group and board members, Cultural Consultants, trainee practitioner psychologists, social work students, assistant psychologists, undergraduate placement students, associate psychologists and therapists, family group conference coordinators, consultants and contractors, and all our staff and employees.

We would also like to thank our funders, commissioners and local partners, including: Rainbow Haven, We Are Survivors, Making Education a Priority, Greater Manchester Immigration Aid Unit, British Red Cross, Seymour Park Primary School, Trafford Housing Trust, Association of Mental Health Providers, National Lottery Community Fund, Livv Housing Group, Trafford Clinical Commissioning Group, Trafford Local Authority, The Fore, Greater Manchester Combined Authority, Social Enterprise Support Fund, School for Social Entrepreneurs, Salford City Council, Seedbed, Henry Smith Charity and Enterprise Development Programme.

We would specifically like to thank the initial supporters who developed the mission, vision and values of Just Psychology, including Carolyn Kagan, Calla Thompson, Amira Hassan, Rhona Brown and Ruth O'Shaughnessy.

Finally, we acknowledge the privilege and honour it has been to work with the children, families and local communities over the years. We thank them for engaging with us and trusting us in our work with them. We will continue to advocate for cultural competence and social justice in services for children, families and communities.

References

Adams, E. A., Kurtz-Costes, B. E. and Hoffman, A. J. (2016) 'Skin tone bias among African Americans: Antecedents and consequences across the life span.' *Developmental Review 40*, 93–116. https://doi.org/10.1016/j.dr.2016.03.002

Ajayi, O. (2021) 'A perspective on health inequalities in Black, Asian and minority ethnic communities and how to improve access to primary care.' *Future Healthcare Journal 8*, 1, 36–39. https://doi.org/10.7861/fhj.2020-0217

Akhurst, J., Kagan, C., Lawthom, R. and Richards, M. (2016) 'Community psychology practice competencies: Some perspectives from the UK.' *Global Journal of Community Psychology Practice 7*, 4, 1–15. www.gjcpp.org/pdfs/6Akhurst-etal.pdf

Alexander, C. and Byrne, B. (2020) 'Introduction.' In B. Byrne, C. Alexander, O. Khan, J. Nazroo and W. Shankley (Eds) *Ethnicity, Race and Inequality in the UK: State of the Nation* (pp.1–14). Policy Press.

Alexander, C. and Shankley, W. (2020) 'Ethnic Inequalities in the State Education System in England.' In B. Byrne, C. Alexander, O. Khan, J. Nazroo and W. Shankley (Eds) *Ethnicity, Race and Inequality in the UK: State of the Nation* (pp.93–126). Policy Press. https://doi.org/10.56687/9781447351269-009

Al-Krenawi, A. and Graham, J. R. (2000) 'Culturally sensitive social work practice with Arab clients in mental health settings.' *Health & Social Work 25*, 1, 9–22. doi: 10.1093/hsw/25.1.9.

Allerton, L. and Bullen, E. (2021) *Children in Manchester: A Profile of Manchester's Children from Birth to 16 Years Old.* Shared Intelligence, PRI, Manchester City Council, England.

Al Shamsi, H., Almutairi, A. G., Al Mashrafi, S. and Al Kabani, T. (2020) 'Implications of language barriers for healthcare: A systematic review.' *Oman Medical Journal 35*, 2, e122. doi: 10.5001/omj.2020.40.

Al-Yateem, N., Hijazi, H., Saifan, A. R., Ahmad, A., *et al.* (2023) 'Quality and safety issue: Language barriers in healthcare, a qualitative study of non-Arab healthcare practitioners caring for Arabic patients in the UAE.' *BMJ Open 13*, e076326. https://doi.org/10.1136/bmjopen-2023-076326

Anderson, H. and Gehart, D. (2007) *Collaborative Therapy: Relationships and Conversations That Make a Difference.* Routledge.

Anderson, K. K., Flora, N., Archie, S., Morgan, C. and McKenzie, K. (2014) 'A meta-analysis of ethnic differences in pathways to care at the first episode of psychosis.' *Acta Psychiatrica Scandinavica 130*, 4, 257–268. https://doi.org/10.1111/acps.12254

Arias, V. S. and Punyanunt-Carter, N. M. (2017) 'Family, culture, and communication.' *Oxford Research Encyclopedia of Communication.* doi: 10.1093/acrefore/9780190228613.013.504.

Arnell, P., Lewis, O., Kalocsányiová, E. and Forrester, A. (2023) 'The UK's illegal migration bill: Human rights violated.' *Medicine, Science and the Law 63*, 4. https://doi.org/10.1177/00258024231186736

Arnett, J. J. (2008) 'The neglected 95%: Why American psychology needs to become less American.' *The American Psychologist 63*, 7, 602–614. doi: 10.1037/0003-066X.63.7.602.

Arnstein, S. (1969) 'A ladder of citizen participation.' *Journal of the American Planning Association 35*, 4, 216–224.

Arogundade, T., Shibib, S., Melton, W. and Younis, A. (2023) 'A service evaluation of referrals to Sheffield Community Child and Adolescent Mental Health Services (CAMHS) by ethnicity and areas of deprivation.' *BJPsych Open 9*, S1, S131–S132. https://doi.org/10.1192/bjo.2023.365

Asen, E. and Scholz, M. (2010) *Multi-Family Therapy: Concepts and Techniques.* Routledge.

Ashley, C. and Nixon, P. (Eds) (2007) *Family Group Conferences: Where Next? Policies and Practices for the Future.* Family Rights Group.

Ashley, C., Halton, L., Horan, H. and Wiffin, J. (2006) *The Family Group Conference Toolkit: A Practical Guide for Setting Up and Running an FGC Service.* Department for Education and Skills, Welsh Assembly and Family Rights Group.

Bains, S. and Gutman, L. M. (2021) 'Mental health in ethnic minority populations in the UK: Developmental trajectories from early childhood to mid-adolescence.' *Journal of Youth and Adolescence 50*, 11, 2151–2165. https://doi.org/10.1007/s10964-021-01481-5

Bamford, J., Klabbers, G., Curran, E., Rosato, M. and Leavey, G. (2021) 'Social capital and mental health among Black and minority ethnic groups in the UK.' *Journal of Immigrant and Minority Health 23*, 3, 502–510. https://doi.org/10.1007/s10903-020-01043-0

Bandura, A. (1977) *Social Learning Theory.* Prentice-Hall.

Bansal, N., Karlsen, S., Sashidharan, S. P., Cohen, R., Chew-Graham, C. A. and Malpass, A. (2022) 'Understanding ethnic inequalities in mental healthcare in the UK: A meta-ethnography.' *PLOS Medicine 19*, 12, e1004139. https://doi.org/10.1371/journal.pmed.1004139

Barn, R. and Das, C. (2016) 'Family group conferences and cultural competence in social work.' *The British Journal of Social Work 46*, 4, 942–959. https://doi.org/10.1093/bjsw/bcu105

Barnes, M., Bauld, L., Benzeval, M., Mackenzie, M., Sullivan, H. and Judge, K. (Eds) (2012) *Health Action Zones: Partnerships for Health Equity.* Routledge. https://doi.org/10.4324/9780203358337

Bateson, G. (2000) *Steps to an Ecology of Mind: Collected Essays in Anthropology, Psychiatry, Evolution, and Epistemology.* The University of Chicago Press.

Bateson, G. (2002) *Mind and Nature: A Necessary Unity.* Hampton Press.

Bateson, N. (2023) *Combining.* Triarchy Press.

Baumrind, D. (1967) 'Child care practices anteceding three patterns of preschool behaviour.' *Genetic Psychology Monographs 75*, 43–48.

BBC News (2017) 'Manchester attack: Islamophobic hate crime reports increase by 500%.' 22 June. www.bbc.co.uk/news/uk-england-manchester-40368668

Bécares, L. and Atatoa-Carr, P. (2016) 'The association between maternal and partner experienced racial discrimination and prenatal perceived stress, prenatal and postnatal depression: Findings from the growing up in New Zealand cohort study.' *International Journal for Equity in Health 15*, 1, 155. https://doi.org/10.1186/s12939-016-0443-4

Begum, S. and Williams, M. (2023) *Dear Stephen: Race and Belonging 30 Years On*. The Runnymede Trust. www.runnymedetrust.org/publications/dear-stephen-race-and-belonging-30-years-on

BEIS (Department for Business, Energy & Industrial Strategy) (2016) 'Creating a Community Interest Company.' In *Information and Guidance Notes* (Chapter 4). Office of the Regulator of Community Interest Companies.

Beiser, M. and Hou, F. (2006) 'Ethnic identity, resettlement stress, and depressive affect among Southeast Asian refugees in Canada.' *Social Science & Medicine 63*, 1, 137–150. doi: 10.1016/j.socscimed.2005.12.002.

Beresford, P. (2019) 'Public participation in health and social care: Exploring the co-production of knowledge.' *Frontiers in Sociology 3*, 41. https://doi.org/10.3389/fsoc.2018.00041

Bernard, C. (2020) 'Understanding the lived experiences of Black and ethnic minority children and families.' www.researchinpractice.org.uk/media/f2scxc5m/kb-understanding-the-lived-experiences-of-black-asian-and-minority-ethnic-children-and-families.pdf

Bernard, D. L., Smith, Q. and Lanier, P. (2022) 'Racial discrimination and other adverse childhood experiences as risk factors for internalizing mental health concerns among Black youth.' *Journal of Traumatic Stress 35*, 2, 473–483. doi: 10.1002/jts.22760.

Berry, J. W. (1992) 'Acculturation and adaptation in a new society.' *International Migration 30*, 1, 69–85. https://doi.org/10.1111/j.1468-2435.1992.tb00776.x

Bertrando, P. (2007) *The Dialogical Therapist: Dialogue in Systemic Practice*. Routledge.

Bhugra, D. (2004) 'Migration and mental health.' *Acta Psychiatrica Scandinavica 109*, 4, 243–258. https://doi.org/10.1046/j.0001-690X.2003.00246.x

Bhui, K. and Bhugra, D. (2002) 'Explanatory models for mental distress: Implications for clinical practice and research.' *The British Journal of Psychiatry 181*, 6–7. doi: 10.1192/bjp.181.1.6.

Bignall, T., Jeraj, S., Helsby, E. and Butt, J. (2019) *Racial Disparities in Mental Health: Literature and Evidence Review*. Race Equality Foundation. https://raceequality foundation.org.uk/wp-content/uploads/2022/10/mental-health-report-v5-2-2.pdf

Birney, A. (2017) *Cultivating System Change: A Practitioner's Companion*. Routledge. https://doi.org/10.4324/9781351274685

Bjornstrom, E. E., Kaufman, R. L., Peterson, R. D. and Slater, M. D. (2010) 'Race and ethnic representations of lawbreakers and victims in crime news: A national study of television coverage.' *Social Problems 57*, 2, 269–293. doi: 10.1525/sp.2010.57.2.269.

Booth, R. (2019) 'Racism rising since Brexit vote, nationwide study reveals.' *The Guardian*, 20 May. www.theguardian.com/world/2019/may/20/racism-on-the-rise-since-brexit-vote-nationwide-study-reveals

Booth, R. and Mohdin, A. (2018) 'Revealed: The stark evidence of everyday racial bias in Britain.' *The Guardian*, 2 December. www.theguardian.com/uk-news/2018/dec/02/revealed-the-stark-evidence-of-everyday-racial-bias-in-britain

Bornstein, M. H. (2012) 'Cultural approaches to parenting.' *Parenting, Science and Practice 12*, 2–3, 212–221. doi: 10.1080/15295192.2012.683359.

Boyd-Franklin, N. and Hafer Bry, B. (2000) *Reaching Out in Family Therapy: Home-Based, School, and Community Interventions*. Guilford Press.

Boyle, D. and Harris, M. (2009) *The Challenge of Co-Production: How Equal Partnerships Between Professionals and the Public Are Crucial to Improving Public Services*.

New Economics Foundation/NESTA. https://media.nesta.org.uk/documents/the_challenge_of_co-production.pdf

BPS (British Psychological Society) (2018) 'Power Threat Meaning Framework (PTMF).' www.bps.org.uk/member-networks/division-clinical-psychology/power-threat-meaning-framework

BPS (2024) 'Expected standards for the recruitment and employment of assistant psychologists (APs).' www.bps.org.uk/guideline/expected-standards-recruitment-and-employment-assistant-psychologists-aps

Branscombe, N. R. and Ryan, M. K. (Eds) (2013) *The SAGE Handbook of Gender and Psychology*. SAGE Publications.

Briggs, S. and Whittaker, A. (2018) 'Protecting children from faith-based abuse through accusations of witchcraft and spirit possession: Understanding contexts and informing practice.' *The British Journal of Social Work 48*, 8, 2157–2175. https://doi.org/10.1093/bjsw/bcx155

Bristow, A. (2021) *Meeting the Housing Needs of Black, Asian and minority ethnic Households in England: The Role of the Planning System*. Heriot Watt University, I-SPHERE (Institute for Social Policy, Housing and Equalities Research) and Oak Foundation. https://i-sphere.site.hw.ac.uk/wp-content/uploads/sites/15/2021/08/A.Bristow-Final-report.pdf

Bronfenbrenner, U. (1992) 'Ecological Systems Theory.' In R. Vasta (Ed.) *Six Theories of Child Development: Revised Formulations and Current Issues* (pp.187–249). Jessica Kingsley Publishers.

Brookfield, S. (2010) 'Critical Reflection as an Adult Learning Process.' In N. Lyons (Ed.) *Handbook of Reflection and Reflective Inquiry* (pp.215–236). Springer US. https://doi.org/10.1007/978-0-387-85744-2_11

Brown, A., Ford, T., Deighton, J. and Wolpert, M. (2014) 'Satisfaction in child and adolescent mental health services: Translating users' feedback into measurement.' *Administration and Policy in Mental Health and Mental Health Services Research 41*, 4, 434–446. doi: 10.1007/s10488-012-0433-9.

Bukowski, W. M. and Adams, R. (2005) 'Peer relationships and psychopathology: Markers, moderators, mediators, mechanisms, and meanings.' *Journal of Clinical Child and Adolescent Psychology 34*, 1, 3–10. doi: 10.1207/s15374424jccp3401_1.

Burnham, J. (2012) 'Developments in Social GRRRAAACCEEESSS: Visible-Invisible and Voiced-Unvoiced.' In I.-B. Krause (Ed.) *Culture and Reflexivity in Systemic Psychotherapy: Mutual Perspectives* (Chapter Seven). Routledge.

Burton, M. H. and Kagan, C. (2003) 'Community psychology: Why this gap in Britain?' *History & Philosophy of Psychology 4*, 2, 10–23. doi: 10.53841/bpshpp.2002.4.2.10.

Cabinet Office (2018) *Race Disparity Audit* (revised March 2018). HM Government, UK.

Cammaerts, B. (2022) 'The abnormalisation of social justice: The "anti-woke culture war" discourse in the UK.' *Discourse & Society 33*, 6, 730–743. https://doi.org/10.1177/09579265221095407

Canadian Race Relations Foundation (2021) *Race Relations in Canada 2021: A Survey of Canadian Public Opinion and Experience*. https://crrf-fcrr.ca/2021/11/race-relations-in-canada-2021-a-survey-of-canadian-public-opinion-and-experience

Casale, L., Seymour, N., Chentite, M. and Zlotowitz, S. (2019) 'People in Their Whole Context: Promoting Social Justice and Community Psychology as a Means to Prevent Psychological Distress and Improve Wellbeing for Children, Young People, and Their Families.' In J. Faulconbridge, K. Hunt and A. Laffan (Eds) *Improving the Psychological Wellbeing of Children and Young People: Effective Prevention and Early Intervention Across Health, Education and Social Care* (pp.190–210). Jessica Kingsley Publishers.

Chan, K. M. Y., Lim, E., Cheung, H., Choo, C. and Fu, C. S. L. (2023) 'The impact and perceived effectiveness of physical punishment: A qualitative study of young adults' retrospective accounts.' https://doi.org/10.31234/osf.io/d843p

Chaney, P. and Wincott, D. (2014) 'Envisioning the third sector's welfare role: Critical discourse analysis of "post-devolution" public policy in the UK, 1998–2012.' *Social Policy & Administration 48*, 7, 757–781. https://doi.org/10.1111/spol.12062

Chen, S. and Mallory, A. B. (2021) 'The effect of racial discrimination on mental and physical health: A propensity score weighting approach.' *Social Science & Medicine 285*, 114308. https://doi.org/10.1016/j.socscimed.2021.114308

Cheng, A. W., Rizkallah, M. and Narizhnaya, M. (2020) 'Individualism vs. Collectivism.' In B. J. Carducci, C. S. Nave, J. S. Mio and R. E. Riggio (Eds) *The Wiley Encyclopedia of Personality and Individual Differences, Volume 4: Clinical, Applied and Cross-Cultural Research* (pp.287–297). John Wiley & Sons.

Chouhan, K. and Nazroo, J. (2020) 'Health Inequalities.' In B. Byrne, C. Alexander, O. Khan, J. Nazroo and W. Shankley (Eds) *Ethnicity, Race and Inequality in the UK: State of the Nation* (pp.73–92). Policy Press.

Chui, Z., Gazard, B., MacCrimmon, S., Harwood, H., *et al.* (2021) 'Inequalities in referral pathways for young people accessing secondary mental health services in south east London.' *European Journal of Child & Adolescent Psychiatry 30*, 7, 1113–1128. doi: 10.1007/s00787-020-01603-7.

Chun, J. and Lee, J. (2006) 'Intergenerational solidarity in Korean immigrant families.' *Journal of Intergenerational Relationships 4*, 2, 6–21. doi: 10.1300/J194v04n02_02.

Coan, J. A. and Sbarra, D. A. (2015) 'Social baseline theory: The social regulation of risk and effort.' *Current Opinion in Psychology 1*, 87–91. doi: 10.1016/j.copsyc.2014.12.021.

Commission for Healthcare Audit and Inspection (2007) *Count Me In 2007: Results of the 2007 National Census of Inpatients in Mental Health and Learning Disability Services in England and Wales.* www.choiceforum.org/docs/countmein2.pdf

Community Psychology Section (2022) 'Using Community Psychology approaches to reduce the impact of inequality through the Community Mental Health Framework.' https://cms.bps.org.uk/sites/default/files/2022-07/Reducing%20the%20impact%20of%20social%20inequalities.pdf

Connolly, M. (1994) 'An act of empowerment: The Children, Young Persons and their Families Act (1989).' *The British Journal of Social Work 24*, 1, 87–100. https://doi.org/10.1093/oxfordjournals.bjsw.a056042

Connolly, M. (2004) *Child Protection and Family Welfare: Statutory Responses to Children at Risk.* Te Awatea Press.

Cornell, S. and Hartmann, D. (1998) *Ethnicity and Race: Making Identities in a Changing World.* Pine Forge Press.

Corrigan, P. W. and Watson, A. C. (2002) 'Understanding the impact of stigma on people with mental illness.' *World Psychiatry 1*, 1, 16–20. PMID: 16946807.

Cougle, J. R. and Grubaugh, A. L. (2022) 'Do psychosocial treatment outcomes vary by race or ethnicity? A review of meta-analyses.' *Clinical Psychology Review 96*, 102192. https://doi.org/10.1016/j.cpr.2022.102192

Cybulski, L., Ashcroft, D. M., Carr, M. J., Garg, S., *et al.* (2021) 'Temporal trends in annual incidence rates for psychiatric disorders and self-harm among children and adolescents in the UK, 2003–2018.' *BMC Psychiatry 21*, 1, 229. doi: 10.1186/s12888-021-03235-w.

Dabiri, E. (2023) *Disobedient Bodies: Reclaim Your Unruly Beauty.* Profile Books.

DaCosta, C., Dixon-Smith, S. and Singh, G. (2021) *Beyond Black, Asian and minority ethnic: Rethinking the Politics, Construction, Application, and Efficacy of Ethnic Categorisation*. April. https://pure.coventry.ac.uk/ws/portalfiles/portal/41898015/Beyond_BAME_final_report.pdf

Dallos, R. (2004) 'Attachment narrative therapy: Integrating ideas from narrative and attachment theory in systemic family therapy with eating disorders.' *Journal of Family Therapy 26*, 40–65. https://doi.org/10.1111/j.1467-6427.2004.00266.x

Das-Munshi, J., Bhugra, D. and Crawford, M. J. (2018) 'Ethnic minority inequalities in access to treatments for schizophrenia and schizoaffective disorders: Findings from a nationally representative cross-sectional study.' *BMC Medicine 16*, 1, 55. https://doi.org/10.1186/s12916-018-1035-5

Dawson, S. and Dargie, C. (2002) 'New Public Management: A Discussion with Special Reference to UK Health.' In K. McLaughlin, S. P. Osborne and E. Ferlie (Eds) *New Public Management: Current Trends and Future Prospects* (pp.34–56). Routledge.

de Shazer, S. (1985) *Keys to Solutions in Brief Therapy*. W. W. Norton & Company.

de Shazer, S. (1988) *Clues: Investigating Solutions in Brief Therapy*. W. W. Norton & Company.

de Shazer, S. and Dolan, Y. (2007) *More than Miracles: The State of the Art of Solution-Focused Brief Therapy*. Routledge.

de Shazer, S., Berg, I. K., Lipchik, E., Nunnally, E., *et al.* (1986) 'Brief therapy: Focused solution development.' *Family Process 25*, 2, 207–221. https://doi.org/10.1111/j.1545-5300.1986.00207.x

De Vos, J. (2009) '"Now that you know, how do you feel?" The Milgram experiment and psychologization.' *Annual Review of Critical Psychology 7*, 223–246.

DeCorby-Watson, K., Mensah, G., Bergeron, K., Abdi, S., Rempel, B. and Manson, H. (2018) 'Effectiveness of capacity-building interventions relevant to public health practice: A systematic review.' *BMC Public Health 18*, 1, 684. https://doi.org/10.1186/s12889-018-5591-6

Deighton, J., Lereya, S. T., Casey, P., Pataly, P., Humphrey, N. and Wolpert, M. (2019) 'Prevalence of mental health problems in schools: Poverty and other risk factors among 28,000 adolescents in England.' *The British Journal of Psychiatry 215*, 3, 565–567. doi: 10.1192/bjp.2019.19.

Denborough, D. (2002) 'Community song writing and narrative practice.' *Clinical Psychology 17*.

Denborough, D. (2008) *Collective Narrative Practice: Responding to Individuals, Groups, and Communities Who Have Experienced Trauma*. Dulwich Centre Publications.

Department for Education (2023) 'GCSE results, Attainment 8: Key stage 4 performance academic year 2021/22.' https://explore-education-statistics.service.gov.uk/find-statistics/key-stage-4-performance/2021-22

Derose, K. P., Escarce, J. J. and Lurie, N. (2007) 'Immigrants and health care: Sources of vulnerability.' *Health Affairs 26*, 5, 1258–1268. doi: 10.1377/hlthaff.26.5.1258.

Deschênes, S. S., Graham, E., Kivimäki, M. and Schmitz, N. (2018) 'Adverse childhood experiences and the risk of diabetes: Examining the roles of depressive symptoms and cardiometabolic dysregulations in the Whitehall II cohort study.' *Diabetes Care 41*, 10, 2120–2126. doi: 10.2337/dc18-0932.

Division of Clinical Psychology (2018) *The Power Threat Meaning Framework*. British Psychological Society. https://explore.bps.org.uk/content/report-guideline/bpsrep.2018.inf299b

Dodd, H. F., Nesbit, R. J. and FitzGibbon, L. (2023) 'Child's play: Examining the association between time spent playing and child mental health.' *Child Psychiatry and Human Development 54*, 6, 1678–1686. doi: 10.1007/s10578-022-01363-2.

Dodd, V. (2023) 'Antisemitic hate crimes in London up 1,350%, Met police say.' *The Guardian*, 20 October. www.theguardian.com/news/2023/oct/20/antisemitic-hate-crimes-in-london-rise-1350-since-israel-hamas-war-met-says

Duncan, B. L., Sparks, J., Miller, S. D., Bohanske, R. and Claud, D. (2006) 'Giving youth a voice: A preliminary study of the reliability and validity of a brief outcome measure for children, adolescents, and caretakers.' *Journal of Brief Therapy 5*, 2, 71–87. www.scottdmiller.com/wp-content/uploads/CORS%20JBT%20(2).pdf

Eberhardt, J., Ling, J., Horsley, L., Cunnett, J., *et al.* (2022) 'Exploring COVID-19 vaccine confidence with people from Black and Asian backgrounds in England.' *Journal of Racial and Ethnic Health Disparities 10*, 4, 1899–1909. doi: 10.1007/s40615-022-01372-w.

Edbrooke-Childs, J. and Patalay, P. (2019) 'Ethnic differences in referral routes to youth mental health services.' *Journal of the American Academy of Child and Adolescent Psychiatry 58*, 3, 368–375. doi: 10.1016/j.jaac.2018.07.906.

Edbrooke-Childs, J., Newman, R., Fleming, I., Deighton, J. and Wolpert, M. (2015) 'The association between ethnicity and care pathway for children with emotional problems in routinely collected child and adolescent mental health services data.' *European Child & Adolescent Psychiatry 25*, 5, 539–546. doi: 10.1007/s00787-015-0767-4.

Edney, C., Alrouh, B. and Abouelenin, M. (2023) *Ethnicity of Children in Care and Supervision Proceedings in England.* Briefing Paper, May. Nuffield Family Justice Observatory. www.nuffieldfjo.org.uk/wp-content/uploads/2023/05/nfjo_briefing_paper_ethnicity_20230518_FINAL.pdf

Edwards, D. (2007) 'Family Group Conferences: The Picture Across the United Kingdom: England.' In C. Ashley and P. Nixon (Eds) *Family Group Conferences: Where Next? Policies and Practices for the Future* (pp.221–228). Family Rights Group.

Epston, D. and White, M. (1992) *Experience, Contradiction, Narrative & Imagination: Selected Papers of David Epston & Michael White.* Dulwich Centre.

Escobar, J. I. and Vega, W. A. (2000) 'Mental health and immigration's AAAs: Where are we and where do we go from here?' *The Journal of Nervous and Mental Disease 188*, 11, 736–740. doi: 10.1097/00005053-200011000-00003.

Expert Advisory Group on Migration and Population (2021) *Family Migration: Understanding the Drivers, Impacts, and Support Needs of Migrant Families in Scotland.* Scottish Government. www.gov.scot/publications/family-migration-understanding-drivers-impacts-support-needs-migrant-families-scotland/pages/3

Falicov, C. J. (1995) 'Training to think culturally: A multidimensional comparative framework.' *Family Process 34*, 4, 373–388. doi: 10.1111/j.1545-5300.1995.00373.x.

Falicov, C. J. (2014) 'Psychotherapy and Supervision as Cultural Encounters: The Multidimensional Ecological Comparative Approach Framework.' In C. A. Falender, E. P. Shafranske and C. J. Falicov (Eds) *Multiculturalism and Diversity in Clinical Supervision: A Competency-Based Approach* (pp.29–58). American Psychological Association. https://doi.org/10.1037/14370-002

Fatimilehin, I. (1999) 'Of jewel heritage: Racial socialization and racial identity attitudes amongst adolescents of mixed African-Caribbean/White parentage.' *Journal of Adolescence 22*, 3, 303–318. https://doi.org/10.1006/jado.1999.0223

Fatimilehin, I. (2007) 'Building Bridges in Liverpool: Delivering CAMHS to Black and minority ethnic children and their families.' *Journal of Integrated Care 15*, 3, 7–16. https://doi.org/10.1108/14769018200700017

Fatimilehin, I. (2018) 'FGCs with Marginalised Communities.' In D. Edwards and K. Parkinson (Eds) *Family Group Conferences in Social Work: Involving Families in Decision-Making* (pp.141–153). Policy Press.

Fatimilehin, I. and Hassan, A. (2016) 'Parenting in Nigeria: Contemporary Families, Extended Family Systems, and Religious Diversity.' In G. Nicolas, A. Bejarano and D. Lee (Eds) *Contemporary Parenting: A Global Perspective* (Chapter 11). Routledge.

Fatimilehin, I. and Hunt, K. (2013) 'Psychometric assessment across cultures.' *Assessment Development Matters 5*, 3, 21–23. https://doi.org/10.53841/bpsadm.2013.5.3.21

Fatimilehin, I., Pilkington, A., McCann, M. and Silfhout, K. (2015) 'Developing a cultural consultancy service.' *Clinical Psychology Forum 273*. https://explore.bps.org.uk/content/bpscpf/1/273/24

Faulconbridge, J., Hunt, K. and Laffan, A. (2019) *Improving Psychological Wellbeing of Children and Young People: Effective Prevention and Early Intervention Across Health, Education and Social Care*. Jessica Kingsley Publishers.

FCA (Financial Conduct Authority) (2022) *Diversity and Inclusion on Company Boards and Executive Management*. Policy Statement PS22/3, April. www.fca.org.uk/publication/policy/ps22-3.pdf

Fernández-Reino, M. (2020) 'Migrants and discrimination in the UK.' Migration Observatory Briefings, University of Oxford. https://migrationobservatory.ox.ac.uk/resources/briefings/migrants-and-discrimination-in-the-uk

Fernando, S. (1991) *Mental Health, Race, and Culture*. Macmillan in association with Mind.

Fernando, S. (2010) *Mental Health, Race and Culture* (3rd edn). Palgrave Macmillan.

Ferragina, E. and Arrigoni, A. (2017) 'The rise and fall of social capital: Requiem for a theory?' *Political Studies Review 15*, 3, 355–367. https://doi.org/10.1177/1478929915623968

Feuerstein, R., Feuerstein, R. S. and Falik, L. H. (2010) *Beyond Smarter: Mediated Learning and the Brain's Capacity for Change*. Teachers College Press, Columbia University.

Firmstone, J., Georgiou, M., Husband, C., Marinkova, M. and Steibel, F. (2009) *Representation of Minorities in the Media: UK. Final Analysis Report*. https://eprints.whiterose.ac.uk/id/eprint/143385/1/FinalAnalysisReportRevisedUK%20-%20with%20pictures.pdf

Foundations (2023) *Randomised Control Trial of Family Group Conferencing at Pre-Proceedings Stage*. June. Foundations – What Works Centre for Children & Families. https://foundations.org.uk/wp-content/uploads/Reports/Randomised-controlled-trial-family-group-conferencing.pdf

Freire, P., Freire, A. M. A. and Barr, R. R. (1999) *Pedagogy of Hope: Reliving Pedagogy of the Oppressed*. Continuum.

Frost, D. (2008) 'Islamophobia: Examining causal links between the media and "race hate" from "below".' *International Journal of Sociology and Social Policy 28*, 11/12, 564–578. https://doi.org/10.1108/01443330810915251

Gajwani, R., Parsons, H., Birchwood, M. and Singh, S. P. (2016) 'Ethnicity and detention: Are Black and minority ethnic (Black and minority ethnic) groups disproportionately detained under the Mental Health Act 2007?' *Social Psychiatry and Psychiatric Epidemiology 51*, 703–711. https://doi.org/10.1007/s00127-016-1181-z

Gearing, R. E., Brewer, K. B., Schwalbe, C. S., MacKenzie, M. J. and Ibrahim, R. W. (2013) 'Stigma and adolescents with psychosis in the Middle East: Implications for engaging in mental health treatment.' *Journal of Nervous and Mental Disease 201*, 1, 68–71.

Gilman, R., Huebner, E. S. and Furlong, M. (2009) *Handbook of Positive Psychology in Schools*. Routledge.

Giuliani, C., Tagliabue, S. and Regalia, C. (2018) 'Psychological well-being, multiple identities, and discrimination among first and second-generation immigrant Muslims.' *Europe's Journal of Psychology 14*, 1, 66–87. doi: 10.5964/ejop.v14i1.1434.

Gone, J. P. and Alcántara, C. (2007) 'Identifying effective mental health interventions for American Indians and Alaska Natives: A review of the literature.' *Cultural Diversity & Ethnic Minority Psychology 13*, 4, 356–363. doi: 10.1037/1099-9809.13.4.356.

Goodman, S. H., Rouse, M. H., Connell, A. M., Broth, M. R., Hall, C. M. and Heyward, D. (2008) 'Maternal depression and child psychopathology: A meta-analytic review.' *Clinical Child and Family Psychology Review 14*, 1, 1–27. doi: 10.1007/s10567-010-0080-1.

Goosby, B. J., Cheadle, J. E. and Mitchell, C. (2018) 'Stress-related biosocial mechanisms of discrimination and African American health inequities.' *Annual Review of Sociology 44*, 1, 319–340. https://doi.org/10.1146/annurev-soc-060116-053403

Goosby, B. J., Malone, S., Richardson, E. A., Cheadle, J. E. and Williams, D. T. (2015) 'Perceived discrimination and markers of cardiovascular risk among low-income African American youth.' *American Journal of Human Biology 27*, 4, 546–552. https://doi.org/10.1002/ajhb.22683

Greeff, A. P. and Holtzkamp, J. (2007) 'The prevalence of resilience in migrant families.' *Family and Community Health 30*, 3, 189–200. doi: 10.1097/01.FCH.0000277762.70031.44.

Green, D. (2016) 'A Power and Systems Approach to Making Change Happen.' In D. Green, *How Change Happens* (pp.235–256). Oxford University Press. https://doi.org/10.1093/acprof:oso/9780198785392.003.0015

Greenfield, P. M., Keller, H., Fuligni, A. and Maynard, A. (2003) 'Cultural pathways through universal development.' *Annual Review of Psychology 54*, 461–490. doi: 10.1146/annurev.psych.54.101601.145221.

Gudykunst, W. B., Yoon, Y.-C. and Nishida, T. (1987) 'The influence of individualism-collectivism on perceptions of communication in ingroup and outgroup relationships.' *Communication Monographs 54*, 3, 295–306. https://doi.org/10.1080/03637758709390234

Gulliver, K. (2016) *Forty Years of Struggle: A Window on Race and Housing, Disadvantage and Exclusion*. Human City Institute. https://hqnetwork.co.uk/download.cfm?doc=docm93jijm4n2932.pdf&ver=5697

Habib, R. R. and Sayed, M. H. E. (2019) 'Cultural perspectives on disability in a sample of Arab families.' *Research in Developmental Disabilities 88*, 49–56.

Hagan, T. and Smail, D. (1997) 'Power mapping: Background and basic methodology.' *Journal of Community and Applied Social Psychology 7*, 4, 257–267. https://doi.org/10.1002/(SICI)1099-1298(199709)7:4<257::AID-CASP428>3.0.CO;2-P

Haidt, J. (2024) *The Anxious Generation: How the Great Rewiring of Childhood Is Causing an Epidemic of Mental Illness*. Allen Lane.

Hall, E. T. (1976) *Beyond Culture*. Anchor Press/Doubleday.

Halpern, D. F. (2013) *Thought and Knowledge: An Introduction to Critical Thinking* (5th edn). Psychology Press.

Halvorsrud, K., Nazroo, J., Otis, M., Brown Hajdukova, E. and Bhui, K. (2018) 'Ethnic inequalities and pathways to care in psychosis in England: A systematic review and meta-analysis.' *BMC Medicine 16*, 1, 223. https://doi.org/10.1186/s12916-018-1201-9

Halvorsrud, K., Nazroo, J., Otis, M., Brown Hajdukova, E. and Bhui, K. (2019) 'Ethnic inequalities in the incidence of diagnosis of severe mental illness in England: A systematic review and new meta-analyses for non-affective and affective psychoses.' *Social Psychiatry and Psychiatric Epidemiology 54*, 11, 1311–1323. https://doi.org/10.1007/s00127-019-01758-y

Hamler, T. C., Nguyen, A. W., Keith, V., Qin, W. and Wang, F. (2022) 'How skin tone influences relationships between discrimination, psychological distress, and self-rated mental health among older African Americans.' *Journals of Gerontology: Series B 77*, 11, 2026–2037. https://doi.org/10.1093/geronb/gbac115

Hankivsky, O. and Cormier, R. (2019) 'Intersectionality and Public Policy: Some Lessons from Existing Models.' In O. Hankivsky and J. S. Jordan-Zachery (Eds) *The Palgrave Handbook of Intersectionality in Public Policy* (pp.69–93). Palgrave Macmillan.

Haque, Z., Becares, L. and Treloar, N. (2020) *Over-Exposed and Under-Protected: The Devastating Impact of COVID-19 on Black and Minority Ethnic Communities in Great Britain.* London: Runnymede Trust. www.runnymedetrust.org/uploads/Runnymede%20Covid19%20Survey%20report%20v3.pdf

Haresnape, S. (2009) *The Use of Family Group Conferences by Black Minority Ethnic Communities.* Family Rights Group.

Harway, M., Kadin, S., Gottlieb, M. C., Nutt, R. L. and Celano, M. (2012) 'Family psychology and systemic approaches: Working effectively in a variety of contexts.' *Professional Psychology: Research and Practice 43*, 4, 315–327. https://doi.org/10.1037/a0029134

Hassan, A., Fatimilehin, I. and Kagan, C. (2018) 'Geedka Shirka (Under the Tree): Cultural, Migratory, and Community Spaces for Preventative Interventions with Somali Men and Their Families.' In L. McGrath and P. Reavey (Eds) *The Handbook of Mental Health and Space: Community and Clinical Applications* (pp.210–225). Routledge.

Hatzidimitriadou, E., Mantovani, N. and Keating, F. (2012) *Evaluation of Co-Production Processes in a Community-Based Mental Health Project in Wandsworth.* Kingston University and St George's, University of London.

Havighurst, S. S., Duncombe, M., Frankling, E., Holland, K., Kehoe, C. and Stargatt, R. (2015) 'An emotion-focused early intervention for children with emerging conduct problems.' *Journal of Abnormal Child Psychology 43*, 4, 749–760. doi: 10.1007/s10802-014-9944-z.

HEE (Health Education England) (no date) *Action Plan to Improve Equity of Access and Inclusion for Black, Asian, and Minority Ethnic Entrants to Clinical Psychology Training.* www.hee.nhs.uk/sites/default/files/documents/Action%20Plan%20to%20Improve%20Equity%20of%20Access%20and%20Inclusion%20for%20Black%2C%20Asian%20and%20Minority%20Ethnic%20Entrants%20to%20Clinical%20Psychology%20Training.pdf

Henrich, J., Heine, S. and Norenzayan, A. (2010) 'Most people are not WEIRD.' *Nature 466*, 7302, 29. https://doi.org/10.1038/466029a

Hervy, C., Cavalli, N., Madia, J. E. and Nicodemo, C. (2022) 'Diverging mental health after Brexit: Evidence from a longitudinal survey.' *Social Science & Medicine 302*, 114993. https://doi.org/10.1016/j.socscimed.2022.114993

Hickman, C., Marks, E., Pihkala, P., Clayton, S., *et al.* (2021) 'Climate anxiety in children and young people and their beliefs about government responses to climate change: A global survey.' *The Lancet. Planetary Health 5*, 12, e863–e873. doi: 10.1016/S2542-5196(21)00278-3.

HM Government (2022) *Inclusive Britain: The Government's Response to the Commission on Race and Ethnic Disparities.* March. https://assets.publishing.service. gov.uk/government/uploads/system/uploads/attachment_data/file/1061421/ Inclusive-Britain-government-response-to-the-Commission-on-Race-and-Ethnic-Disparities.pdf

Hoffman, L. (1993) *Exchanging Voices: A Collaborative Approach to Family Therapy.* Karnac Books.

Hofstede, G. (1980) *Culture's Consequences: International Differences in Work-Related Values.* SAGE Publications.

Holman, D. M., Ports, K. A., Buchanan, N. D., Hawkins, N. A., *et al.* (2016) 'The association between adverse childhood experiences and risk of cancer in adulthood: A systematic review of the literature.' *Pediatrics 138*, Suppl. 1, S81–S91. https:// doi.org/10.1542/peds.2015-4268L

Home Office (2018) 'Hate crime, England and Wales, 2017 to 2018.' Statistical Bulletin 20/18. www.gov.uk/government/statistics/hate-crime-england-and-wales-2017-to-2018

Home Office (2023) *Illegal Migration Act 2023.* www.gov.uk/government/collections/ illegal-migration-bill

Hood, C. (1991) 'A public management for all seasons?' *Public Administration 69*, 1, 3–19. https://doi.org/10.1111/j.1467-9299.1991.tb00779.x

Horvat, L., Horey, D., Romios, P. and Kis-Rigo, J. (2014) 'Cultural competence education for health professionals.' *Cochrane Database of Systematic Reviews 5*, CD009405. doi: 10.1002/14651858.CD009405.pub2.

Howes, O. D., Whitehurst, T., Shatalina, E., Townsend, L., *et al.* (2021) 'The clinical significance of duration of untreated psychosis: An umbrella review and random-effects meta-analysis.' *World Psychiatry 20*, 1, 75–95. doi: 10.1002/wps.20822.

Huckfield, L. (2021) *How Blair Killed the Co-ops: Reclaiming Social Enterprise from Its Neoliberal Turn.* Manchester University Press.

Huey, S. J., Jr, Park, A. L., Galán, C. A. and Wang, C. X. (2023) 'Culturally responsive cognitive behavioral therapy for ethnically diverse populations.' *Annual Review of Clinical Psychology 19*, 51–78. https://doi.org/10.1146/annurev-clinpsy-080921-072750

Humphrey, A., Wilson, H. and Ford, R. (2024) *Immigration: Changing Attitudes, Policy Preferences and Partisanship: British Social Attitudes 41.* National Centre for Social Research. https://natcen.ac.uk/sites/default/files/2025-04/british-social-attitudes-41-%7C-immigration-1297.pdf

Hutchins, H. J., Barry, C. M., Wanga, V., Bacon, S., *et al.* (2022) 'Perceived racial/ ethnic discrimination, physical and mental health conditions in childhood, and the relative role of other adverse experiences.' *Adversity and Resilience Science 3*, 2, 181–194. https://doi.org/10.1007/s42844-022-00063-z

Hwang, W.-C., Wood, J. J. and Fujimoto, K. (2010) 'Acculturative family distancing (AFD) and depression in Chinese American families.' *Journal of Consulting and Clinical Psychology 78*, 5, 655–666. doi: 10.1037/a0020542.

Individual Differences Research Labs (no date) *White Privilege Test.* www.idrlabs. com/White-privilege/test.php

Johnstone, L. and Boyle, M. with Cromby, J., Dillon, J., Harper, D., Kinderman, P., Longden, E., Pilgrim, D. and Read, J. (2018) *The Power Threat Meaning Framework: Towards the Identification of Patterns in Emotional Distress, Unusual Experiences and Troubled or Troubling Behaviour, as an Alternative to Functional Psychiatric Diagnosis.* British Psychological Society.

Johnstone, L. and Dallos, R. (2013) *Formulation in Psychology and Psychotherapy: Making Sense of People's Problems.* Taylor & Francis Group.

Just Psychology (2018) *Just Psychology Social Impact Report 2016–2017.* https://hubble-live-assets.s3.amazonaws.com/justpsychology/redactor2_assets/files/69/Just_Psychology_Social_Impact_Report_2016-17_final.pdf

Kagan, C. (2007) 'Working at the "edge": Making use of psychological resources through collaboration.' *The Psychologist 20*, 4, 224–227.

Kagan, C. and Duggan, K. (2009) *Breaking Down Barriers: Universities and Communities Working Together.* Community Cohesion Thematic Evaluation Report, February. Research Institute for Health and Social Change, Manchester Metropolitan University. https://e-space.mmu.ac.uk/83457/1/978-1-900139-29-8.pdf

Kagan, C., Burton, M., Duckett, P., Lawthom, R. and Siddiquee, A. (2020) *Critical Community Psychology: Critical Action and Social Change* (2nd edn). Routledge.

Kaiser, P. (2016) 'Spirituality and Religion in Life Story Work.' In P. Kaiser and R. Eley (Eds) *Life Story Work with People with Dementia: Ordinary Lives, Extraordinary People* (pp.210–225). Jessica Kingsley Publishers.

Kakişim, C. (2019) 'Racism in Russia and its effects on the Caucasian region and peoples.' *Tesam Akademi Dergisi 6*, 1, 97–121. https://doi.org/10.30626/tesamakademi.528002

Katan, D. and Taibi, M. (2021) *Translating Cultures: An Introduction for Translators, Interpreters and Mediators.* Routledge.

Kauhanen, L., Yunus, W. M. A. W. M., Lempinen, L., Peltonen, K., *et al.* (2023) 'A systematic review of the mental health changes of children and young people before and during the COVID-19 pandemic.' *European Child & Adolescent Psychiatry 32*, 6, 995–1013. doi: 10.1007/s00787-022-02060-0.

Kaur-Ballagan, K., Cereso, I., and Kamvar, R. (2020) *World Refugee Day 2020.* Ipsos MORI Public Affairs: UK.

Keating, F., Robertson, D. and McCulloch, A. (2002) *Breaking the Circles of Fear: A Review of the Relationship Between Mental Health Services and African and Caribbean Communities.* 15 July. Centre for Mental Health. www.centreformentalhealth.org.uk/publications/breaking-circles-fear

Kelley, N., Khan, O. and Sharrock, S. (2017) *Racial Prejudice in Britain Today.* NatCen Social Research. https://cdn.prod.website-files.com/61488f992b58e687f1108c7c/61c209424ce8cec640976cfb_racial-prejudice-report_v4.pdf

Kelly, Y., Bécares, L. and Nazroo, J. (2012) 'Associations between maternal experiences of racism and early child health and development: Findings from the UK Millennium Cohort Study.' *Journal of Epidemiology and Community Health 67*, 1, 35–41. doi: 10.1136/jech-2011-200814.

Kim, J. S. and Franklin, C. (2009) 'Solution-focused brief therapy in schools: A review of the outcome literature.' *Children and Youth Services Review 31*, 4, 464–470. https://doi.org/10.1016/j.childyouth.2008.10.002

Kim, S. Y., Schwartz, S. J., Perreira, K. M. and Juang, L. P. (2018) 'Culture's influence on stressors, parental socialization, and developmental processes in the mental health of children of immigrants.' *Annual Review of Clinical Psychology 14*, 343–370. doi: 10.1146/annurev-clinpsy-050817-084925.

Kinouani, G. (2021) *Living While Black: The Essential Guide to Overcoming Racial Trauma.* Ebury Press.

Kirmayer, L. J. and Minas, H. (2000) 'The future of cultural psychiatry: An international perspective.' *The Canadian Journal of Psychiatry 45*, 5. https://doi.org/10.1177/070674370004500503

Klassen, C. L., Gonzalez, E., Sullivan, R. and Ruiz-Casares, M. (2022) '"I'm just asking you to keep an ear out": Parents' and children's perspectives on caregiving and community support in the context of migration to Canada.' *Journal of Ethnic and Migration Studies 48*, 11, 2762–2780. https://doi.org/10.1080/1369183X.2019.1707647

Kleinman, A. (1980) *Patients and Healers in the Context of Culture: An Exploration of the Borderland between Anthropology, Medicine, and Psychiatry*. University of California Press.

Knight, S., Jarvis, E., Ryder, A. G., Lashley, M. and Rousseau, C. (2021) 'Ethnoracial differences in coercive referral and intervention among patients with first-episode psychosis.' *Psychiatric Services 73*, 1, 2–8. https://doi.org/10.1176/appi.ps.202000715

Kowalewska, H. (2018) *Ethnicity and Social Housing Allocation in England: An Exploratory Analysis of CORE*. Ministry of Housing, Communities and Local Government. https://helenkowalewska.uk/publication/2018-ethnicity-and-social-housing-report

Krzyżanowski, M. and Ekström, M. (2022) 'The normalization of far-right populism and nativist authoritarianism: Discursive practices in media, journalism, and the wider public sphere.' *Discourse & Society 33*, 6, 719–729. doi: 10.1177/09579265221095406.

Kulakiwicz, A., Foster, D., Danechi, S. and Clark, H. V. (2022) *Children's Social Care Workforce*. Research Briefing. House of Commons Library. https://commonslibrary.parliament.uk/research-briefings/cdp-2022-0142

Landy, R., Cameron, C., Au, A., Cameron, D., *et al.* (2016) 'Educational strategies to enhance reflexivity among clinicians and health professional students: A scoping study.' *Qualitative Social Research 17*, 3, Art. 14. http://eprints.lse.ac.uk/68328

Lansford, J. E. (2021) 'Cross-cultural similarities and differences in parenting.' *Journal of Child Psychology and Psychiatry 63*, 4, 466–479. doi: 10.1111/jcpp.13539.

Law, D. and Jacob, J. (2015) *Goals and Goal-Based Outcomes: Some Useful Information* (3rd edn). CAMHS Press.

Lawrence, V., McCombie, C., Nikolakopoulos, G. and Morgan, C. (2021) 'Ethnicity and power in the mental health system: Experiences of White British and Black Caribbean people with psychosis.' *Epidemiology and Psychiatric Sciences 30*, e12. https://doi.org/10.1017/S2045796020001043

Lawthom, R. (2011) 'Developing learning communities: Using communities of practice within community psychology.' *International Journal of Inclusive Education 15*, 1, 153–164. https://doi.org/10.1080/13603116.2010.496212

Lazaridou, F. B., Heinz, A., Schulze, D. and Bhugra, D. (2023) 'Racialised identity, racism and the mental health of children and adolescents.' *International Review of Psychiatry 35*, 3–4, 277–288. doi: 10.1080/09540261.2023.2181059.

Lehane, D. and Campion, P. (2018) 'Interpreters: Why should the NHS provide them?' *British Journal of General Practice 68*, 677, 564–565. doi: 10.3399/bjgp18X699905.

Lekas, H.-M., Pahl, K. and Lewis, C. F. (2020) 'Rethinking cultural competence: Shifting to cultural humility.' *Health Services Insights 13*, 1178632920970580. doi: 10.1177/1178632920970580.

Levitas, R., Pantazis, C., Fahmy, E., Gordon, D., Lloyd, E. and Patsios, D. (2007) *The Multi-Dimensional Analysis of Social Exclusion*. January. University of Bristol. https://dera.ioe.ac.uk/id/eprint/6853/1/multidimensional.pdf

Lewis-Smith, H., Pegram, G., White, P., Ward, L. M. and Diedrichs, P. C. (2023) 'A short-form drama series created for the digital media environment: A randomised controlled trial exploring effects on girls' body satisfaction, acceptance of appearance diversity, and appearance-related internalised racism.' *Body Image* 47, 101610. doi: 10.1016/j.bodyim.2023.08.002.

Lopez, S. J. and Snyder, C. R. (Eds) (2009) *Oxford Handbook of Positive Psychology* (2nd edn). Oxford University Press.

Lwembe, S., Green, S. A., Chigwende, J., Ojwang, T. and Dennis, R. (2017) 'Co-production as an approach to developing stakeholder partnerships to reduce mental health inequalities: An evaluation of a pilot service.' *Primary Health Care Research & Development 18*, 1, 14–23. doi: 10.1017/S1463423616000141.

MacAlister, J. (2022) *Independent Review of Children's Social Care: Final Report.* Department for Education. www.gov.uk/government/publications/independent-review-of-childrens-social-care-final-report

Maccoby, E. E. and Martin, J. A. (1983) 'Socialization in the Context of the Family: Parent–Child Interaction.' In P. H. Mussen (Ed.) *Handbook of Child Psychology: Vol. IV. Socialization, Personality, and Social Development* (4th edn, pp. 1–101). John Wiley & Sons.

Macpherson, W. (1999) *The Stephen Lawrence Inquiry.* Home Office. www.gov.uk/government/publications/the-stephen-lawrence-inquiry

Madanes, C. (1981) *Strategic Family Therapy.* Jossey-Bass Publishers.

Malek, M. (2011) *Enjoy, Achieve and Be Healthy: The Mental Health of Black and Minority Ethnic Children and Young People.* The Afiya Trust.

Mann, F., Fisher, H. L., Major, B., Lawrence, J., *et al.* (2014) 'Ethnic variations in compulsory detention and hospital admission for psychosis across four UK Early Intervention Services.' *BMC Psychiatry 14*, 256. https://doi.org/10.1186/s12888-014-0256-1

Marmot, M. and Allen, J. (2020) 'COVID-19: Exposing and amplifying inequalities.' *Journal of Epidemiology & Community Health 74*, 9, 681–682. doi: 10.1136/jech-2020-214720.

Marmot, M., Allen, J., Boyce, T., Goldblatt, P. and Morrison, J. (2020) *Health Equity in England: The Marmot Review 10 Years On.* Institute of Health Equity. www.instituteofhealthequity.org/the-marmot-review-10-years-on

Marmot, M., Allen, J., Boyce, T., Goldblatt, P. and Morrison, J. (2021) *Build Back Fairer in Greater Manchester: Health Equity and Dignified Lives.* Institute of Health Equity. www.instituteofhealthequity.org/resources-reports/build-back-fairer-in-greater-manchester-health-equity-and-dignified-lives

Marsh, P. and Crow, G. (1998) *Family Group Conferences in Child Welfare.* Blackwell Science Ltd.

Maslow, A. H. (1943) 'A theory of human motivation.' *Psychological Review 50*, 4, 370–396. https://doi.org/10.1037/h0054346

Maté, G., with Maté, D. (2022) *The Myth of Normal: Trauma, Illness, and Healing in a Toxic Culture.* Penguin.

Maza, M. T., Fox, K. A., Kwon, S., Flannery, J. E., *et al.* (2023) 'Association of habitual checking behaviors on social media with longitudinal functional brain development.' *JAMA Pediatrics 177*, 2, 160–167. doi: 10.1001/jamapediatrics.2022.4924.

McDonald, J. T. and Kennedy, S. (2004) 'Insights into the "healthy immigrant effect": Health status and health service use of immigrants to Canada.' *Social Science & Medicine 59*, 8, 1613–1627. doi: 10.1016/j.socscimed.2004.02.004.

McFarlane, M. (2014) *Ethnicity, Health and the Private Rented Sector*. Race Equality Foundation. https://raceequalityfoundation.org.uk/wp-content/uploads/2018/02/Housing-Briefing-25.pdf

McGrath, L., Griffin, V., Mundy, E., Curno, T., Weerasinghe, D. and Zlotowitz, S. (2016) 'The psychological impact of austerity: A briefing paper.' *Educational Psychology Research and Practice 2*, 2, 46–57. https://doi.org/10.15123/uel.885xw

McLeod, M., King, P., Stanley, J., Lacey, C. and Cunningham, R. (2017) 'Ethnic disparities in the use of seclusion for adult psychiatric inpatients in New Zealand.' *The New Zealand Medical Journal 130*, 1454, 30–39. PMID: 28449014.

McNamee, S. and Gergen, K. J. (Eds) (1992) *Therapy as Social Construction*. SAGE Publications.

Memon, A., Taylor, K., Mohebati, L. M., Sundin, J., *et al.* (2016) 'Perceived barriers to accessing mental health services among Black and minority ethnic (Black and minority ethnic) communities: A qualitative study in Southeast England.' *BMJ Open 6*, 11, e012337. doi: 10.1136/bmjopen-2016-012337.

Mesquita, B. (2022) *Between Us: How Cultures Create Emotions*. W. W. Norton & Company.

Messent, P. and Murrell, M. (2003) 'Research leading to action: A study of accessibility of a CAMH service to ethnic minority families.' *Child and Adolescent Mental Health 8*, 3, 118–124. doi: 10.1111/1475-3588.00057.

Miller, S. D., Duncan, B. L., Brown, J., Sparks, J. and Claud, D. (2003) 'The Outcome Rating Scale: A preliminary study of the reliability, validity, and feasibility of a brief visual analog measure.' *Journal of Brief Therapy 2*, 91–100. https:// scottdmiller.com/wp-content/uploads/documents/OutcomeRatingScale-JBTv2n2.pdf

Mind (2020) *The Mental Health Emergency: How Has the Coronavirus Pandemic Impacted Our Mental Health?* June. www.mind.org.uk/media-a/5929/the-mental-health-emergency_a4_final.pdf

Mind (2021) *Coronavirus: The Consequences for Mental Health*. July. www.mind.org.uk/media/8962/the-consequences-of-coronavirus-for-mental-health-final-report.pdf

Minuchin, S. (1974) *Families and Family Therapy*. Harvard University Press.

Mitic, M., Woodcock, K. A., Amering, M., Krammer, I., *et al.* (2021) 'Toward an integrated model of supportive peer relationships in early adolescence: A systematic review and exploratory meta-analysis.' *Frontiers in Psychology 12*, 589403. doi: 10.3389/fpsyg.2021.589403.

Mokuria, V. G., Morris, B. J., Lino Correa, A. S., Vu, T. and Lowery, K. L. (2023) 'Out of the frying pan and into the fire: The emotional labor of excavating internalised racism.' *Whiteness and Education 9*, 2, 310–331. https://doi.org/10.1080/2379340 6.2023.2220719

Monk, G., Winslade, J., Crocket, K. and Epston, D. (Eds) (1997) *Narrative Therapy in Practice: The Archaeology of Hope*. Jossey-Bass.

Moore, K. (2010) 'The three-part harmony of adult learning, critical thinking, and decision-making.' *Journal of Adult Education 39*, 1. https://files.eric.ed.gov/fulltext/EJ917394.pdf

Morgan, A. (2000) *What is Narrative Therapy?* Dulwich Centre Publications.

Morgan, C., Fearon, P., Lappin, J., Heslin, M., *et al.* (2017) 'Ethnicity and the long-term course and outcome of psychotic disorders in a UK sample: The AESOP-10 study.' *The British Journal of Psychiatry 211*, 2, 88–94. doi: 10.1192/bjp.bp.116.193342.

Morris, R. M., Sellwood, W., Edge, D., Colling, C., *et al.* (2020) 'Ethnicity and impact on the receipt of cognitive-behavioural therapy in people with psychosis or bipolar disorder: An English cohort study.' *BMJ Open 10*, e034913. https://doi.org/10.1136/bmjopen-2019-034913

Mrug, S., Barker-Kamps, M., Orihuela, C. A., Patki, A. and Tiwari, H. K. (2022) 'Childhood neighborhood disadvantage, parenting, and adult health.' *American Journal of Preventive Medicine 6*, 1, Suppl. 1, S28–S36. https://doi.org/10.1016/j.amepre.2022.01.028

Mulder, P. (2018) 'Soft systems methodology (SSM).' Toolshero, 29 April. www.toolshero.com/problem-solving/soft-systems-methodology-ssm

Mulholland, H. (2005) 'Counting on change.' *The Guardian, 7* December. www.theguardian.com/society/2005/dec/07/mentalhealth.socialcare

Multilingual Manchester (2013) *Multilingual Manchester: A Digest.* University of Manchester. http://mlm.humanities.manchester.ac.uk/wp-content/uploads/2015/12/MLMDigest.pdf

Murray, A. (2024) 'Unemployment by ethnic background.' House of Commons Library. https://researchbriefings.files.parliament.uk/documents/SN06385/SN06385.pdf

Naeem, F. (2015) 'Disability in South Asia: Knowledge and experience.' *Disability and Rehabilitation 37*, 22, 2043–2047.

National Centre for Social Research (2022) *British Social Attitudes Survey*, London.

Ncube, N. (2006) 'The Tree of Life Project: Using narrative ideas in work with vulnerable children in Southern Africa.' *The International Journal of Narrative Therapy and Community Work 1*, 3–16. https://narrativetherapycentre.com/wp-content/uploads/2020/12/Tree-of-Life-by-Ncazelo-Ncube-2006.pdf

NHS Digital (2023) *Mental Health of Children and Young People in England, 2023 – Wave 4 Follow-Up to the 2017 Survey.* https://digital.nhs.uk/data-and-information/publications/statistical/mental-health-of-children-and-young-people-in-england/2023-wave-4-follow-up/part-1-mental-health

NHS England (2019) *The NHS Long Term Plan.* https://digital.nhs.uk/data-and-information/publications/statistical/mental-health-of-children-and-young-people-in-england

Noyce, R. and Simpson, J. (2018) 'The experience of forming a therapeutic relationship from the client's perspective: A metasynthesis.' *Psychotherapy Research 28*, 2, 281–296. https://doi.org/10.1080/10503307.2016.1208373

Ocloo, J. and Matthews, R. (2016) 'From tokenism to empowerment: Progressing patient and public involvement in healthcare improvement.' *BMJ Quality & Safety 25*, 8, 626–632. https://doi.org/10.1136/bmjqs-2015-004839

OECD (Organisation for Economic Co-operation and Development) (2023) *Health at a Glance 2023: OECD Indicators.* OECD Publishing. https://doi.org/10.1787/7a7afb35-en

Olabi, Y., Waheed, H., Fatimilehin, I. and Begum, F. (2022) 'Family Reunion and Parenting Project: Supporting families through separation, reunification, and serial migration.' *Clinical Psychology Forum 1*, 357. doi: 10.53841/bpscpf.2022.1.357.44.

Oliver, K., Kothari, A. and Mays, N. (2019) 'The dark side of coproduction: Do the costs outweigh the benefits for health research?' *Health Research Policy and Systems 17*, 1, 33. doi: 10.1186/s12961-019-0432-3.

Oluwoye, O., Davis, B., Kuhney, F. S. and Anglin, D. M. (2021) 'Systematic review of pathways to care in the US for Black individuals with early psychosis.' *npj Schizophrenia 7*, 58. https://doi.org/10.1038/s41537-021-00185-w

ONS (Office for National Statistics) (2020) 'Coronavirus (COVID-19) related deaths by ethnic group, England & Wales: 2 March 2020 to 15 May 2020.' www.ons.

gov.uk/peoplepopulationandcommunity/birthsdeathsandmarriages/deaths/
articles/coronaviruscovid19relateddeathsbyethnicgroupenglandandwales/2ma
rch2020to15may2020

ONS (2023a) 'Child and infant mortality in England and Wales: 2022.' www.gov.uk/
government/statistics/child-and-infant-mortality-in-england-and-wales-2022

ONS (2023b) 'Ethnic group differences in health, employment, education and
housing shown in England and Wales' Census 2021.' www.ons.gov.uk/
peoplepopulationandcommunity/culturalidentity/ethnicity/articles/ethnicgro
updifferencesinhealthemploymenteducationandhousingshowninenglandand
walescensus2021/2023-03-15

ONS (2023c) 'Sociodemographic inequalities in suicides in England and Wales: 2011
to 2021.' www.ons.gov.uk/peoplepopulationandcommunity/healthandsocialcare/
healthinequalities/bulletins/sociodemographicinequalitiesinsuicidesinengland
andwales/2011to2021

Otaye-Ebede, L. and Shaffakat, S. (2023) *Promoting Race Representation and Culture
Change*. North West Business Leadership Team, University of Liverpool.

Otu, A., Ahinkorah, B. O., Ameyaw, E. K., Seidu, A. A. and Yaya, S. (2020) 'One country,
two crises: What COVID-19 reveals about health inequalities among Black, Asian
and minority ethnic communities in the United Kingdom and the sustainability of its health system.' *International Journal for Equity in Health 19*, 1, 189. doi:
10.1186/s12939-020-01307-z.

Paradies, Y., Ben, J., Denson, N., Ellas, A., *et al.* (2015) 'Racism as a determinant of
health: A systematic review and meta-analysis.' *PLoS One 10*, 9, e0138511. doi:
10.1371/journal.pone.0138511.

Parkinson, K. P. (2018) 'An International Perspective.' In D. Edwards and K. Parkinson
(Eds) *Family Group Conferences in Social Work: Involving Families in Social Care
Decision Making* (pp. 99–120). Bristol University Press.

Parlatini, V., Frangou, L., Zhang, S., Epstein, S., *et al.* (2024) 'Emotional and behavioural outcomes among youths with mental disorders during the first COVID
lockdown and school closures in England: A large clinical population study using
health care record integrated surveys.' *Social Psychiatry and Psychiatric Epidemiology 59*, 1, 175–186. doi: 10.1007/s00127-023-02517-w.

Patel, N., Bennett, E., Dennis, M., Dosanjh, N., *et al.* (Eds) (2000) *Clinical Psychology,
'Race' and Culture: A Training Manual*. Blackwell.

Pedersen, M. L., Gildberg, F., Baker, J., Brammer Damsgaard, J. and Boldrup, E. (2023)
'Ethnic disparities in the use of restrictive practices in adult mental health inpatient settings: A scoping review.' *Social Psychiatry + Psychiatric Epidemiology 58*,
505–522. https://doi.org/10.1007/s00127-022-02387-8

Peirson, L. J., Boydell, K. M., Ferguson, H. B. and Ferris, L. E. (2011) 'An ecological
process model of systems change.' *American Journal of Community Psychology 47*,
3–4, 307–321. https://doi.org/10.1007/s10464-010-9405-y

Pérez, I. E., Wu, R., Murray, C. B. and Bravo, D. (2021) 'An interdisciplinary framework
examining culture and adaptation in migrant children and adolescents.' *New
Directions for Child and Adolescent Development 176*, 13–39. doi: 10.1002/cad.20405.

Perspective Economics (2022) *The Role of Voluntary, Community, and Social Enterprise
(VCSE) Organisations in Public Procurement*. Department for Digital, Culture,
Media, and Sport, August. https://assets.publishing.service.gov.uk/govern-
ment/uploads/system/uploads/attachment_data/file/1100749/The_role_of_
Voluntary__Community__and_Social_Enterprises_in_public_procurement.pdf

Philips, B. A. (2007) *The Clash of Civilisations: An Islamic View*. International Islamic Publishing House.

Phinney, J. S., Horenczyk, G., Liebkind, K. and Vedder, P. (2001) 'Ethnic identity, immigration, and well-being: An ineractional perspective.' *Journal of Social Issues 57*, 3, 493–510. doi: 10.1111/0022-4537.00225.

Phoenix, A. (1996) *Constructing Ethnicities, Obscuring Racisms: Issues for the Study of Identities*. Paper presented at the British Psychological Society Conference, Brighton.

Piaget, J. (1952) *The Origins of Intelligence in Children* (M. Cook, Trans.). International Universities Press.

Plackett, R., Sheringham, J. and Dykxhoorn, J. (2023) 'The longitudinal impact of social media use on UK adolescents' mental health: Longitudinal observational study.' *Journal of Medical Internet Research 25*, e43213. https://doi.org/10.2196/43213

Poehner, M. E., Davin, K. J. and Lantolf, J. P. (2017) 'Dynamic Assessment.' In E. Shohamy, I. Or and S. May (Eds) *Language Testing and Assessment. Encyclopedia of Language and Education* (pp.1–18). Springer. https://doi.org/10.1007/978-3-319-02261-1_18

Powdthavee, N., Plagnol, A. C., Frijters, P. and Clark, A. E. (2019) 'Who got the Brexit blues? The effect of Brexit on subjective wellbeing in the UK.' *Economica 86*, 343, 471–494. https://doi.org/10.1111/ecca.12304

Priest, N., Paradies, Y., Trenerry, B., Truong, M., Karlsen, S. and Kelly, Y. (2013) 'A systematic review of studies examining the relationship between reported racism and health and wellbeing for children and young people.' *Social Science & Medicine 95*, 115–127. doi: 10.1016/j.socscimed.2012.11.031.

Proto, E. and Quintana-Domeque, C. (2021) 'COVID-19 and mental health deterioration by ethnicity and gender in the UK.' *PLoS One 16*, 1, e0244419. https://doi.org/10.1371/journal.pone.0244419

Purwati, D., Mardhiah, A., Nurhasanah, E. and Ramli, R. (2022) 'The six characteristics of andragogy and future research directions in EFL: A literature review.' *Elsya: Journal of English Language Studies 4*, 1. https://doi.org/10.31849/elsya.v4i1.7473

Quintana, S. M., Aboud, F. E., Chao, R. K., Contreras-Grau, J., *et al.* (2006) 'Race, ethnicity, and culture in child development: Contemporary research and future directions.' *Child Development 77*, 5, 1129–1141. doi: 10.1111/j.1467-8624.2006.00951.x.

Qureshi, A., Collazos, F., Revollo, H. W., Valero, S., Ramos, M. and Delgadillo, C. (2009) 'Cultural bias in psychiatric and psychological testing.' *European Psychiatry 24*, S1, 24–69. https://doi.org/10.1016/S0924-9338(09)70302-5

Rad, M. S., Martingo, A. J. and Ginges, J. (2018) 'Toward a psychology of *Homo sapiens*: Making psychological science more representative of the human population.' *Psychological and Cognitive Sciences. Proceedings of the National Academy of Sciences 115*, 45, 11401–11405. doi: 10.1073/pnas.1721165115.

Ramasubramanian, S., Riewestahl, E. and Ramirez, A. (2023) 'Race and ethnic stereotypes in the media.' *Oxford Research Encyclopedia of Communication*. https://doi.org/10.1093/acrefore/9780190228613.013.1262

Rapley, M., Moncrieff, J. and Dillon, J. (Eds.). (2011). *De-Medicalizing Misery: Psychiatry, Psychology and the Human Condition* (1st ed.). Palgrave Macmillan.

Rapp, C. A. (1998) *The Strengths Model: Case Management with People Suffering from Severe and Persistent Mental Illness*. Oxford University Press.

Rapp, C. A. and Goscha, R. J. (2012) *The Strengths Model: A Recovery-Oriented Approach to Mental Health Services* (3rd edn). Oxford University Press.

Recto, P. and Champion, J. D. (2020) 'Psychosocial factors associated with paternal perinatal depression in the United States: A systematic review.' *Issues in Mental Health Nursing 41*, 7, 608–623. https://doi.org/10.1080/01612840.2019.1704320

Reynolds, V. and Wilson, J. (2024) 'Deconstructing the trauma industry: Dialogue with Vikki Reynolds and John Wilson.' YouTube. www.youtube.com/watch?v=xDAlaTjCbl8

Rivas-Drake, D., Seaton, E. K., Markstrom, C., Quintana, S., *et al.* (2014) 'Ethnic and racial identity in adolescence: Implications for psychosocial, academic, and health outcomes.' *Child Development 85*, 1, 40–57. https://doi.org/10.1111/cdev.12200

Rochester, C. and Zimmeck, M. (2011) 'The Compact: We've lost it!' ARVAC (Association for Research in the Voluntary and Community Sector) Bulletin, 115. www.vahs.org.uk/2011/09/the-compact-weve-lost-it

Rodrigues, R., MacDougall, A. G., Zou, G., Lebenbaum, M., *et al.* (2020) 'Risk of involuntary admission among first-generation ethnic minority groups with early psychosis: A retrospective cohort study using health administrative data.' *Epidemiology and Psychiatric Sciences 29*, e59. https://doi.org/10.1017/S2045796019000556

Rogers, C. R. and Freiberg, H. J. (1994) *Freedom to Learn* (3rd edn). Merrill.

Ruiz-Casares, M., Nazif-Muñoz, J. I., Iwo, R. and Oulhote, Y. (2018) 'Nonadult supervision of children in low- and middle-income countries: Results from 61 national population-based surveys.' *International Journal of Environmental Research and Public Health 15*, 8, 1564. https://doi.org/10.3390/ijerph15081564

Ruphrect-Smith, H., Davies, S., Jacob, J. and Edbrooke-Childs, J. (2023) 'Ethnic differences in treatment outcome for children and young people accessing mental health support.' *European Child & Adolescent Psychiatry 33*, 4, 1121–1131. doi: 10.1007/s00787-023-02233-5.

Saleebey, D. (2012) *The Strengths Perspective in Social Work Practice* (6th edn). Pearson.

Satir, V. (1964) *Conjoint Family Therapy.* Science and Behavior Books, Inc.

Satir, V. S. (1972) *Peoplemaking.* Science and Behavior Books, Inc.

Scheppers, E., van Dongen, E., Dekker, J., Geertzen, J. and Dekker, J. (2006) 'Potential barriers to the use of health services among ethnic minorities: A review.' *Family Practice 23*, 3, 325–348. doi: 10.1093/fampra/cmi113.

Scott-Samuel, A., Bambra, C., Collins, C., Hunter, D. J., McCartney, G. and Smith, K. (2014) 'The impact of Thatcherism on health and well-being in Britain.' *International Journal of Health Services 44*, 1, 53–71. https://doi.org/10.2190/HS.44.1.d

Seikkula, J. and Olson, M. E. (2003) 'The open dialogue approach: Its poetics and micropolitics.' *Family Process 42*, 3, 403–418. doi: 10.1111/j.1545-5300.2003.00403.x

Seligman, M. E. P. and Csikszentmihalyi, M. (2000) 'Positive psychology: An introduction.' *American Psychologist 55*, 1, 5–14. https://psycnet.apa.org/doi/10.1037/0003-066X.55.1.5"https://doi.org/10.1037/0003-066X.55.1.5

Selvini Palazzoli, M., Boscolo, L., Cecchin, G. and Prata, G. (1980) 'Hypothesizing – circularity – neutrality: Three guidelines for the conductor of the session.' *Family Process 19*, 1, 3–12. https://doi.org/10.1111/j.1545-5300.1980.00003.x

Shankley, W. and Williams, P. (2020) 'Minority Ethnic Groups, Policing and the Criminal Justice System in Britain.' In B. Byrne, C. Alexander, O. Khan, J. Nazroo and W. Shankley (Eds) *Ethnicity, Race and Inequality in the UK: State of the Nation* (pp.51–72). Policy Press.

Silove, D., Steel, Z. and Watters, C. (2000) 'Policies of deterrence and the mental health of asylum seekers.' *JAMA 284*, 5, 604–611. doi: 10.1001/jama.284.5.604.

Singal, S., Howell, D., Hanna, L., Tang, S. X., *et al.* (2023) 'Race-based disparities in the frequency and duration of restraint use in a psychiatric inpatient setting.' *Psychiatric Services 75*, 4, 308–315. https://doi.org/10.1176/appi.ps.20230057

Skinner, R. (2019) 'Traditions, paradigms, and basic concepts in Islamic psychology.' *Journal of Religion and Health 58*, 4, 1087–1094. doi: 10.1007/s10943-018-0595-1.

Skokauskas, N., Dunne, M., Gallogly, A. and Clark, C. (2010) 'Ethnic minority populations and child psychiatry services: An Irish study.' *Child and Youth Services Review 32*, 10, 1242–1245. doi: 10.1016/J.CHILDYOUTH.2010.04.014.

Smart, A. and Harrison, E. (2017) 'The under-representation of minority ethnic groups in UK medical research.' *Ethnicity & Health 22*, 1, 65–82. https://doi.org/10.1080/13557858.2016.1182126

Smith, C. and Adamczyk, A. (2021) 'How Family Life Shapes Religious Parenting: The Role of Parents, Grandparents, Spouses, and Ex-Partners.' In C. Smith and A. Adamczyk, *Handing Down the Faith: How Parents Pass Their Religion on to the Next Generation* (pp.151–176). Oxford University Press. https://doi.org/10.1093/oso/9780190093327.001.0001

Smith, C. M., Turner, N. A., Thielman, N. M., Tweedy, D. S., Egger, J. and Gagliardi, J. P. (2022) 'Association of Black race with physical and chemical restraint use among patients undergoing emergency psychiatric evaluation.' *Psychiatric Services 73*, 7, 730–736. https://doi.org/10.1176/appi.ps.202100474

Smith, E. P., Atkins, J. and Connell, C. M. (2003) 'Family, school, and community factors and relationships to racial-ethnic attitudes and academic achievement.' *American Journal of Community Psychology 32*, 1–2, 159–173. doi: 10.1023/a:1025663311100.

Smith, L. T. (2006) *Decolonizing Methodologies: Research and Indigenous Peoples* (2nd edn). Zed Books.

Social Enterprise UK (2023) 'All about social enterprise.' www.socialenterprise.org.uk/all-about-social-enterprise

Social Work England (2019) *Professional Standards*. www.socialworkengland.org.uk/standards/professional-standards

Sorrentino, M., Sicilia, M. and Howlett, M. (2018) 'Understanding co-production as a new public governance tool.' *Policy and Society 37*, 3, 277–293. https://doi.org/10.1080/14494035.2018.1521676

Stevens, A., Kingdon, C. and Devakumar, D. (2023) 'The UK Illegal Migration Bill: A child rights violation and safeguarding catastrophe.' *The Lancet. Child & Adolescent Health 7*, 7, 445–447. doi: 10.1016/S2352-4642(23)00104-9.

Stone, L. L., Otten, R., Engels, R. C. M. E., Vermulst, A. A. and Janssens, J. M. A. M. (2010) 'Psychometric properties of the parent and teacher versions of the strengths and difficulties questionnaire for 4 to 12-year-olds: A review.' *Clinical Child and Family Psychology Review 13*, 3, 254–274. doi: 10.1007/s10567-010-0071-2.

Su, S., Jimenez, M. P., Roberts, C. T. and Loucks, E. B. (2015) 'The role of adverse childhood experiences in cardiovascular disease risk: A review with emphasis on plausible mechanisms.' *Current Cardiology Reports 17*, 10, 88. doi: 10.1007/s11886-015-0645-1.

Suárez-Orozco, C. and Suárez-Orozco, M. M. (2001) *Children of Immigration*. Harvard University Press.

Sudo, M., Won, Y. Q., Chau, W. W. Y., Meaney, M. J., *et al.* (2023) 'Physical discipline as a normative childhood experience in Singapore.' *Child and Adolescent Psychiatry and Mental Health 17*, 81. https://doi.org/10.1186/s13034-023-00632-9

Sue, D. W. and Sue, D. (2013) *Counseling the Culturally Diverse: Theory & Practice* (6th edn). John Wiley.

Sue, D. W. and Sue, D. (2016) *Counselling the Culturally Diverse: Theory & Practice* (7th edn). John Wiley.

Sunak, R. and Rajeswaran, S. (2014) *A Portrait of Modern Britain*. Policy Exchange. https://policyexchange.org.uk/publication/a-portrait-of-modern-britain

Szreter, S. (2012) 'Britain's Social Welfare Provision in the Long Run: The Importance of Accountable, Well-Financed Local Government.' In A. Ishkanian and S. Szreter (Eds) *The Big Society Debate: A New Agenda for Social Welfare?* (pp.39–49). Edward Elgar.

Tell MAMA (2023) *A Decade of Anti-Muslim Hate.* https://tellmamauk. org/a-decade-of-anti-muslim-hate

Triandis, H. C. (1995) *Individualism & Collectivism*. Westview Press.

The Maori Perspective Advisory Committee (1988) *Puao-te-ata-tu (Day Break): The Report of the Ministerial Advisory Committee on a Maori Perspective for the Department of Social Welfare.* www.msd.govt.nz/documents/about-msd-and-our-work/ publications-resources/archive/1988-puaoteatatu.pdf

Triandis, H. C. (2001) 'Individualism-collectivism and personality.' *Journal of Personality 69*, 6, 907–924. https://doi.org/10.1111/1467-6494.696169

Tribe, R. and Thompson, K. (2021) 'Working with Interpreters in Mental Health: Good Practice Guidelines.' In D. Moussaoui, D. Bhugra, R. Tribe and A. Ventriglio (Eds) *Mental Health, Mental Illness and Migration* (pp.489–511). Springer Nature. https://doi.org/10.1007/978-981-10-2366-8_38

UK Parliament (2021) Nationality and Borders Bill. https://hansard.parliament.uk/ Commons/2021-07-06/debates/21070641000012/NationalityAndBordersBill

Ungar, M. (Ed.) (2005) *Handbook for Working with Children and Youth: Pathways to Resilience across Cultures and Contexts.* SAGE Publications.

UNHCR (2022) 'Asylum in the UK.' www.unhcr.org/uk/asylum-in-the-uk.html

Vahdaninia, M., Simkhada, B., van Teijlingen, E., Blunt, H. and Mercel-Sanca, A. (2020) 'Mental health services designed for Black, Asian and minority ethnics (Black, Asian and minority ethnic) in the UK: A scoping review of case studies.' *Mental Health and Social Inclusion 24*, 2, 81–95. https://doi.org/10.1108/ MHSI-10-2019-0031

Venter, G. J. and Stoker, H. G. (2020) 'Young age faith in light of developmental psychology.' *Unio cum Christo: International Journal for Reformed Theology and Life 6*, 1. https://doi.org/10.35285/ucc6.1.2020.art11

Vygotsky, L. S. (1978) *Mind in Society: The Development of Higher Psychological Processes.* Harvard University Press.

Walsh, F. (1996/2003) *Strengthening Family Resilience*. Guilford Press. (Revised in 2016.)

Wampold, B. E. (2015) 'How important are the common factors in psychotherapy? An update.' *World Psychiatry 14*, 3, 270–277. https://doi.org/10.1002/wps.20238

Watt, N. and Mason, R. (2015) 'Cameron rebukes Farage over "fifth column" Charlie Hebdo comments.' *The Guardian*, 8 January. https://www.theguardian.com/ world/2015/jan/08/paris-attack-nigel-farage-gross-policy-multiculturalism

Watters, E. (2011) *Crazy Like Us: The Globalization of the Western Mind*. Little, Brown.

Wenger, E. (1998) *Communities of Practice: Learning, Meaning, and Identity*. Cambridge University Press.

Whaley, A. L. and Davis, K. E. (2007) 'Cultural competence and evidence-based practice in mental health services: A complementary perspective.' *American Psychologist 62*, 6, 563–574. doi: 10.1037/0003-066X.62.6.563.

White, M. (2007) *Maps of Narrative Practice*. W. W. Norton & Company.

White, M. and Epston, D. (1990) *Narrative Means to Therapeutic Ends*. W. W. Norton & Company.

WHO (World Health Organization) (2022) *World Mental Health Report: Transforming Mental Health for All*. www.who.int/publications/i/item/9789240049338

Wilkinson, R. G. and Pickett, K. E. (2017) 'The enemy between us: The psychological and social costs of inequality.' *European Journal of Social Psychology 47*, 1, 11–24. https://doi.org/10.1002/ejsp.2275

Williams, M., Burnap, P., Javed, A., Liu, H. and Ozalp, S. (2020) 'Hate in the machine: Anti-Black and Anti-Muslim social media posts as predictors of offline racially and religiously aggravated crime.' *The British Journal of Criminology 60*, 1, 93–117. https://doi.org/10.1093/bjc/azz049

Williams, O., Sarre, S., Papoulias, S. C., Knowles, S., *et al.* (2020) 'Lost in the shadows: Reflections on the dark side of co-production.' *Health Research Policy and Systems 18*, 1–10. https://doi.org/10.1186/s12961-020-00558-0

Wood, S., Scourfield, J., Au, K., Evans, R., *et al.* (2022) *A UK-Wide Survey of Family Group Conference Provision*. CASCADE Infrastructure Partnership, University of Cardiff, December. https://cascadewales.org/wp-content/uploads/sites/3/2022/12/CASCADE-Family-VOICE-survey-findings.pdf

World Bank (2023) 'Mortality rate, under-5 (per 1,000 live births) – Nigeria.' https://data.worldbank.org/indicator/SH.DYN.MORT?locations=NG

York, K. (2019) 'Black, Asian and minority ethnic representation and psychology.' British Psychological Society, 2 December. www.bps.org.uk/psychologist/bame-representation-and-psychology

Young Manchester Partnership (2020) *State of the Youth and Play Sector in Manchester: Risks and Challenges During Covid-19*. Submitted to Department for Digital, Culture, Media & Sport (DCMS).

Zavattaro, S. M. and Bearfield, D. (2022) 'Weaponization of wokeness: The theater of management and implications for public administration.' *Public Administration Review 82*, 3, 585–593. https://doi.org/10.1111/puar.13484

Zimmeck, M., Rochester, C. and Rushbrooke, B. (2011) *Use It or Lose It: A Summative Evaluation of the Compact*. Commission for the Compact, March. https://baringfoundation.org.uk/wp-content/uploads/2011/12/CompactUIOLI.pdf

Author Biographies

All the chapter authors have contributed to Just Psychology's work either as employees, associates, trainees, board/advisory group members or Cultural Consultants.

Fateha Begum is a qualified Social Worker and was the Project Lead for Just Psychology's Family Reunion and Parenting Project from its inception. She oversaw the management and delivery of the project and took a lead role with the Cultural Consultancy service. Prior to that she worked for Freedom from Torture Northwest.

Nic Bonham holds a BA (Hons) in Sociology and Criminal Justice and is a qualified Probation Officer and accredited coach. With a diverse background spanning youth justice and intensive family intervention, Nic has spent her career working at the intersection of social care, justice and restorative practice. She played a pivotal role in the development and delivery of the Family Group Conference (FGC) element within the nationally recognized, innovation-funded Family Valued programme at Leeds City Council. Her work focused specifically on embedding restorative approaches in responses to domestic abuse, placing FGCs at the heart of family-led decision making. As FGC Lead at Just Psychology, she championed culturally competent approaches to family decision making. Passionate about empowering families and promoting systemic change, Nic brings both strategic insight and hands-on experience to the evolving field of restorative practice.

Emcee Chekwas is a Consultant Forensic Psychologist with additional specialisms in clinical and counselling psychology as well as mental health law. He is a registered expert witness in both criminal and family law psychological practice and is the Lead Psychologist of MindSpace Clinics. He is often instructed by Courts and Local Authorities to provide expert psychological witness testimony.

With over 23 years of clinical and therapeutic experience, Emcee has worked extensively in the rehabilitation of individuals convicted of serious criminal offences, as well as those affected by mental health trauma. His practice has spanned the UK Prison Service and Mental Health Services, including therapeutic communities and the Bermuda Correctional Services. His primary area of focus is the influence of cultural factors on psychological theory and practice, particularly in relation to minority ethnic populations in Western European and North American contexts. He is an Associate of Just Psychology.

Emcee is statutorily regulated by the UK Health and Care Professions Council (HCPC) and the Bermuda Health Council (BHEC). He holds Chartered Scientist status with the UK Science Council and is an Associate Fellow of the British Psychological Society (BPS). In addition, he is a registered member of the European Federation of Psychologists' Associations (EFPA), an Accredited Test User, and holds the European Certificate in Psychology (EuroPsy).

Deanna Edwards is a Lecturer in Social Work at the University of Salford. She is a qualified counsellor and Social Worker with an interest and background in Family Group Conferences (FGCs) and Restorative Practice. Her previous roles have included managing FGC services and policy adviser for Family Rights Group. She is an experienced FGC trainer and Social Work Practice Educator with over 30 years' experience of teaching, training and social work with children and families.

Iyabo Fatimilehin is a Consultant Clinical Psychologist and Director of Just Psychology CIC, a social enterprise she founded in 2011 to address the psychological and mental health needs of children and families with a particular emphasis on cultural diversity, cultural competence and social justice. She worked in the National Health Service for over 20 years and was service lead for an award-winning specialist Child and Adolescent Mental Health Service for Black and minority ethnic children and families. She has presented at national and international conferences on racial and ethnic identity development, community-based initiatives, social exclusion, attachment and working with culture. Iyabo is an Associate Fellow and chartered member of the British Psychological Society and is a registered practitioner psychologist with the Health and Care Professions Council.

Michael Galbraith is a Clinical Psychologist and Systemic Psychotherapist. He jointly set up and is the clinical lead for the Liverpool Parent-Baby Service at PSS. Michael's passion for early years was fuelled by his experience of working in Sure Start centres and he holds on to the fourth objective of the Sure Start local programmes, which was/is to 'strengthen families and strengthen communities'.

Amira Hassan is a retired Chartered Counselling Psychologist with extensive experience in child and adolescent mental health. Before retiring, she served as Head of Psychology for a paediatric service in Qatar, supporting children with developmental delays and social communication difficulties.

Amira previously worked for over a decade in the UK's National Health Service, where she focused primarily on working with Black and minority ethnic communities. Her leadership included pioneering intergenerational projects with Black and Muslim fathers and sons, addressing the challenges of acculturation and strained family relationships shaped by migration and cultural transitions.

Her areas of expertise include culturally informed psychological assessment and intervention, service development, supervision and professional training. Amira has presented at national and international conferences and contributed to published work on race, identity and culture in mental health. Amira was a founding member of Just Psychology's Advisory Group.

She remains a Chartered member of the British Psychological Society and is registered with the Health and Care Professions Council.

Kate Hellin is an Associate Fellow of the British Psychological Society and a Health and Care Professions Council registered Consultant Chartered Clinical Psychologist in the United Kingdom. She worked for 30 years in the UK National Health Service with those affected by chronic trauma, with personality-based problems and substance misuse, in psychotherapy, forensic and general community mental health services. For the last 18 years, she has been working for the UK courts, mainly for the family court, undertaking psychological assessments of parents. She has a particular interest in cultural factors in parenting and is an Associate of Just Psychology. Her assessments focus not only on achieving the psychological understanding of parents, but also of the relationships between them and the professionals and organizations with whom they are involved, the dynamics of the system around families. She has spoken at national conferences about this, and about personality disorder, attachment and staff welfare.

Carolyn Kagan is Professor Emerita, Community Social Psychology at Manchester Metropolitan University and Honorary Fellow of the British Psychological Society. During her working life she was a chartered Counselling Psychologist and qualified social worker. She was Director of the Research Institute of Health and Social Change and is widely published on collaborative projects with marginalized communities. She continues to work on community projects in the community, voluntary and social enterprise sectors and has been a trustee of a number of organizations. She was a part of Just Psychology from its inception until 2024.

Rohan Morris is a Principal Clinical Psychologist working in a large adult mental health hospital for Greater Manchester Mental Health Trust. Previously Rohan was the clinical lead for an award-winning specialist service for people aged 16–25. Rohan was awarded his PhD in Psychology at Manchester Metropolitan University in 2014, before working as research assistant at the University of Manchester. Rohan was awarded his Doctorate in Clinical Psychology from Lancaster University in 2020 and subsequently gained registration as a practitioner psychologist with the Health and Care Professions Council. As a trainee Rohan undertook a specialist placement for Just Psychology where he was supervised by Dr Iyabo Fatimilehin. Rohan has published research looking at treatment disparity based on ethnicity and delivered workshops and presentations on the subject area.

Modupe Odebunmi is an accomplished professional proudly associated with Just Psychology, where she has trained and contributed as a Cultural Consultant. Her key interests lie in understanding how individuals and families from diverse cultural and ethnic minority backgrounds adapt and thrive when navigating contrasting cultural environments outside their countries of origin. She is particularly passionate about how neurodiversity and disabilities affect individuals and their families within the cultural contexts of ethnic minority communities. This includes exploring how cultural beliefs and systemic challenges influence access to care, education and social inclusion. Modupe actively volunteers as a Parent School Governor, where she advocates for inclusive education, and is especially interested in how students with Special Educational Needs are supported compared to those in mainstream settings. She currently works in an administrative role within the NHS, and is looking to pursue a future career in Psychological Wellbeing Practice and Health Psychology, where she hopes to integrate her lived experience, cultural insight and professional skills to positively influence holistic healthcare delivery.

Catherine O'Neill is a Clinical Psychologist and Principal Lecturer at Teesside University. Catherine has a specialist interest in community-based interventions, with particular reference to suicide prevention, loneliness and mental health. Her orientation to community work is based on Asset Based Community Development principles, community power and place-based approaches to health creation. As a trainee Catherine undertook a specialist placement for Just Psychology where she was supervised by Dr Iyabo Fatimilehin. Catherine is currently working with local neighbourhood and peer support organizations to examine factors which enhance emotional wellbeing and address suicide in the community.

Aneela Pilkington is a Clinical Psychologist in the United Kingdom. She has a specialist interest in working with families from different cultural groups, with a particular focus on cultural diversity and developing cultural competence. She completed her doctoral thesis looking at barriers to accessing mental health support for minority groups. She worked in Child and Adolescent Mental Health Services in the NHS for seven years. Over the last 10 years she has been working as an Expert Witness for the Family Courts. Her assessments look at systemic issues within families alongside developing an understanding of cultural factors. She delivers regular training on cultural competence to different organizations within the public and private sector and has worked with Just Psychology over many years. Aneela is a registered practitioner with the Health and Care Professions Council.

Hasan Waheed is a Principal Clinical Psychologist and Training Lead at Just Psychology CIC, and also holds roles as Principal Clinical Psychologist at Ihsaan CIC and Clinical Psychologist at Freedom from Torture. Alongside clinical practice, Hasan also serves as a Board Member for Inspirited Minds and has previously served on the Equality, Diversity and Inclusion Board for the British Psychological Society. He is passionate about working within the Voluntary, Community and Social Enterprise (VCSE) sector, with a focus on early intervention, prevention and asset-based approaches that recognize and build upon the strengths, skills and resources within communities, and is particularly interested in integrating creative approaches within psychological practice to enhance engagement and accessibility.

Subject Index

Author Index